THE
WORLD
OF
PAUL
CRUME

THE WORLD OF PAUL CRUME

EDITED BY
Marion Crume

FOREWORD BY
Lon Tinkle

INTRODUCTION BY
Frank Tolbert

SMU PRESS · DALLAS

Design: Chiles & Chiles, Dallas

Library of Congress Cataloging in Publication Data

Crume, Paul, 1912–1975.
The world of Paul Crume.

Essays originally published in the Dallas morning news.
I. Crume, Marion W.   II. Dallas morning news.   III. Title.
AC8.C78   081   80-14072
ISBN 0-87074-176-4

To
CHRIS

CONTENTS

CONTENTS

CONTENTS

CONTENTS

FOREWORD

FOR the third quarter of this century, from about 1948 to 1975, Paul Crume was, with little doubt, the most quoted newspaper columnist in the state of Texas, the most reprinted by other papers in the Southwest.

His was a voice heard throughout the region but with a message important for the nation, even though the meaning of Paul's comments was directed primarily at a specific and small segment of the country's population.

For anyone who knew Paul, to be told that hearing him in person presented a problem will be considered an understatement. In truth, it was an ordeal. One of the quirks about this lovable man, who otherwise had few quirks, was that in talk he either came on loud and clear or so low you had to resort to lip-reading to know what he was saying. He claimed he had no middle register to his voice, and this must have been so. Regardless of that, his friends were always cheering for him, feeling that if he ever failed he didn't deserve to. Rarely has any Texan ever inspired more loyalty.

Out of such loyalty, I wish this volume had a more evocative title, but in this case to call it, say, "The Pure Gold of Crume," implies the existence of impure gold as an opposite, and the same objection applies to silver and platinum — and Paul Crume was too natural a man for anything else. In the long run, *The World of Paul Crume* says enough.

Paul Crume was trained at the University of Texas, whose two "superstar" professors at the time were J. Frank Dobie and Walter Prescott Webb. Crume studied with both and was Webb's student grader and assistant. Both Webb and Dobie were nationally known and their books were regarded as significant contributions to scholarship. Through his association with these two men, Crume was strengthened in his belief that the history of the American

Southwest, so sadly neglected or ignored by national historians, was central to the American dream — central to our notion of a freedom that guaranteed human beings the right to move on if they wished and begin life all over again as a challenge to which the proper response was courage and bravery.

As much as Crume admired those now unfashionable heroic virtues, he never ranked them above intellectual achievement. He was a believer in logic. If his targets were hypocrisy and cant and bunkum, his weapon was laughter and his ammunition was ironic, rarely sardonic, tolerance of human frailty.

Crume's bedrock wisdom was specifically rural American, or pioneer. There are pages here worthy of Mark Twain, as there are a good many superior to Will Rogers. But the stance is the same. The humor comes from a broad, generous understanding of the gap between what people are and what they ought to be, above all of the gap between what dream promises and what reality forks over. For Crume the perception of this gap results in thigh-slapping guffaws far more often than in the melancholy tear.

He believed in the existence of good and evil, of good tutelary angels and of fallen ones like Lucifer. One of his best essays, stating this view, forms in a way the climax of this book, as the reader will discover.

It is time now for the maître d' to end his introduction and to invite the reader to a feast.

Lon Tinkle

Dallas, Texas
September, 1979

PREFACE

ONE February evening in 1952 Paul came home from the *Dallas News* and said, "They've asked me to start writing a new column." "What kind?" I asked, and he answered, "They're not exactly sure, but they want something that will add a personal touch to the front page. We're going to try a few ideas and see what works."

What "worked" was a six-day-a-week, five-hundred-word column called "Big D." It appeared on the front page of the *Dallas News* for almost twenty-four years. As a rule, five columns a week were devoted to what Paul referred to as "anecdote and oddity," and the sixth was what he called his "thumbnail essay."

The personal touch that the *News* had wanted was more than adequately provided. "I've never met Paul Crume," readers said to me again and again over the years, "but I feel as if I know him."

They were right, for from the beginning "Big D" *was* Paul Crume. The column mirrored his extraordinary range of interests — folklore, philosophy, politics, science, history, foreign affairs, literature, music, the English language, and sports, to name a few. It revealed his fascination with people: old-timers and children, public figures and bums, women, businessmen, artists, all kinds of people. Paul believed that human dignity and decency were important, and every line he wrote reflected this. He thought laughter was the best way to deal with the frustrations of life, and his columns were filled with wit and humor. Yet he never quite lost his own awareness of the tragedy of human existence, and this, too, is there.

It was my hope in planning this collection that I could assemble a group of the columns which would at least in some small measure re-create "The World of Paul Crume." There was no difficulty with finding enough material; in fact, the chief problem was that there was so much. More than eight thousand "Big D" columns were published between February 17, 1952, and November 13, 1975. Two decisions seemed necessary. The first was to limit the collection to the thumbnail essays. Second, since an earlier collection (*A Texan at Bay*, published by McGraw-Hill in 1961) had used columns printed between 1952 and 1960, it was decided to limit this second volume to those printed between 1960 and 1975.

Once final selections of the columns had been made, a plan for how to arrange them was needed. Paul's readers had had a way of saying, "My favorites are the ones about politics," or, "I save all the columns about words," or, "Why doesn't he do more on Lariat?" With this in mind, it seemed appropriate to gather the 254 final selections into five favorite subject areas, subdividing them into more specific topics for convenience in locating particular columns. Each selection also was given a title, drawn wherever possible from the text of the column.

A very light hand was used in editing. Two rules were followed in accordance with Paul's practice. When an occasional piece was rerun, he preferred to delete names of private people whose letters or comments had been used in the original column, as he felt it would be taking unfair advantage of them to have their names suddenly appear in print long after they had forgotten their contact with Paul. Also, he never hesitated to update or generalize a reference, if necessary, to keep it timely.

Additional minor editing for spelling, punctuation, syntax, slips of the typewriter, occasional repetition, etc., has been done in conformity with the publisher's standard practice.

Many people have helped to make this collection possible. I would like to express my appreciation, first of all, to Joe M. Dealey, publisher of the *Dallas Morning News*, for permission to use the "Big D" columns. Other *News* friends who kindly gave their time and good suggestions include Thomas J. Simmons, vice president and executive editor, and Jack Krueger, former executive editor.

Two of Paul's long-time friends and co-workers on the *News*, Frank X. Tolbert and Lon Tinkle, have written introductory material for the collection. I am deeply grateful to them for the love and insight which their words so eloquently reflect.

A number of other friends and relatives have given greatly appreciated assistance. I would like to thank Erik Jonsson for the helpful advice which he so generously gave. In addition, valuable help in reading through and selecting from the columns was given by Paul's brother, Bill Crume, and his wife, Sandy; our friends, Gordon and Mary Alice Brown; my sister, Nancy Curry, and my mother, Marion G. White. To my mother, in particular, I give special thanks; her love for Paul, together with her sensitive and honest appraisal of the various stages of work which have gone into the collection, have contributed more than I could ever adequately describe.

No publication is likely to be of any lasting merit without the guidance of skilled editors. I was fortunate in being able to work with three of the best: Allen Maxwell, SMU Press director, whose steadfast belief in the collection has sustained me in times of considerable despair; Margaret L. Hartley, SMU Press editor, whose unflagging drive for perfection has been an inspiration to me during our months of proofreading together; and Charlotte T. Whaley, assistant to the director, whose patient, cheerful aid has been provided instantly and freely whenever it was needed.

Last of all, and most of all, I would like to thank the many, many people — friends, acquaintances, strangers — who have repeatedly said in the years since Paul's death: "I never open my morning paper without missing his column. Please make a collection of them."

MARION CRUME

Dallas, Texas
March, 1980

INTRODUCTION

PAUL CRUME'S father, Charles Crume, was a restless man for most of his 87 years. He was a locomotive engineer in the late 1890s, a U.S. marshal in Indian Territory, a mountain farmer, and a horse and mule trader.

Charles Crume once declared his attitude about life in general with these words: "Things ought to be decent."

Paul Crume tried to live with his father's philosophy. And Paul had the exquisite skills with written words to express his thoughts in deeper terms.

Crume figured it almost a sin to miss a deadline. Even when he was away from the *Dallas News* on brief vacations he left columns to cover.

His last illness was a terrible thing. Still, from his home or from a hospital, he continued to meet the deadlines for his page 1 column, "Big D," up until three days before he died on November 16, 1975. And here are some of his last written words:

> The courts continue their gradual enslavement of the people. That judge who tried the Karen Quinlan case up in New Jersey has declared that nobody has a constitutional right to die . . . We have searched the Constitution diligently and can find in it no constitutional right to be born. We are talking here about the United States Constitution; nobody can find anything in the Texas Constitution . . . Since a man has no constitutional right to be born or to die, his whole life appears to be unconstitutional.

You can read all of this last column in the back of this book, next to one about angels which the *Dallas News* reprints sometimes at Christmas.

One of Paul's ancestors, Ralph Crume, was said to have been a close friend of Abraham Lincoln's parents. Paul resembled Abraham Lincoln physically. He also resembled the sixteenth President in compassion and native wit and wisdom.

Like Lincoln, Crume was born in February and in a log cabin. Paul's birthdate was February 24, 1912. And the scene was his parents' farm in the Ozarks near the village of Alpena Pass, Arkansas.

When Paul was six his parents sold the mountain farm. And in a covered wagon the family (five boys and one girl) headed westward, followed by a remuda of horses and mules for swapping along the way. After a year of wandering in Colorado and New Mexico the Crumes settled in Parmer County, Texas, on the New Mexico border.

Crume often wrote about the people of the hamlet of Lariat in Parmer County, although he usually explained that he didn't grow up in metropolitan Lariat and much of his boyhood was spent in "the suburbs of Lariat."

Once, after Paul's death, I stopped in Lariat (population 200) and spoke with an elderly farmer who was lounging in front of the store. This old guy may have been one of Crume's characters. Anyway, he talked like one. I told him I didn't know how to pronounce the name of the village. (Actually, I did know how.) He said: "That's easy. Say they is this boy named Larry and he has just et. You just say 'Larry et.'"

Paul's section on Lariat in this book starts with a recital of how the afternoon Santa Fe passenger train used to slow down to take a mail sack while underway with a mechanical mail grabber, the mail sack strung loosely on a crane at the side of the right-of-way. After that, Crume wrote, the new mail sack for Lariat was "heaved into the nearby cotton field" from the moving train. And Crume said: "That was all for the day. And that was good. After all that excitement, we had had about all we could take of the Santa Fe Railroad for one day."

Paul spoke of his immense talents in this offhand way: "If a humorous newspaper column serves any purpose it is to contribute a bit of temperate climate in a world too often hot-headed. We have in this country an intense ability to get serious — to differ with each other. We forget that our differences are only about five percent of our ideas, and we believe alike on the other 95 percent."

Joe Dealey, publisher of the *News*, has said: "Readers still miss him keenly. He had a way of lifting the spirits of people disturbed by today's bad news."

Paul's word magic could also make the preposterous seem logical. For a sample read the section in which he declares that "air conditioning robs the ordinary sleeper of participating in nature. It is also responsible, I believe, for destroying family history as it used to exist." The essays in this book are mostly fun ones. But Paul could be more somber, as in his 1974 New Year's Eve column (not included here) which began:

INTRODUCTION

Time stands still and never changes. The human race moves rapidly around it and thus the illusion of the passage of time. Time is like the cosmos, infinite in concept, uncaring, inert. We merely think we measure time because man invented the clock and had to invent some purpose for his machine. Time is really a vast and deep dark thought which the human race swims in like a bunch of golden minnows, putting down a January 1 here and there to mark its progress, it thinks.

Reading Paul could get your head "on straight." He had a genius for making logical deductions in a few words, such as: "The man who robbed from the rich and gave to the poor was a much better redistributor of wealth than the government. Instead of robbing from the rich and giving to the poor, the government robs from the middle class and gives to the rich and the poor."

Crume was graduated from the University of Texas at Austin, near the top scholastically, in 1936. His journalism classmates had included Walter Cronkite and Lady Bird Johnson. Paul worked his way through school with jobs such as washing dishes in cafés until his last year when he was a "grader" for one of his professors, the great historian, Walter Prescott Webb.

After graduation Crume planned to go to New York and try to get a job on a newspaper. Webb had other ideas for his brilliant student's career. Slyly, he told Crume: "Stop by the *Dallas News* on your way. Maybe one of the *News'* editors can help steer you to a job in New York."

Paul didn't know that Webb had called Ted Dealey, vice-president of the *News*, and told him one of the real stars of his classroom, Paul Crume, was going to visit the *News* on a certain day en route to job-seeking in New York. "Ted," Webb said, "sign him up with the *News*, if you can. Talk him out of going to New York. We need his talent in Texas."

Crume was surprised on his arrival in the *Dallas News* building when he asked to talk with the editors and, instead, was escorted to the executive offices. There Ted Dealey ended a long conversation with this: "Go to work tomorrow."

And, except for four years as a Navy officer during World War II, Crume performed brilliantly for Dealey's newspapers, from that day in June, 1936, to the sad time in November, 1975, when he wrote his final column, a wryly humorous one. The subject was death.

FRANK TOLBERT

Dallas, Texas
March, 1980

As It Was

BOYHOOD DAYS

---

*The wild geese were stirring on
the night I was born, and it is said
that their honks were like a chorus
of celebration. Ever since I have
distrusted goose judgment.
They just might celebrate anything
at all on impulse.*

BOYHOOD DAYS

AN IMPULSIVE CELEBRATION

A RECENT unwary admission that George Washington, Abraham Lincoln, and I share February as a natal month has brought in a spate of Happy Birthday cards, too many to answer. I hope that I have not unduly disturbed the other two gentlemen.

I found the cards very cheering. It has been a long time since anybody remembered that I was ever born. Most people now seem to think that I have always been here like the primordial basalt beneath the earth's crust and the traffic foul-up at the Triple Underpass.

As a matter of fact, I was born so long ago that I myself can barely remember it. I remember that there was a lot of stir around the house. My mother was there, of course. My father seemed to be in and out running errands. My grandmother was keeping a sharp and suspicious eye on the doctor.

Unfortunately, there is no written record of the event. It falls under the classification of the things that writers always refer to as "History does not record . . ."

I WAS born in this log house under which already lived the blacksnake which became my first childhood pet.

People were not born in hospitals then. Hospitals among our people were regarded as something like the Swift & Company butcher house, bloody places which were mere way stations on the way to Mr. Fry, who dealt in furniture, coffins, and fine undertaking.

When you had to send a person to the hospital, you never expected to see him again outside the Pearly Gates.

Doctors then did not like to practice in hospitals. It was too lonely.

The man who presided at my initiation was Dr. McCurry, a cynically kindhearted man who always had a "humph" and a sneer for the things that the practitioners of folk medicine knew were bedrock medicine. In later years he made his rounds in an old high-wheeled Dodge, but at the time of my emergency he had a handsome buggy and a spirited pair of horses.

He did not, however, go around whipping his horses into a gallop like the doctor in the famous Family Doctor picture. He had too much respect for his horses.

He arrived in time at our house, and even my grandmother conceded that, despite his ignorance in practical practice, he did a good job.

It wasn't until years later that people began to wonder whether I was all there.

THE wild geese were stirring on the night that I was born, and it is said that their honks were like a chorus of celebration. Ever since I have distrusted goose judgment. They just might celebrate anything at all on impulse.

Probably, this is the reason they were dying out until the goose hunters organized to protect them. Now, if you shoot two geese, you have to put one back.

Some day, by the way, I am going to write my reminiscences about Noah.

THE WANDERING BOY

DURING the autumn that I was four, a wandering boy appeared at our farm in the Ozarks.

His kind were common enough in that time and place, orphans without family or friends, possessed only of the hand-me-down clothing on their backs and what they could carry in a bundle, uneducated, untrained. They worked at whatever farm jobs they could get for food and a few pennies, slept in the hayloft in the barn, and disappeared, God knows where, beyond the edges of the American Dream.

This one was a good, big, husky, hearty boy, friendly and given to laughter. He could do a lot of hard work. In my memory, he is gigantic, though not of the Jovian proportions of my father. If you live on a lonely farm where there

are not many new people, you can quickly become fond of a newcomer. This one played with me a lot when he wasn't shocking fodder. It is easy to see now that he was living half the time in the world of a boy and half in the world of an adult; but he wasn't permitted to be a boy then.

He arrived at harvesttime, and my dad had work to do. My mother had a conscience that went off easily and she tried to move him into the upstairs room, but he wanted to stay in the hayloft. She compromised by overfeeding him.

Everybody grew fond of this boy. He was a sunny, noncomplaining person, and my dad would boast about the work he could do.

BUT the harvest ended, and on a small farm, you either have the money for a hired hand or you don't. We didn't. The last evening of Jake, if we may call him that, was almost one of weeping at our house.

Next morning, before anyone knew it, he was gone, vanished from our familiar earth. As the day advanced, my father also missed Shep, a trained livestock dog. He was not long in learning things. A neighbor reported that Jake had gone walking off down the road with Shep following. Jake had his belongings in a bandanna bundle. People suddenly remembered that Shep and Jake had occupied the hayloft together. My dad was fonder of Shep than he was of Jake.

Other people volunteered to round up a posse. At that time, a constable in an Ozark precinct was permitted only to serve legal papers with a humble apology, touching his forelock to his neighbor as he did so. Officers of the law were twelve miles away in the county seat, where they meant to stay.

*The posse was formed. It saddled up
and rode away, twelve or fifteen men in
search of a fourteen-year-old.*

THE memories that live with a man until the
day he dies are odd and unpredictable
ones. I will never forget that day.

It was gray, wet, chilly November weather.
They came back by our house late in the
afternoon, the posse self-consciously stern
aback the prancing horses and the boy in a
spring wagon, bound and tied to the seat where
all could see.

The landscape looked gray and slick. I will
never forget it. Rain dripped drearily from the
eaves, falling with little notes of music into the
water at the foot of the walls. The air bit into
you as the procession swept by.

I will never forget the sick, shamed,
hopeless look on the face of that boy, bound
and tied to the spring seat.

My mother was mad for a week.

THE YEAR THE SNAKES CAME

WITH no intention of shaking anybody up, I
would like to say that this dry spring has
left me with a sense of foreboding. It has the
feel of the spring of the year that the snakes
came.

All this happened long ago, almost half a
century ago, when I was very small. That year
began with little rain, too, and a sense of
foreboding that deepened as summer came.
The corn blades burned tawny at the edges
while they were still green that June. The
livestock grew fretful and bony on the dry grass
of the hillsides. In the brassy sunlight, the tall
weeds stood motionless and white-heavy with
dust.

The world was already grim and sad with the
feel of financial ruin that came to a farmer with
a drought in those days. Even the children
sensed the mood and attuned themselves to it.

Then, in early summer, the snakes came.

*Thousands of snakes, millions of them,
big jet black chicken snakes, as large as
a fire hose, took over chicken roosts,
horse troughs, the shade under a porch
stoop, everything.*

MOSTLY, they appeared by night, though
you could see their traces by the
daytime, small faint tire tracks that ran
everywhere over the powdery dust of the
roads and the field rows. A traveler walking
one of the dusty country roads occasionally
would spot a black snake slithering across the
road ahead of him, six feet long perhaps with a
body as thick as a man's arm. But when night
came, the snakes really came out.

The nights that I remember from that
summer were pitch black and blanket warm.
The air packed in about you, closed in your
eyes, and assailed your senses. Even grown
men had company on those evenings if they
could find anyone to stay. The kerosene lantern
stayed lit. There would be low hushed talk on
the dark veranda until the idiot squawk of a hen
or a sudden thunder from the horse barns
would sound the alarm. The men would trot off
with the lantern. There would be distant
excited talk around the barns. Finally, the men
would return with a story of having killed not
only the one snake but perhaps half a dozen
others encountered on the way to the barns
and back. The ground was alive with them.

They kept nightlong vigils, the adults did. A
bag of twenty-five or thirty snakes a night was
common. Farm folk aged four to six went finally

and unwillingly to bed and fitful sleep, with dreams full of snakes and sudden screaming awakenings.

With snakes everywhere else, it was hard not to see them writhing in the dark beside your bed.

SLOWLY, that sad summer dragged past. Sometime during it the snakes disappeared, though if you were small, you did not feel safe until September sharpened the air over the ruined fields and the desolate land.

To this day I still cannot believe that a chicken snake is harmless, though I know that it is. I know there is some explanation for why the snakes sought out the habitations of men, a need for comparative coolness and water perhaps, but I do not welcome them back. As I said, this year has that certain feel about it. I am keeping the lantern lit.

A THREE-MILE WALK

THREE of us were swapping yarns around the lunch table the other day about testing out cars on Chalk Hill thirty years ago. In those days if you had a car that could climb the hill on the west edge of Dallas in high, you had a jet thrust pure and simple.

The tales seemed somehow as far distant in time as Galileo, and the feel of the experience, the quality of it, suddenly reminded me of a summer day when I was six. On that day the parents decided a six-year-old boy was old enough to walk by himself the three miles from our Ozark farm to the small village where a favorite grandmother lived.

It was the longest journey I ever made, and it remains the most memorable.

THE road I traveled doglegged back and forth, following the edges of fields instead of section lines. I took to it with thunder in my heart and my senses keened by excitement.

The iron tires of wagons and buggies had cut the dirt of the road into soft dust a foot deep. It was pleasantly hot to the skin of bare feet. The road drowsed. It lay in silence. A crow flapped its way across a nearby field without cawing. At a spot in a fencerow where blackberry vines grew, one could all but hear the slither of snakes crawling across the dusty grass.

I crossed the footlog over Long Creek. I stopped at a house by the way and talked with Mrs. Ed Jones. She gave me a dipper of water and asked hintingly whether my parents knew where I was. Assured they did, she said I was getting mighty big and brave to undertake such a journey alone.

Once a man named Clyde Tabor waved to me from his field. And once the Smith who was called Cussing Smith gave me a ride in his Model T, one of those old-timers with tie rods that ran down from the windshield to the square front fenders. Cussing Smith was a little fat man with a beaming red face and walrus moustaches. He was generally equated in the community with Sin and Whiskey.

When I had got in, he pulled the gas lever on the Model T and really tore out. It was a long, wild, wonderful ride, and the whole half-mile before he turned off the road flew beneath us like the wind.

WHEN I got to town, I found that my grandmother was absent. An uncle arrived, took charge of me, and informed me that she would be back the next day.

What seems odd is that she had been gone

from home a week and I, three miles away, knew less about all these things than a man in Dallas now knows about the plans of a friend in Washington. Only yesterday that was, and three miles was a world away. Now, they say, the moon is next door.

THE WOODCUTTERS

AN Austin man was a little scandalized recently at finding that firewood was selling at $28 a cord and that the seller offering it was selling it by the "chord." At $28, it probably was music to somebody's ears.

It raised the question in my mind of whether the professional cordwood cutters still exist. I never knew but two of them. One fall and winter, when I was a very small boy in the Ozarks, Pete and Ellis set up camp in the woods beyond our north pasture. At that time, a landowner who wanted some new ground cleared commonly turned it over to a woodcutter who cleared the trees for the wood.

Pete and Ellis spent that fall and winter clearing a hillside beyond the pasture.

They also served as hosts twenty-four hours a day for small boys who discovered in their way of life an existence that finally made sense.

PETE and Ellis had the best of all possible worlds for a small boy. When they moved in, they spent a few days cutting saplings, out of which they constructed a framework over which they stretched a tarp for a roof. It was called a wagon sheet in those days. They also framed a couple of bunks out of saplings with a rope webbing for springs. Other saplings supported a couple of short 1 x 12s, which

served as a table, and another 1 x 12, which was a bench.

Thus, they had a small house open on three sides. They cooked on a fire which never went out in front of the lean-to, and they had marvelous food — flapjacks with molasses two or three times a day, beans, lots of fried slab bacon. They had a single-barrel shotgun, and it often produced a squirrel or a quail to vary the menus.

They also had a pet raccoon, which was kept chained to one of the bunk posts.

Here were all the comforts of home without the worry of being clean.

It was a privilege to be allowed to sit around these camps of a morning and watch their bean pot while they were off cutting wood.

THE real fun at the woodcutters' camp was at night. They kept a huge fire going at the front of the lean-to, and the men and boys of the neighborhood would gather there to stay late, sometimes until 9:00 P.M., and listen to talks about old hunts and the odd occurrences that had taken place around somebody's deathbed.

Pete was the leader in all this. He was a lean, enormously tall, lantern-jawed man who had been everywhere. He had even been to the county seat four or five times, and by his own account, women had always found him irresistible. He also played the five-string banjo, accompanying himself on a French harp which he tucked away in his left jaw. His repertoire was limited to "Sally Goodin" and "Walk along, Johnny, with your leather britches on," but so far as it went, it was perfect.

Ellis usually just sat there and smoked and admired Pete.

Long before the winter was out, the woods had been cut down. The wood was neatly stacked in cords, and Pete and Ellis were forever gone.

Wood of that kind is worth $28 a cord.

BOTTLE BROKERS

THE big thing in Dallas these days, they say, is the bottle — not the full bottle, which has been popular for some time, but the empty bottle.

People used to collect rare gems or blondes or Don Meredith autographs. Nowadays, they are hunting unusual bottles. The cosmetic and liquor trades especially seem to have sensed the current unhinging of the public mind. They are creating more and more unusual bottles. It doesn't even worry most of the buyers that the bottles don't have much in them.

A lower downtown liquor dealer waved an arm toward the curious collection of canisters and crockery jars containing his Christmas items.

"They'll pay $25 for one of those, and they don't even drink the whiskey. They give it away," he said unbelievingly.

Apparently, the feeling is abroad that a man might make a killing in unusual bottles if he buys and holds, that a $25 bottle may shoot up to $35 or even $50. People used to feel this way about the franc.

As an old bottle broker, I would like to warn the public that there is no investment so fragile as a bottle.

AS a small boy of seven, I spent awhile in an Ozark town where the local druggist, a Mr. Watkins, bought bottles.

He put out several patent medicines of his own manufacture which were good for man or beast, the main one being a liniment which cured the heaves in horses and asthma in man and was also beneficial in the treatment of bog spavin and iron-poor blood. Bottles were hard to come by in that small town, and Mr. Watkins needed them. He would pay one cent for any usable bottle and two cents for the ones with the graduated ounces marked.

A small, boot-tough, seven-year-old entrepreneur named Cannonball Sawyer, who was usually up to something, came up with the big idea. We would pool our bottles, corner the bottle supply of the town, and jack the price up to a nickel a bottle.

This prospect of instant great wealth was breathtaking, and we went instantly to work.

WE rummaged all the trash piles behind the stables for bottles, searched the alleyways, and then stole all the liquid medicines in our houses. We emptied the bottles and added them. This sudden disappearance of home remedies undoubtedly increased Mr. Watkins's business and put him in a bottle squeeze. He asked some of us whether we couldn't find him some bottles, and we promised to try.

After a few days, a delegation headed by Cannonball called on him with the news that we knew where there was an absolute trove of bottles available at a nickel each.

"No thanks, boys," he said. "I had to order a supply from Kansas City."

It taught me a lesson. Never trust a get-rich-quick scheme. Stick with the small and safe.

So far as I know, all those bottles are still safely stowed in the cave by the creek, which was a deep, dark secret place to the small boys of that town for three generations.

MAKING FRIENDS WITH THE BEES

I HEARD that a Britisher has invented an electronic gadget with which you can listen inside a beehive and get advance warning of swarming or queen failure.

Undoubtedly, queen failure is a bad thing, and anything that would reduce the hazard to life and limb of opening up a beehive ought to be welcomed by the human race. We doubt that this is going to work, however. A man concentrating on a listening device around a beehive is likely to get a bee in his bonnet. When you are around bees, you had better keep whirling your head around, or one will creep in on your blind side.

At an early age, I aspired to be a hive robber. I was influenced in this by an elderly man named Mr. Mills who was always called in to rob hives or handle swarms. Mr. Mills would wade right in among the bees, and they would settle over him in a great fuzz while lesser mortals had to stand back about a half-mile and watch in admiration.

It was an occupation full of dash and drama. I was naturally attracted to dashing occupations, and this one looked as impressive as bronc riding without being half as dangerous — if you knew the trick.

I SOUGHT Mr. Mills's advice on his profession, and he gave it gladly. Mr. Mills wasn't in a hurry to get anything done, and he always had plenty of time for advice. He said the trick was to make friends with the bees.

"A bee will never hurt a friend," he said.

I decided to take measures in case the bees did not appreciate my friendliness in robbing the hive. I acquired an old metal colander as a tin hat and attached to it a length of mosquito bar so that it would drape over my shoulders. I acquired some long women's gloves from my mother's dresser drawer and pulled them up over my shirt cuffs. I dogged down all the hatches in my pants.

If the bees didn't have sense enough to know a friend when they saw one, I wasn't going to bear the consequences.

I WAS all set to wade in and let the bees settle on me when there came a sudden whine that was unmistakable. While I was concentrating on protecting myself, some bees had got inside the mosquito netting. This was no time to stand on friendship. I tried to yank off the colander and throw it away, but the netting tangled around my neck. Before I could get it straightened out, the bees mistook me for an enemy — twice.

I doctored the spots with wet clay from the creek, and except for having a lopsided head for awhile, I came out all right.

That is the extent of my beekeeping, if you can call it keeping. It is enough to be suspicious of a bee listening device.

A SHOAT NAMED LOUELLA

THE most maligned beast of the animal kingdom is the hog.

This affectionate, wise, and lively animal is invariably depicted as a lazy, stupid, and insensate glutton. He is said to love filth and to like to wallow in mud and to wolf down any victuals that will add to his waistline.

Anybody who has been closely associated all his life with hogs, as I have, knows this to be a canard. Far from being filthy, the hog is probably instinctively the cleanest of animals. He does wallow in the mud of the ordinary pigpen because this is the only way he can keep his hide wet, and this is a necessity with hogs. Given the chance, the ordinary hog would much prefer to be sprayed by a garden hose and to be cleaned of any kind of dirt. He is not a glutton. The hog's stomach is very small, relatively, and he eats only a little. He is very efficient in converting this small amount of food into waistline.

He is not slow or lazy, either. If you've ever tried to hem up a hog in a bunch of bushes, you will discover just how slow and lazy the human race is.

The pig as an animal is a lot more adequate than the man.

AS a small boy, I had the privilege of being a close friend of a shoat named Louella. He had got this name before somebody found out that he wasn't a gilt, and he never got mad about it.

Louella had become mine by a strange route. He had been the runt of the litter, and my mother had got him over his doldrums by feeding him from a bottle and keeping him in a basket on the back porch next to the sauerkraut crock. Louella got to have a great advantage over his siblings. He outgrew them all, but he never considered the house off limits. He was likely to wander into the living room, a five-hundred-pound pig, if he could follow me in through the screen door. This usually shattered the composure of any visitors and made my mother mad for days.

Anyhow, Louella belonged to me and followed me wherever I went. We had one cherry tree then which produced black cherries so sweet that they demanded to be eaten. When I was up in the limbs eating them, I had to throw a share down to Louella. If I didn't, he would set up that insane squealing that pigs do which would bring the adults running to find a pig caught in a fence. After the first time, I never did this.

Louella was too shrewd, even while dealing with my dad, to monkey with. You had to stay on his good side.

LOUELLA was the playmate of a generation of small boys. We learned to ride on him. Two people would hold up Louella until a rider was aboard. Louella, turned loose, would sit there a minute and then take off like a jet, sending a small boy pinwheeling into the air. He would then come back and root under the fallen rider to see whether he wasn't going to get up.

In time, Louella grew great in size and girth. My father persuaded me to sell him to the commission merchant. Even at the prices in those days, Louella brought $30.

For thirty pieces of silver I sold him, and I still think that was the beginning of original sin with me.

THE FORBIDDEN LEAF

MAYBE you have already been disgusted to notice that they are now making a menthol chewing tobacco.

Pretty soon there will be no men left, just sweet menthol-smelling escorts of ladies. This new tobacco advises you merely to take a pinch and place it between cheek and gum. "No chewing!" it advertises. Why, in Pete's sake, if you aren't going to chew, do you want a chewing tobacco?

Any good tobacco chewer knows that you do not place the cud between cheek and gum until it has been pretty well tamped down by the teeth and you wish to preserve it for awhile. This is a perfect place, for instance, to preserve the cud for eight or ten hours while you are asleep. Juice seeps slowly from it, enough juice to keep you alive until you awaken in the morning and cut yourself off a new and flavorful chew.

This new tobacco is called Skoal, which sounds as if it was invented by a drinker instead of a tobacco chewer.

I WAS lectured at the age of eight on the dangers of tampering with the pure and undefiled chewing tobacco.

At the time, my dad grew his own tobacco. This was the pure leaf, dried worms and all, not the leavings and bits of stems and wood shavings that they put into cigarettes now. When it was harvested, my dad hung the tobacco in a special section of the barn loft. It was forbidden to us, so naturally my brother and I used it all the time.

It was easy enough to smoke. Though it could not be ground into flakes small enough for cigarettes, we could use a piece of newspaper as a wrapper and roll it into a fat cigar. It was safe enough to smoke this if you took a heavy drag at it and then dodged before the smoke got to you. If you failed to dodge, the smoke produced a state amply described by Shakespeare as swooning.

Some of the older citizens around could twist these leaves into a twist and chew them, but my brother and I had never been able to

chew until he finally hit upon an invention.

It was late in the season, and we had many jars of elderly sorghum molasses. As anybody familiar with molasses knows, sorghum at this stage threatens to turn to sugar and has a smell very like two-week-old feet.

My brother hit upon the idea of soaking a tobacco leaf with this syrup, putting another leaf upon it, cementing this with molasses, and so on until he had a good thick cut plug. He weighted the whole thing down with a two-by-four surmounted by a brick and let it set.

It was a capital idea. When you chewed the stuff, you could barely taste the molasses.

UNFORTUNATELY, our Uncle Tobey came upon us while my brother and I were gushing forth great slobbers of this tobacco juice. "Aren't you ashamed?" he asked.

Thinking that he was shaming us for chewing tobacco, we nodded.

It turned out, though, that Uncle Tobey's concern was for the tobacco. By soaking it with these rancid molasses, he pointed out, we had destroyed the delicate taste of the tobacco. Uncle Tobey's white teeth wore a constant lens of yellow from the stuff. He yanked out a tobacco twist and bade us taste it after sampling the molasses plug.

"Notice the difference," he said.

"It sure is different," agreed my brother, turning green and sprinting for the barn.

Neither of us has been in favor of flavoring chewing tobacco since.

CAUGHT BETWEEN TWO FIDDLERS

I ONCE had the misfortune to get caught in a tug of war between two country fiddlers who were determined to teach me to play the fiddle if it killed me.

This all happened because my dad swapped a single-shot Stevens .22 for a fiddle. He didn't have any use for the fiddle, but apparently he had even less use at the moment for the target gun, and he believed that the only way for a man to get ahead was to keep "trading up" as he called it, to keep swapping things and increase the quality of his possessions.

Since we had a fiddle, he figured we might as well do something with it, and he made the mistake of mentioning to a couple of family friends that they might teach me to play it.

We quickly found out you had better not mention even a fiddler's name to another fiddler.

ORDINARILY these men got along very well together. Frank Edwards was a big man, dark of hair and skin. John McCall was a little redheaded man who wore a scraggly, sandy moustache that always looked as if it was about to weep. It quickly became evident, though, that neither man could stand the sight of a fiddle in the other's hands.

Fiddlers then did not know notes. They knew "pieces." Frank was very strong on "Hell Among the Yearlings," while John's strong piece was "The Robert E. Lee." Neither man could play the other's pieces, and each let you know that it was hardly worth learning to play them.

Frank would get my dad off to the side. He would mention that John McCall was a fine man. Best hearted man in the world, but, of course, he didn't know beans about fiddling. Or John would mention casually that Frank Edwards was one of the best workers in the county but simply didn't have any talent for music. They were both insistent on having the monopoly of teaching me to fiddle.

As a result, I had to saw that thing morning and night. Since neither fiddler could bear the fiddle in the other's hands, I had to sit there between them and fiddle away. I never produced anything that sounded remotely like "Hell Among the Yearlings" or "The Robert E. Lee," but my father pretended to admire my music no end.

He said it was wonderful how I was taking on the best characteristics of both Frank's and John's pieces.

WELL, I never did learn to play the fiddle, and never did really want to. My dad finally solved the problem of preventing a duel between his two old friends. He swapped the fiddle for a shoat. As he pointed out, all the fiddle was doing was lying around there deteriorating. A man could hardly get ahead sticking with trades like that. The shoat was bound to get bigger and improve its chances.

Of course, later on, he swapped the shoat for a Marlin .22 rifle.

All this did something to my psyche.

A COVERED WAGON TREK

ONE of these days some archeologist is going to unearth a huge cache of Rocky Mountain Indian arrowheads at a spot near Garden City, Kansas, and establish a theory that these dwellers of the high places often ventured far onto the plains for to hunt the buffalo.

I mean here only to head off the waste of scientific brainpower that will ensue. It happened differently.

Almost fifty years ago my dad and his brother decided to migrate by covered wagon from eastern New Mexico to Grand Junction, Colorado, to find new range, to break out new ground, and to get rich quick. My father was burdened by five very active small boys, of whom I was one.

It was a long trip through country that was barely settled, and the best run that we could make in good weather on level ground was thirty miles a day. It should have been a boy's paradise. Each family had a wagon with bunks rigged at the back and a small stove set up in the front for cooking. At night, when we could find the wood, there were campfires with the coyotes yapping somewhere out there in the dark. My uncle had an old Edison cylinder-record phonograph, and sometimes we would sit listening to beautiful music like "Redwing" and "My Silver Star."

It wasn't paradise, though. It was pure boredom.

IN theory, the five of us were supposed to stay quiet back in the bunk area of the wagon. We were too small to be allowed to wander around on the prairie. My older cousin, Lyle, was privileged to saddle a pony when he wanted to gallop around ahead of the line of march, bringing back reports of conditions. It seemed unfair that we were not also allowed to ride. If there was anything we had, it was plenty of horses.

So we invented our own forms of amusement. We fought. We played very active games that once tore the canvas cover of the wagon. My dad stayed very irritable all this time. On the few stretches of road where autos traveled, we would imitate the old Locomobile klaxon, and my dad would obligingly pull off to the side. After the third or fourth time, he would always get very mad.

Also, the glass jar in which my brother kept his tarantulas broke. At the insistence of my mother, we lost half a day while the cargo was unloaded and the wagon fumigated.

WE traveled mostly over trackless prairies, forded rivers with quicksand, snaked up dry creek beds, and hauled wagons by main force up hills and mesas. Indian artifacts were everywhere, and my mother, out of self-defense, interested us in collecting them.

As the trip wore on, my dad kept complaining that the horses just could not pull as much as they had. He worried. At Pueblo, he decided to give up eldorado at Grand Junction and turn back to the familiar farming country in the Ozarks. Still, the horses didn't seem able to pull as well as they had.

We were near Garden City when he discovered something between five hundred and a thousand pounds of Indian arrowheads stowed beneath the bunk.

They were unloaded right there in a deep borrow ditch. He delivered a heated lay sermon, and many tears were shed. It was all right the next morning, though. We started collecting other things.

The Indians have been blamed for a lot, but they didn't do this.

CAREERS BY CORRESPONDENCE

THERE was a time in my life when I was all torn up trying to decide whether to be a taxidermist or a fingerprint expert. It started on a day when I was answering the ads in *Popular Mechanics*.

At the time, this was a monthly chore. I was still within the eleven-year-old age bracket, but I had already discovered that one way to break the daily boredom in a small town was to answer all the ads in *Popular Mechanics.* Back would come enough reading matter each morning to last a day, prospectuses on itch powder, treatises on esoteric machines to turn weaklings into muscle men, and plans for miniature prairie schooners.

My daily take had already grown beyond the capacity of my day's lockbox. Each day I showed up at the post-office window to take charge of my bushel basket of loot, and once the postmaster, Old Man Wulfman, a rather tired soul, asked whether I wasn't thinking about ordering a kitchen stove in the mail.

At the time, you could train for any career by correspondence. I remember a full-page ad in "Scribner's" showing a woman remarking to her husband about the commanding figure another man made at a party, and the husband was saying: "Yes, my dear, he knows The Law."

TWO careers caught my eye in this issue of *Popular Mechanics,* however. One ad said: "Earn Big Money! BE A TAXIDERMIST. Taxidermists earn up to $10 a day."

The other said: "BE A DETECTIVE. Learn fingerprinting, the scientific method of crime detection. Excitement! Travel! Romance! Conversations with women!"

As you can see, the appeals in these ads are different, and a man has to give long thought to the conflicting attractions. The detective ad made no promise whatsoever of approaching $10 a day in income, and the taxidermy ad spoke nothing of conversations with women.

I sent for material on both jobs. In due time, I got a six-inch-thick portfolio from taxidermy showing pictures of fierce animals which had been stuffed and including letters from people who said they had never stuffed a kangaroo in their lives and then they took this course and stuffed a kangaroo.

The fingerprinting kit included the secret reports of a detective. They clearly showed he traveled. He went from Philadelphia to Pittsburgh, but he seemed to be handicapped by having to carry always in his pocket a glass which he would hand people to get their fingerprints.

THEN began a three-week wrestle with the conscience over the career I wanted to choose. It was aided by mailings from the two schools. After the third follow-up mailing, the taxidermy institute bluntly wanted to know whether I was chump enough to pass up the field and stated that it would mail no more.

For six months, though, I got printed letters from fingerprints implying that open detective jobs were being filled fast. I would have taken the course if I had had any money after paying the stamp bill for answering the ads in the new month's issues of magazines.

Of such slender things is a career in journalism made.

CULTURE SHOCK

A DALLAS man has raised the question. He read a newspaper story about the "cultural shock" that Indian kids get when they go away to school. He wonders whether I experienced any cultural shock when I moved as a child from Arkansas to Lariat.

I experienced something, although there wasn't much culture involved. I decided to use the move as an opportunity to promote myself two grades, from the fifth to the seventh. The new principal looked at me and seemed to be in an awfully good humor. He asked me what was one-fourth of one-fourth.

"There's no such number," I told him.

He said I could stay in the fifth grade for the moment and progress rapidly through the year. He said that he didn't see any reason why a student of my ability couldn't progress all the way to the eleventh grade before the year was over.

I had the idea that his good humor wasn't entirely pleasure at seeing me, but I couldn't say anything.

THE kids then all hung their coats on a long rack along the hall between the classrooms. I found out before the day was over that the principal took a dim view of students who left hog snakes in their coat pockets.

This was after I had my first fight. It happened just two minutes after the first recess began. I decided to establish my authority and took offense at another fifth grader who seemed to be bemused.

He wouldn't stand up and fight with his fists. Instead, he would turn his back and seem to be running away and would then deliver a mule-kick backward. I got damaged a bit. When recess was over, I still hadn't figured out how to handle the kick.

This was certainly a shock. It wasn't supposed to happen this way. I was supposed to win this fight because the other kid was smaller than I was.

When classes were called back, the principal got me out of class, took me to his office, and asked whether anything was bothering me.

I looked him squarely in the eye through my black eye and said nothing was.

IT was just a bad day. Before it was over a girl who was a head taller than I was decided to flirt with me, and this caused snickers among all the boys.

When I got home, my dad asked where I got the black eye, and I told him I ran into the school. That was the truth.

Things got better. The kid with whom I had picked the fight became my bosom buddy and taught me how to do the kick. I got in some good licks. The girl who was a head taller whipped another boy because she thought he was abusing me.

Gradually, it became a pretty good school. It was a shock, though I doubt that it was very cultural.

TWO-DOLLAR RIDE IN A FLYING MACHINE

THE U.S. astronauts may have got man a lot farther toward the moon, but they didn't risk their lives the way I did.

One day early in the 1920s a flying machine, as they were then called, circled the water tower several times in our town in West Texas and then headed for the cow pasture at the edge of town and landed. The entire township, all 262 of them, gathered there as instantly as a mule can run.

The aviator was waiting beside the flying

machine, a tall, slim young man with a little pencil moustache. He wore one of those tight, soft-leather helmets, and he had goggles pushed up above his eyes. In his leather jacket, his lace-legged, moleskin boot pants, and his English boots, he seemed to a twelve-year-old to be a man of infinite dash, making the rest of us look like clodhoppers. A real devil, obviously. As soon as the fathers had spotted him, they made their daughters go back and sit in the car.

The aviator made a little speech. He said that for two dollars he was offering one and all the chance to ride in this flying machine, the marvel of the ages.

HE didn't exactly get an enthusiastic response. Most of the men frowned at the flying machine and fingered their money and decided that buying rides in a flying machine was a foolish frivolity. But I had two dollars, barely, and a great temptation.

As I remember that plane, I shudder. It was an old spruce and cloth biplane. The cloth on the wings and the fuselage had been sewn in a hundred places, and a few slits had been patched with tire tape.

The wings were kind of loose, too; but at the time, that didn't bother me. I thought they were supposed to flap. Anyhow, I didn't see any danger in going up. After all, I had fallen off the top of Charlie Dycus's commission barn without any ill effects.

Just as the aviator seemed to be getting dispirited in his sales pitch, I stepped forward and presented my two dollars—a dollar bill, a quarter, a few nickels and dimes, and quite a few pennies. The aviator kept a poker face, but it seemed to me his eyes were grinning as he boosted me up into the front seat.

I remember hearing, as I was climbing aboard, a neighbor woman yelling at me, "Your daddy will hear about this."

THE plane had a rotary motor. I think they called it a Wright Whirlwind. The aviator started it by flipping the propeller, and as the plane started forward, he ran around to the side and mounted into the cockpit as you would mount a horse. I remember thinking wildly that he would miss it, and I would be up in the air without any way to get down. He didn't.

We had quite a flight, and he did something that I think used to be called an Immelmann. It would have been better if I hadn't been eating the peanuts. I couldn't stand up very well when we got down.

The aviator handed me back the dollar bill.

"Keep it, sport," he said. "I'd give you the whole two dollars back, but I'd hate to have to count the rest of it."

Sure enough, my dad heard about this, and I heard about it plenty from him. In the words of our town, I had completely blowed the wages of a week's weed-cutting on something as silly as shooting at the moon.

SIX WEEKS WITH SHAKESPEARE

SHAKESPEARE got to be four hundred years old last week. In absentia, of course.

There are quite a few old boys out of the seventh grade of forty years ago out in the Lariat country who will still swear that Shakespeare once lasted a lot longer than four hundred years in just one six-week period. This happened when a gentle, patient English teacher locked the seventh grade in away from their ponies and burros and a .22 rifle and RJR tobacco and tried to lead them through *Julius Caesar.*

It caused near mutiny. To begin with, part of the stuff was in poetry, and that was suspicious enough. Also, argued the seventh grade long and angrily, Shakespeare couldn't use the English language.

"Why don't he say what he means?" demanded Bully Edwards. "Spit it out."

"'Yon Cassius,'" snorted Harlan Kelly. "Why don't he say, 'Cassius over yander' like anybody would?"

JULIUS CAESAR lasted just about forever. It wasn't progressing very well either until Miss Walker, the teacher, played a sly card. The principal, she said, had heard of our project and had suggested we dramatize a few selected scenes from *Julius Caesar* for the school assembly.

This put a different light on the play. Nobody ever suspected Miss Walker of duplicity. Honor was now at stake. It was the seventh grade against the world, and if the school was to miss out on Shakespeare, it wasn't going to be the seventh grade's fault.

As a crew, we started rewriting Shakespeare, pointing him up, throwing in a few more "Beware the Ides of March" than he had called for and dropping Marc Antony altogether. Miss Walker started us memorizing lines at a furious rate, and the character who forgot took some coaching in words of Shakespearean pungency from the rest of the cast.

Right at the beginning, the seventh grade committed itself firmly to a modern dress production with no appearances in bed-sheet togas before the whole school.

"It would be ridiculous," declared Harlan Kelly, "just ridiculous."

THE details of the performance are dim now except that there were no props on the stage and no togas.

"Beware the Ides of March" was well received whenever it was shouted, and the audience got actually enthusiastic during the assassination scene. In the melee, Caesar got an accidental lick from a 2×2 doubling as broadsword. He let out a bawl and put on a furious fight for life until the rest of the cast subdued him before he could disgrace the performance.

As a whole, the audience seemed a little bewildered by the production, but it applauded.

So we laid Caesar's ghost to rest and got back to the ponies.

THE CASE OF THE MAUVE COLORED GARTER

IN January, 1971, the local school superintendent lost his fight to keep school kids from wearing armbands to protest the Viet Nam war, and I believe he made the tactical error of attacking the practice instead of the individual kid.

I have had some experience at this. Forty-odd years ago the high school principal out in West Texas roared at me, "Crume, get that girl's garter off your arm." I was wearing a mauve colored thing with black lace edgings.

"Sir," I replied, "how would you know this is a girl's garter?"

He sputtered for a minute and began to turn red. When he got mad he always turned very red and puffed up at the neck; and he was pretty puffed up at the moment.

"Upstairs to the office," he roared. When we were there, he took out the section of a tractor belt that he used on the big boys and laid it down in a sinister manner on the desk.

"Now," he said, "which girl did you take this garter off of?"

YOU note that he did not lay down the general principle that nobody could wear garters in school. All the girls would probably have lost their socks under that policy. He specifically attacked me for wearing a garter.

Also, he wasn't too worried about my wearing it. He wanted to know where I had got it. Since the boys and girls at every recess were herded to different sides of the school building, my acquiring a garter was some kind of coup.

I wasn't going to tell him. The fact was that the garter had come loose on Miss Haley, a pretty, young, and shy English teacher. It had dropped around her ankle in the hall. She was too prim and proper to reach down and replace the gadget. She had eased her foot out of a shoe, kicked the garter off to the floor, and walked away, all in her most dignified manner, unaware that she had been seen.

I had decided to wear the garter as an armband knowing that every time she saw it Miss Haley would cringe. This kind of cruelty to shy people was high humor in our set. Now that the garter was officially noticed, I wasn't going to tell on Miss Haley. She was a good sort, a gentle person. In the phrase of the day, she would have been mortified if she thought anybody actually knew about the garter.

The principal could whale away if he wanted to, and I knew from experience that he could whale.

LUCKILY, the women teachers had been conducting a massive investigation to find a girl with a missing garter. They couldn't. Every girl had at least two garters if she had any.

This left the principal without a leg to stand on and a mauve garter in his hand.

"All right," he said. "Get out of here. But don't wear this any more."

"Oh, that's all right, sir," I said. "You can have it if you want it."

He started turning red and bulging at the neck again.

I got out of there.

STANDING TALL AT SEVENTEEN

ONE of my Dallas friends is a thin man. He stands 6 feet and 2 inches but weighs 125 pounds. His wife has always bought boys' Size 20 T-shirts for him because they fit and they are twenty-five cents cheaper than men's Small. The other day the salesman at a Dallas store suggested they measure the Size 20 against the men's Small. "The Small might be the same width," he said, "but it might be longer." They carefully measured the two shirts and found the boy's shirt was an inch longer than the man's. It didn't seem reasonable even to the salesman. However, it may represent abstract truth.

It may indicate the steady erosion of self-esteem that a man experiences as he becomes more and more of a man.

I NEVER again stood as tall as the year when I was seventeen and was a senior in high school, nor did my classmates. We were suddenly as tall as men. Furthermore, we had it made. We had whipped the system. We could go around ordering the younger students about, offering them free advice, and passing judgments on their problems.

It was an intoxicating time, but we were generous people and never rubbed it in on inferior folks. We were capable of a lordly generosity toward the faculty people, who after all had to grub away at polishing our records, and toward our parents, who meant well but hardly had the intelligence to understand us.

The old men of the town made snide remarks about yearlings who thought they had become bulls, but we were lordly enough to overlook that. Obviously, the old men were envious.

Shortly after that, I entered a college and found I was dirt under everybody's feet. Nobody seemed to appreciate the magnanimity of my character or the extent of my ability, and one mere English instructor once accused me of committing a comma blunder.

It would have been the same if I had gone directly to work. I would have started as a copyboy, and it is hard to show everybody how superior you are if you can't begin at the top.

Over the years, it seems to me, I have steadily declined in relative importance.

THIS happens to most men after their senior year. They gradually lose stature. They work under an editor who doesn't have the sense to recognize genius. They approach a banker who demands that somebody else go on their note. They work under an admiral or an old gray captain who has a sarcastic opinion of a gifted ensign's ideas. They marry a wife who quickly shows that she hasn't bought the whole bill of sale, though she may be very happy with him, and his kids are always telling him that Bobby's father can throw a baseball farther than he can.

This is the reason clothing designers slowly let their customers sag toward the earth.

And at the end of a life, every man, no matter how big he has been, is reduced to size in the eyes of the universe.

FLESHING OUT THE AMERICAN STORY

You may be of an age when you suddenly realize that you have lived personally through about one-third of all the history of the United States of America, and I can tell you there is small profit in it. The demand for eyewitness consultants is very small.

FLESHING OUT THE AMERICAN STORY

FLESHING OUT THE AMERICAN STORY

YOU may be of an age when you suddenly realize that you have lived personally through about one-third of all the history of the United States of America, and I can tell you there is small profit in it. The demand for eyewitness consultants is very small.

The average man-of-the-street patriot is not interested in knowing what George Washington and Benjamin Franklin were doing two hundred years ago. Average patriot wants people to know what he is doing. He perhaps is building a red, white, and blue birdhouse with a Cape Cod roof in honor of the Bicentennial. He is not interested in those of us who settled and built this country back in the pioneer days before 1950.

When this Bicentennial thing started, I had in mind cashing in. I was going to bring out a book called "History of the World as I Have Known It." I could see chances at last of making my million if only inflation would keep growing. But when I talked to a young scholar of American history, he looked me up and down with some disdain and advised against it. "You will give historical research a bad name," he said.

He wouldn't even listen to how I almost saw Teddy Roosevelt and would have if the grown-ups hadn't all rushed up to the front of the crowd.

ACTUALLY, we old-timers who won the West have a lot to tell the youngsters. We could tell them, for instance, how to shoot an anvil, except that youngsters now don't seem to want to shoot an anvil. They want to take hostages.

We could inform them on the little details of pioneer life, such as striped madras shirts. We could educate them in the ways of old-time speech.

When a friend wanted you to speed up your Model T, for instance, he didn't yell, "Floorboard it." He said, "Pull her ears down," a reference to the gas and spark levers on either side of the steering column. When you cranked a Model T, you choked it by hooking your hand through a wire loop at the side of the radiator and jiggling — except that it wasn't called choking it. It was called goosing it. People seem uninterested in such matters. They want to know what went on in rumble seats, which is unimportant.

The same thing went on in the rumble seat as went on before and after the rumble seat.

OLD-TIMERS could flesh out the story of America by furnishing the little details about life in those hard times. They are about to be lost because there were no columnists or TV commentators at the time to record them.

The founding fathers did not believe in the public's right to know. They regarded newspapermen as lowlifes and would not talk to them. After all, they might print the story if you got drunk and started throwing dollars away across the Rappahannock River.

Also, many of the fine things of modern America came out of the trials and hardships of us noble pioneers. Our family doctor's Model T, for instance, was once hopelessly bogged down in the rut road where Terrapin Creek ran into Long in the Ozarks. While waiting there with nothing to do, the doctor suddenly had an idea.

"There ought to be a highway here," he thought.

Sure enough, there is a highway there now, though the bog has long since dried up.

DRENCHING A HORSE

A DENTIST was telling me the other day that one of the great hazards of his profession is the human tongue. Just when he had got everything fixed right, the tongue was likely to dart over involuntarily and get in front of the drill.

It brought to mind the ancient ritual of drenching a horse. This always happened about two o'clock on a frigid morning. A strange sound would come from the horse lot, a sound

which would awaken your dad out of a sound sleep and send him running out there in his long underwear.

"Old Sam is foundering," he would report on the run, and the household would go into emergency routine.

This meant that Old Sam had broken into the watering trough too soon after eating alfalfa or had broken into the cow barn and eaten too much bran.

EVERYBODY would get mad. Your dad was mad at Old Sam and also at your mother because she was slow in getting the fire started and fixing the melted lard and ginger that was the remedy. She was mad because the younger kids were underfoot. They usually gathered in a nearby corner and cried fearfully at the doom that was befalling the family. The small boys were mad because they had to help.

Here was this Shire or Belgian standing six inches higher at the withers than a tall man. Your dad snapped a rope to a halter and threw it over a rafter of the horse barn. If you were ten years old, you had to haul back and wrap yourself up in it to keep Old Sam's head in the air.

If you were seven or eight, you had to get up on another rafter and pull Old Sam's tongue down and to the side so that your dad could thrust the quart whiskey bottle full of hot lard down his gullet and drain it.

Old Sam's tongue was about the size of a collapsed football that wouldn't quite deflate. Also, it was very slick and hard to hold. If you dug your fingernails into it, Old Sam struggled and screamed through his nostrils.

The milk cows woke up and started mooing around. The rooster, thinking it was morning, began to crow. Dogs for half a mile around began to bark.

Neighbors began to show up asking anxiously whether anything was wrong.

This always angered your father, who explained patiently that he was only going through the usual routine of drenching a horse.

FINALLY, gastric rumblings would start inside the horse that sounded like distant thunder. The tongue-holder would be shooed out of the horse yard instantly. Your dad would give Old Sam about six hard kicks in the ribs. He would then shoo the halter rope-holder out of the yard, take over himself, and release Old Sam, who only respected your dad among all people.

"That Old Sam," your dad would say happily, "is quite a horse."

If dawn was breaking and you had to get ready for school pretty quick, you didn't think so.

A PLAINS BOY'S FEET

THE modern kid is spared one problem as he goes back to school this year. He does not have to reconcile his feet again to shoes.

Modern kids feel somehow naked without shoes. Years ago, on the high baldies of West Texas, barefoot time coincided roughly with the vacation from school. Reliable warmth came a little late out there, so not many scholars were tempted to take off their shoes before the first of May. Of course, some toughies who wished to demonstrate their independence of the principal would wade barefoot through snow in March.

Most parents, who had to compare doctor's bills with the price of leather, elected for May 1, however. After this, you were required as a kid only to wear shoes at Sunday school, and many of us cultivated broad feet during this period. If you could no longer get your feet in your winter shoes, common household thrift dictated that maybe you wouldn't be required to go to Sunday school and hear again about Little David and Goliath.

Appearing in Sunday school without shoes was not regarded as indecorous, but the ordinary boy's ham-sized feet usually had a granular dirty look. Mammas often thought that this look was not conducive to an air of godliness, much less saintliness. As a result, many of us were spared the ordeal.

Broad, unmitigatedly dirty-looking feet in those days often saved the fourteen-year-old boy from unwanted social obligations.

ALONG about the last two weeks of August, an active boy's feet could furnish him with material for profound philosophical thought. This would be the time of the summer when everything was dead. You ached for school to start and stir up something. Along in the afternoon, when it was still too early to cut the watermelons, you could lie back against the shady side of the cow shed and contemplate your feet.

Stevenson's mirror of damned reminders of past sins and follies never equaled a plains boy's feet. You could study them and see in the dirt and rust the reflection of a summer. The grass-burr sores did not count. Here was the scar where you had jumped out of Old Man Jones's cherry tree and landed on the hoe that he had negligently failed to turn down. Here was the enlarged big-toe joint which came from an ill-advised sally in tin-can shinny.

You could look upon your begrimed feet and see there the whole mirror of a fine summer.

WITH the coming of school, you had to get these gigantic pads back into shoes somehow. At that time, boys' shoes tended to be either brown or tan, and when you put them on, they were enormous. This was beside the fact that feet which have been allowed to roam free resent confinement.

You looked down at your newly shod feet and felt as if you were a toothpick standing in two pumpkin pies. You felt especially this way around girls. It is not true that boys are more conscious of girls now. It would be an impossibility. But boys then were a lot more self-conscious.

THE DANGERS OF LEAP YEAR

ONE of the advantages of being an old-timer is that you no longer have to dread Leap Year and February 29.

A man of fifty is hardly likely to be grabbed and forced into marriage by some impetuous female. At the age of twelve, however, Leap Year was a clear and worrisome danger until February was torn off the calendar. Even at twelve, you did not really believe that the girl next door was foolish enough to force matrimony on a guy who couldn't afford more than one ice cream soda a week.

However, we all knew that the law conferred special powers on girls on February 29, and that if a girl laid claim on you and could defend you against all her fellow girls, she owned you body and soul.

Bruz Peters once ran two miles trying to escape a skinny, stringy-haired little girl who had terrific stamina and a kind of long, loping stride that ate up the ground. As he was giving out, he whirled and faced her.

"April Fool," he shouted at her.

It wasn't, of course, but the gambit confused her enough that he escaped.

At age twelve, Leap Year's Day was a good time to play hookey and go off on a stag party.

VALENTINE'S Day used to be bad enough for the twelve-year-old boy. Usually, he was secretly smitten with a twelve-year-old charmer who sat with the other girls across the room. Great emotional affairs like this generally transmit themselves to their participants, even if the participants do lift their chins haughtily and stare in opposite directions.

For two weeks before Valentine's Day, the small boy worried that he wouldn't get a Valentine from his girl and worried that he would. He would be desolate if she overlooked him, but he was in danger, if she sent a Valentine and anybody ever found out about it, that he would lose his standing among his peers, all of whom professed much scorn for female entanglements.

He hoped, if she sent him a Valentine, that she would have the ordinary common sense to decorate it with a horse or a cow rather than a heart.

I remember one small girl who was adept at drawing ropes, horses, and cow horns on her Valentines. She kept twenty small boys on the string through two Valentine boxes.

I don't know what finally happened to her, but she deserved it. Jezebel!

WHEN a man was twelve, he believed that a girl waited to trap him behind every corner or bush. Luckily, our country was one of empty distance which afforded plenty of room for caution. By the time the twelve-year-old reached twenty, he had discovered that not as many girls were lying in wait for him behind bushes as he had hoped. A lot of young bachelors even planted shrubs.

This is the standard man-woman equation. Men and women of any age seldom are thinking about the same thing at any given moment. It is a good thing. It has probably prevented a number of devastating events all through history.

SUNDAY IN THE OLD DAYS

A DALLAS old-timer was discoursing a few days ago on the fun that people used to have on Sunday before pandemonium took over all human life.

It used to be, he said, that a family in good weather would get on the open-air trolley after church and take a ride "around the belt" at a nickel apiece. Or they might walk to the city cemetery and read the inscriptions on the tombstones. Some took a trolley that dead-ended at a place called Violet Hill.

"And violet picking was a pastime not easily forgotten," says my friend, raising a suspicion that there is more going on in his memory than meets the eye.

At any rate, he says, all these pleasant excursions invariably wound up at the neighborhood soda fountain for a lemon ice cream soda or a lemonade and the end of a perfect day.

And what, declares he with some show of indignation, do people do now on Sunday?

Well, people now do a lot on Sunday. At times, it seems, they mostly drown.

AT any rate, Sunday in the old days wasn't quite the idyll that my friend describes. At least, it wasn't in the small West Texas town where I grew up. Proper people might be found at home on Sunday afternoon fighting the effects of the big Sunday dinner and engaging in learned religious debates on the front porch with visiting friends and neighbors. Their dressed-up children would be miserably trying to while away the time with hide-and-seek in the yard.

But Sunday afternoon has always been a time of utter boredom for restless people, and the restless had their way of fighting ennui. You could go down to the piles of railroad ties beyond the depot and watch the big boys of the town hide behind the ties and shoot at each other with Roman candles. A big boy was any boy between sixteen and twenty-five who was unmarried. A married man of eighteen was an adult.

At other times, the restless would gather in a pasture near town, and everybody from ten to twenty-five would ride broncs. This was a jolly recreation, a welcome change from the riding of tamer horses all through the week. And if broncs were scarce, you could turn any horse into a bronc by looping a short rope around his body at the flanks and yanking it tight.

Or, you could go down to the Santa Fe work train on the siding by the stockyards and risk twenty-five cents in a monte game on one of the many blankets spread out beside the track.

IF you get right down to it, people are probably doing on Sunday afternoon just about what they always did.

Probably nobody has time to read tombstones anymore. With modern traffic, they are too busy making them. Also, bronc riding seems to lack the element of danger to interest the modern restless breed. They put on shorts or a bikini and climb on water skis.

Undoubtedly, thousands of people still have sedate and pleasant Sunday afternoons and stop for a lemonade.

But sedate people are sedate, and restless people are restless. It is probably best that the twain don't meet.

JUGGING BUMBLEBEES

AN old Hopkins County boy has asked whether I ever engaged in the sport of jugging bumblebees.

Certainly, I have jugged bumblebees, though it is not my favorite form of bumblebee hunting. I have jugged them with tight jugs and loose jugs. In jugging bumblebees, of course, you will fill a jug about half full of water and set it down next to a bumblebee nest. Then you stir up the nest with a stick, and run. Run for your life.

The bumblebees come out in an angry swarm. The theory is that they all identify the jug as the offending object, dive into it, and are drowned.

I can tell you from experience, though, that not all the bumblebees are fooled by the jug every time.

AS I was saying, this is not the kind of bumblebee hunting preferred by us active types. It is too much like sitting in a heated stand and waiting for a deer to walk by so you can shoot him. It is too much like trapping sparrows by standing inside the window and pulling the trip string on a dishpan deadfall.

We active sportsman types prefer to get right out there with the sparrow, or snowbird, as he is properly called, and sprinkle some salt on his tail and catch him.

When deer hunting, we prefer to go out and lasso the deer and bring him up to the stand to be shot.

After all, sport is sport.

The active bumblebee hunter, the bumblebee stalker as opposed to the bumblebee still hunter, goes forth equipped only with a fairly wide wooden paddle of a heft that swings easily to him. He had best also go equipped with six or eight companions fully paddled, because this is dangerous sport.

When you stir up the bumblebee nest with a stick, you run as is normal for the average sensible person.

HOWEVER, you do not run too far because the swarm of bees is gaining on you. At the proper moment, you whirl and start work with the paddle, hoping that each swing has increased your bumblebee bag by one. If it hasn't, you will know it. Six or eight lively boys swinging paddles can almost hold their own, but it is best to allow some ground for a slow retreat while fighting.

Inevitably, you don't get them all, and you pay for it. But after the tears are dried and the stings have been plastered with good clean mud, you know that you have had a wonderful time.

Anyway, beestings are good for the rheumatism.

Because of my active bumblebee hunting as

a boy, I didn't have a single rheumatism attack before I was twenty-one.

GETTING IN THE HAY

ALIBIS, alibis, that's all we ever get. Now they are saying that the farmers can't get in the hay crop because there is no baling wire. My lord. West Texas is full of baling wire. You can find old unused wooden windmill towers which are wound around with baling wire. The trouble is that the hay farmers want nice shiny new baling wire, and they may not ever get it again.

Anyhow, whatever happened to the old hay barn? There would come a haying time when I was a boy when the weather would be so dry that the contracting shingles on the barn would start popping out the nails. All human beings would be sitting in the shade panting. The rooster, having delivered a crow from the fence, would have fallen off and be lumped up in a coma by a post.

The stock tank would be losing water to the sun at about an inch a minute. My dad would study this and look at his watch.

"This proves," he would say, "that there is going to be rain. Everybody out and get in the hay."

Everybody meant everybody, men, women, and children. It also meant any neighbor who was willing to swap work and anybody's guests in the neighborhood.

Guests were especially valuable because you didn't have to trade back work with them.

THE hay, when it hadn't been baled, would have been raked into long windrows along which the wagons could drive. The women and children and guests would heave this up with pitchforks into the wagons. The men would stay in the wagons and tramp down the hay, they being the only experts at this.

They would sing a lot as they stamped, but the rest of us didn't have breath enough to sing. We were being constantly reminded under that brassy sun that the rain was about to ruin the hay.

Sure enough, just as we had thrown up the last fork in late afternoon, a black cloud would boil up over the hill, and a bolt of lightning would explode on the meadow.

The men would start tramping harder and exhorting us to save the hay.

ALL the women and children would find purchase places and push while the horses heaved to get the haywagon to the barn. A few drops of rain would start horses, women, and children at work on the double while the men called down advice.

Just in time, we would shove the loaded haywagon inside the big runway of the barn. The rain would start to pour. The thunder would rattle the boards. Everybody would set up a cheer because the hay had been saved.

"That is the way to get in the hay," my dad would say.

During haying season, the women always kept great quantities of lemonade and cake on hand. They would break out the reserve supplies. Everybody would feast. The men, though, would go to the back of the barn where there was a crockery jug with a corncob cork which was supposed to hold a remedy for bog spavin. They would drink out of this and feel better by the minute.

They were just being gallant, of course, and allowing the women and children their fill of the lemonade.

"WARSHING" THE CLOTHES

WHEN the final history of our sad era is written, the judgment may well be that the worst polluting agent of our time was not the auto but the automatic washing machine. The downfall of mankind, if anybody is left to record it, may date from the time that man decided he was supposed to be clean.

Anybody who was a small boy fifty or sixty years ago can remember when people concentrated all their attention on cleanliness on the area behind the ears. If you were clean behind the ears, you had attained the necessary social status in school. You could be as dirty as you liked elsewhere, and small boys have an affinity with dirt. They feel more comfortable if they are dirty.

A man was responsible then for his own pollution. He kept it with him. The reason was that washing things then involved a great deal of labor which nobody liked. The streams were pure and drinkable and the human being was a real individual with his own smell.

He didn't get rid of his smell on other people downstream. He liked it.

WASHING clothes in the old days was a major task which involved the work of half a dozen women for a whole day, and they utilized whatever child labor they could coerce.

"Punch the clothes," the adults were always telling you. Here, right in the middle of tops season or maybe marble season, you were handed a large stick and put to work on the black iron kettle in the back yard where the clothes were boiling. The steam from the boiling water always caused huge blubbers of broadcloth and chintz to inflate above the boiling, soapy water. "Punch the clothes," you were told, and you had to punch and keep the clothes underwater.

Afterward, you carried boiling water from another pot to the washtubs, and the women hand-scrubbed the clothes on brass washboards. "Wrench the clothes," they would order later, and you would have to transfer the scrubbed-down clothes to a tub or a kettle of hot, clear water.

"Warshing" the clothes at that time was heavy work on everybody, and no reasonable person wanted to do the work very often.

As a result, people then invented ingenious devices such as the celluloid collar, which could be wiped clean with a wet handkerchief. A man could wear the same shirt for a week.

WHEN it was hard to wash clothes, a human being didn't dump his pollution lightly into the sewers. Mostly, decent people held that a working man ought to change his overalls once a week. Some very sissy people held that you ought to change your long underwear at least once a week, but people who have ever had to live in the cold and the rain know better.

Every time we have a war, the experts discover that the human body secretes oil which, stored up in clothing, helps to protect the human animal against the elements.

The automatic, electric washer is the demoniac influence which has ruined man's environment and diverted man from his normally happy, dirty existence.

We need a lot less warshing and wrenching.

SMELLING LIKE A MAN

A COMPANY which manufactures an aftershave lotion has been plugging an ad that makes fun of the sissy perfumes which are being foisted off on men these days. In the ad, a suspicious-looking character bellows, "A man wants to smell like a man."

The company had better hope not. If its idea catches on, the market may vanish for all kinds of stink waters.

There are those of us still alive who remember what a man smelled like before people acquired civilized noses. His smell was an amalgam varying with the individual. His smell might be a mixture of the smell of Bull Durham tobacco, the camphor from the horse liniment with which he was treating his cold bum shoulder, some hint of last winter's mustard plaster, the sharp blue smell of the last shotgun shell he had exploded, and, of course, the smells of his trade.

Old-time natural man did not have to run to the bathroom every hour and smell himself to find out whether he needed more nard and attar of roses. The old-timer had no body odor. The sun and the wind had encased him in a kind of olfactory enamel and had cleaned away the excretory smells which keep a city man from smelling like a man.

Modern city man's skin is seldom exposed to the cleansing effect of fresh air. As a result, he smells like something not quite dead and has to hide it.

IN the old days you didn't have to be Sherlock Holmes to deduce what a man's occupation was. You could smell it out in an instant. Our town blacksmith was always surrounded by a faint pungent hint of coke smoke and occasionally by the funny, edgy smell of heated steel. The barber smelled of bay rum. The introduction of bay rum as an aftershave may have been the beginning of the decline in man's innocence.

Mr. Snyder, the grocer, always smelled of the latest merchandise that had been unloaded. He smelled best when it was bananas. Mr. Cansler, who ran the livery, had an indescribable aroma.

In our town, only the town banker and the undertaker had no smells, which was only fair. They were already working under professional handicaps.

Skunk Williams, who made his living in the winter by trapping polecats, was a slight exception to the rule. He did not have an aroma. He stank. His occupation was an honorable one, though, and nobody looked on Skunk with disrespect. They just respected him from a distance.

Sometimes you could trace a man's recent activities by his smell. You could always tell when he had been at the saloon.

A MAN'S smell used to be so individual that his wife could be working in the kitchen a block away when he arrived at the barn, and she would say, "George is here."

Nowadays, George's smell is pallid. If he didn't bathe himself in loud-smelling perfume, his wife wouldn't even bother to notice his presence except on payday. We need to get back to fundamental smells, the kind that flesh is heir to. Let us leave the witch hazel and the rose water to the girls. Before altering the balance of nature's odors, always ask yourself, "What would Ralph Waldo Emerson have thought of this?"

THE DEGENERATION OF STORE WINDOW ADVERTISING

ON the whole, you would have to say that store window advertising has degenerated in the last twenty-five or thirty years. The merchants seem to think that the customers wish to see merchandise. Actually, the customer knows that the store has merchandise already. He wants to see something he might not have to buy.

The modern store window usually contains only a bunch of lifelike women dummies all decked out in a lot of fashionable clothes. The average man, when he looks at a window like this, is apt to let his attention stray to some real girl nearby who is considerably less adequately dressed. The stares which these dummy women all wear do not impress the average man, as women have stared at him this way before.

A store window ought to contain something to peg down a man's interest. One of the better windows of our West Texas boyhood was in the town drugstore. Those were Prohibition days. The window merely contained dozens of bottles of Virginia Dare tonic with a penciled sign which read: "Although This Tastes Like Wine and Acts on You Like Wine, It Is Not Wine."

Doc Curry, the druggist, said he liked to display Virginia Dare in the window because it didn't stay around and collect dust.

AS a general all-around attention-getter for show windows, probably nothing has ever quite matched Tanglefoot flypaper. The Plains grocery had a whole window full of it and nothing else. People would stand around it by the hour counting the flies and trying to decide whether there was any new catch.

Even in the winter months when flies were no problem the Plains management kept the display in the window. It would work just as good the next spring as a new batch of paper, and besides it showed that the store was sanitary.

Only the window at Mr. Craig's real estate office ever rivaled the Plains window. Mr. Craig occupied the front quarter of an old building that had an enormous plate glass window. Since he had no use for the window, Mr. Craig let the agriculture students put in the county agricultural exhibit they had collected after the State Fair had done with it. In addition to the canned garden truck, ear corn, and needlework, it included several shocks of maize and kafir.

After the first few weeks, a family of mice took up residence in the shocks, and half the town used to gang up in front of the window to watch the mice work away at their trade.

It is hard to remember whether Mr. Craig finally took out the display or whether it burned up in the fire.

DMITTEDLY, in comparison with these windows, the modern big city store works under a handicap. It would be hard to find enough flies in any of them to make a decent Tanglefoot display.

They ought to be able to do better than they do, though. Some of us suspect that merchandising nowadays has run afoul of the modern fetish of cleanliness, a highly overrated virtue. Cleanliness is supposed to be next to godliness, but anybody who has studied the subject knows that people, as they have become cleaner, have also become a lot more worldly.

THE OLD SYSTEM OF TELEPHONY

A FRIEND of mine recently tried to dial me from Fort Worth, a distance of thirty (three, oh, that is) miles. Under today's system where every man is his own long-distance operator, he found that he was having to memorize and dial 12,147,474,611, which is hard even for a mind accustomed to readying the modern income tax return.

Then, he had to ask for extension 397.

It was having to remember this last number, he says, that finished him. His overtaxed mind rebelled. It is easier arithmetically to walk from Fort Worth to Dallas than it is to telephone, he says. He longs for the good old days when the drugstore in his hometown had the number of 22.

In the old days in Lariat, we had things even better. True, the Fox Drug Store had a telephone number of 3, but high-handed callers like Judge McGill, a peppery lawyer, would simply lift the receiver and say, "Operator, get me the Fox."

After he had talked a minute or two, the judge would always say to the operator, "Dammit, Louella, get off the line."

IT was this kind of direct, down-to-earth communication with the telephone that made the industry what it is today, and it is high time that the telephone people got their numbers back to two-digit figures instead of confusing them with light years. After all, Alexander Graham Bell barely thought up the telephone, much less trying to think in nine-digit numbers.

Doubtless it will do no good to object. The telephone company has thousands of scientists who have already thought up the answers to all my objections, probably. Still, there is a valid objection which they have not answered because I haven't made up my mind what it is yet; I just object.

Maybe the phone company thinks it is saving money on long-distance operators. Probably it is, but it is also losing money on directories. In the old days, the phone directory did not attempt to compete with the Sears catalog, a mistake because Sears has more interesting material. Our directory, for instance, was a simple 8×10 placard with names on both sides. If a number changed, you did not reprint the directory. People were expected to change it with a pencil.

Some of these directories became priceless and illegible heirlooms before they were retired, their owners having long before learned to pick up the phone and ask some eavesdropper how to make a call.

THE old system of telephony had other advantages, too. Nowadays, there is a concerted effort everywhere to make the customer do as much of the work on everything as possible. The philosophy then was different. People like Judge McGill did not need to keep a record of their important calls. If they needed to remember what they had said, Louella, our operator, would chime in and tell them.

It made for a cozy, intimate community. The telephone then was indeed a marvel of progress, not a necessary irritant.

Somehow, I doubt that the modern system is ever going to work entirely right. Some of us are geniuses and can add forty-three and seventeen in our heads, but people generally are going to fail area codes just like they failed arithmetic.

HOT NIGHTS AND FAMILY HISTORY

THE present heat wave has uncovered some defects in modern education as well as some weaknesses in the modern degenerate character. All people know to do about the heat now is stay in air conditioning, which is the worst thing in the world you can do unless you want to be comfortable.

To beat the heat really you have to meet it face to face and eyeball it down. Our ancestors, who were always singing, "If it was good for Paul and Silas, it's good enough for me," knew how to do this. They had various tricks to outwit the sultry antagonist. When I first came to Dallas, for instance, and lived in a rickety apartment on Ross, you made your hot weather bed on a hard mattress with a single tightly drawn sheet.

You directed on this mattress a fan. If you were rich, you owned something called an oscillating fan, but we didn't. You wet and wrung out a couple of large towels, spread them over you under the fan, and settled down,

being careful to sleep spread-armed and spraddle-legged so that no part of you would impart its heat to another part. After a night of this, you woke up with a wonderful feeling of having been purged of everything, especially energy.

Air conditioning robs the ordinary sleeper of the chance of participating in nature.

AIR conditioning, I believe, is also responsible for destroying family history as it used to exist.

Family history used to be kept by word of mouth. On a farm in those days, the hot weather bed was a pallet, a single quilt spread for each sleeper on the big front porch that ran the length of the house. When it was still too hot to sleep, which was anytime before 2:00 A.M., the elders lay there and discussed what had happened to the family. They went into elaborate analyses of motives. What made Cousin Clint quit his wife and move with the children to the remote wildernesses of Mineral Wells? What made Aunt Crecy a witch, though a benevolent one bent mostly on curing erysipelas?

The recurring quotation was, "Nobody will ever know why he done what he did."

Along about dawn, when you could have expected to sleep, you were roused out to get to work. Nobody was worried about the effects of heat on human beings, but working in the full of the day might be hard on the horses.

As a result of these nighttime seminars, I learned very early that there were few saints in our family.

ACTUALLY, I do not remember as much of the family history as I might have if I had slept on more pallets. I learned a lot about my uncles that I was too chicken to use against them. Mostly I remember incidents.

There was the time when Uncle Uriah, a pillar of the Baptist church, was mad because the minister, a man contemptibly soft of hands, had asked him to call his go-devil a plowing sled. The preacher thought the correct name smacked of strong language.

"I told him," said Uncle Uriah from the pallet that night, "that no matter what you call it, it's still a go-devil."

And air conditioning or not, heat is still heat.

THE UNIQUE HORN

THE big town has no excitement to match that generated in a small West Texas town a generation ago when a railroad locomotive killed one of the town cows.

The townspeople generally regarded this as an attack by a heartless corporation on the citizenry of the town. When a cow was killed, nearly everybody knocked off business at the store or ice plant and went down to view the ground and to offer sympathy to the cow's owners. Almost everybody offered the opinion that the engineers were getting awfully careless in the way they were throwing their locomotives about in the city limits.

The Santa Fe had a bunch of old foxes on its legal staff, all right. They seldom let a cow damage case come to trial, knowing that any jury which could sit on the case was already convinced that the Santa Fe had plenty of money and might as well share some with their neighbors and fellow citizens.

Had it not been for this Santa Fe habit, you would have had proof in the court records that the most valuable cows ever bred in the world were the ones killed by the Santa Fe.

NEARLY every cow that was killed turned out to have five or six ragged, near-orphan children utterly dependent on her milk, and to have a mysterious pedigree that could not be replaced.

Tom Moore, the school janitor in our town, had a cow, a mean, rawboned, black-and-white bossy with a right horn that curved downward and pointed into her right eye. One day the cow became irritated at a passing locomotive and charged the intruder head-on.

The locomotive not only killed her but destroyed the unique horn.

The horn became important in the legal dickering with the railroad over the next few months. Mr. Moore had paid $25 for the cow and secretly valued her at $50 because he considered himself a sharp trader, but he sued the railroad for $150. The lawyer who handled the cow cases in the town went further in his correspondence with the railroad than stressing the deprivation which had come to a fine West Texas family. He pointed out that it was nigh impossible to find a cow with the deceased's unique horn structure.

Mr. Moore became so impressed with the arguments that he wished he had sued for $300.

"The more I think about her," he said of the cow, "the more valuable she gets."

Tuffy Landrum advised Mr. Moore to stick to his demands on the railroad because the company had it in for small towns. "If this had happened in Amarillo," said Tuffy, "they would have paid off plenty."

IN time, the railroad sent down a lawyer, a fancy city fellow with an expensive celluloid collar and an elk's tooth watch chain, to talk with the local cow lawyer. Mr. Moore had the habit of breaking into tears when anybody mentioned the word *mother,* and the cow lawyer took occasion to mention the mother of Mr. Moore's children often, while Mr. Moore was present.

The railroad lawyer squirmed in his chair and finally halfheartedly offered to settle for $50. The cow lawyer privately advised Mr. Moore later to take it because these sharp lawyers had ways of cheating honest folk.

The unique horn, though, was lost to the world forever.

THE HEARTY "A-MEN"

I WENT to church one day not long ago and discovered that while I have been away they have changed the pronunciation of "amen."

It is no longer pronounced "A-men!" with a heavy emphasis on the "A" and a kind of jubilant whip to the "men." That was the way it was when ladies went to church in starched calico and their best sunbonnet. Now that the ladies have nearly all acquired a string of cultured pearls and a silk dress, people pronounce it "ah-men," very softly and without any exclamation marks.

Obviously, this new pronunciation is a product of the effete East which was always too cowardly and flabby to go West and break out some new ground, shoot a Comanche, or meet a hard *a* face to face.

For all I know, the pronunciation may have been framed up by that diabolical crowd which we used to call "the crowned heads of Europe."

THE suspicion is that while watering down "amen," the church has also watered down religion somewhat and almost banked the fires of hell. In my childhood, it was different. Religion hung over your head from dawn to night. On many a lonely prairie farm, God was the only outsider that the family got to talk to for days on end. The average man, whether he admitted it or not, knew that he had one foot in hell already and that it would take an awful lot of praying to keep him from teetering as he skirted the rim of the brimstone lake.

A Mr. Gilly of our town, who ran an excellent small dry-goods store in the few intervals that he wasn't drinking, once summed it up.

"If there is any justice at all in the hereafter, I know I am going to hell," he said. "But I am hoping for mercy instead of justice."

Few people were as candid as Mr. Gilly, who always gave generously to the First Baptist Church in our town. It was also the only Baptist church. He regarded himself as unworthy to say, "Amen."

I AM by way of being an expert on the old-time pronunciation of "A-men!" My Great-Aunt Martha, although she didn't invent the phrase, undoubtedly carried it to greater lengths than anybody else.

She was one of the self-appointed claque who were to yell a hearty "A-men" after every sentence of a sermon. These built up into a kind of rhythm, like a college cheer, until they had a manic crowd effect. People would stalk up to the front and shout out their sins tearfully for everybody to enjoy.

I was almost "convicted" of my sins once or twice, but I wisely held back. After all, for my most recent sins, I would have got a whipping if I had admitted them.

A PROPER RELIGIOUS REVIVAL

ONE reason that the world is going to the hot place in a handbasket may be that nobody knows how to run a proper religious revival anymore. True, Billy Graham can call fifty thousand people into the Cotton Bowl, but a sinner in a hurry to get to the mourner's bench has to leap over the stadium rail. By the time he gets to the mourner's bench he is too breathless to mourn, let alone confess his sins to the multitude.

These confessions were what made the old-time West Texas revival go. A confession was good for the soul of the sinner and also interesting to his neighbors.

In retrospect, it seems that those old-timers were holding back some. Usually they confessed to drinking bootleg whiskey and playing cards. Everybody knew they had done more than that, but this was enough to remind the town that Satan was in our midst and that the sirens of temptation lurked behind every unripened tumbleweed.

These meetings were not called revivals. They were called protracted meetings, and they were protracted enough to flagellate the community.

THESE meetings were held after the crops were laid by and the harvest had not started. It was a short period of time when people had leisure for the higher things.

Every church had its own revival, but they were staggered so that the members of all churches could attend. It was a good way to keep up with sin in the town and would also be the only entertainment until the yearly visit of Harley Sadler's tent show.

The sinner at these meetings was supposed to repent, confess his sins aloud, and be convicted. Sometimes people were convicted in more than one church.

Poke Wilson, a harmless drunk, was convicted at nearly every meeting. Nobody objected because he was in need of it. He also could spin a convincing confession. His trip to the mourner's bench often started others, and Poke generally was sober a day or two after each conviction.

The most shocking confession of our time was made by Clyde Carter, a big, genial lout of a boy, who broke down and admitted that he had once visited a dance hall while in Amarillo buying a tractor part.

Some suspected that old Clyde was putting the people on and playing to the audience.

OUR churches usually brought in evangelists from Cookson Hills or South Austin or some other place close enough to hell so that the minister knew brimstone when he smelled it in a small town.

The minister had to have a loud voice, loud enough to be heard by the people listening on their front porches within a quarter of a mile. He had to be able to deliver two three-hour sermons daily and an extra one on Sunday morning. He had to lead the singing and baptize the converts.

Uplift, that was his job.

WITCH'S SABBATH IN BOVINA, TEXAS

IT seems that witches are coming back into fashion after a couple of hundred years. So, if you see a well-dressed young woman walking through the downtown and carrying a broom, think nothing of it. She is merely taking care of her transportation.

The prevalence of witches right now, however, raises the question of whether we the public are getting authentic witches. Anybody can claim to be a witch and carry a broom. She cannot necessarily take the hair of an enemy and rub it against her pet cat and send him to his grave. Probably, Ralph Nader should start an investigation to find out whether the consuming public is getting the best quality witch for its money. There are some very inferior witches who loaf on the job half the time.

Luckily, the ordinary householder can test his witch if he likes. All he has to do is truss up the witch from shoulder to ankles and throw her in the swimming pool. If she floats, she is a witch. If she sinks, you may as well walk off and forget her; you don't have a witch of value at all.

I learned all this from a close study of Matthew Hopkins, a great English witch-hunter of the sixteenth century, who executed all his witches on the basis of this evidence.

Later, people gave him the same kind of bound-up trial, and he floated, and they chopped off his head for being a sorcerer.

AS a child, I actually had very small experience with witches. Getting caught by your dad was bad enough.

As a teen-ager, I believe I once observed one witch's coven. It was called Barney's Dance Hall and Soda Pop and was located several miles outside Bovina, Texas, where it wouldn't disturb the town's morning prayer.

It was a long, unfinished hall, the studs still bare to the sight, with a three-man bandstand at one end and an office and ticket-taking structure at the other. Here a kind of Witch's Sabbath was held every day of the week except on the Sabbath, which was a closed down day in our county. People cavorted around in unrestrained orgies of the fox-trot and ducked out occasionally to sample hell's brew out of a fruit jar with one of Barney's pops as a chaser.

It was a witch's Sabbath, all right, according to the dictates of Bovina, Texas.

AS early teen-agers, we were not permitted to join the witches and the warlocks on the floor, but a rude stair led up over Barney's office to a small balcony from which you could watch.

This was for free except that Barney charged you an outrageous price for a pop before you could go up. He charged a dime a bottle for Cokes.

When I look back at it, I think Barney's place was a coven. Covens are supposed to be run over by snakes and hellhounds. There were plenty of snakes around Barney's place. When a booted man went out to get some hell's brew, he would often kick a rattler away from his feet.

Barney also had a three-legged wolfhound, who was probably a hellhound, though he traveled incognito on a pallet outside Barney's office.

As for Barney, he was thin, knotheaded, and equipped with a thin white goatee. He might have been The Goat.

MULES AND OTHER ANTIQUES

Back when the mule was great in America, food was so cheap that beer taverns gave the food away free…
I have made a scientific graph of this, one line showing the number of mules and the other showing the food supply. The two lines go off in all directions, and only when the mule line and the food line are together has America been happy.

MULES AND OTHER ANTIQUES

THE TEN-GALLON HAT

A LONGVIEW man says that he is a Kentuckian but has been visiting in Texas for about twenty years.

"I figure that is enough time to form an opinion about a matter that bothers me a lot," he adds. "It is the cost of those ten-gallon hats that Texans wear.

"A lot of Bowling Green citizens will back me up when I say that those ten-gallon hats only cost three gallons back home." Three gallons of what Kentuckians usually swap for something might be a pretty fair price at that.

It is doubtful, however, that anybody in a short twenty-year visit has actually seen a real ten-gallon hat. A lot of things connected with modern living such as the cramped interior of Cadillacs and the width of the ordinary city door have tended to reduce the acreage of the Texas hat.

The modern ten-gallon hat probably won't hold over six or seven gallons at the most.

THE old-time ten-gallon hat was a thing of majesty. For years the ten-gallon had what was the most imposing edifice on the plains. It was high-crowned, and the old-timer usually wore it without creasing. The brim was larger than a lot of California ranches and it tended to curl up at the edges.

The old-timer wore this hat squared away even on his head or perhaps tilted backward a little. He would no more think of tilting it to one side than he would have allowed his picture to be made while he was smiling. Tilting the hat to the side of the head was indicative of a smart-alecky nature. It signified the kind of feller who would probably waste his time playing dominoes.

And when the old-timer acquired a hat, he wore it. It was the last thing he took off at night, and when he got up in the morning in his long-handled drawers, he reached first for his hat and put it on and then continued dressing.

It was regarded as immodest to go unhatted even in the company of other men.

THE real ten-gallon hat was worth however many gallons it cost. It was not only shade and shelter to the owner; it was one of his most useful tools. It could be used, for instance, as a water dipper. The old-timer didn't eat out of his hat, but he fed his horse from it on occasions. The ten-gallon hat could be used to fan the blacksmith's fire when the bellows was broken, or to shoo off a stray herd of buffalo.

A man's hat in those days was his castle, not a mere frill to hide his bald spot.

THE PRINCE ALBERT TIN

PROGRESS nearly always throws the cart away before the horse and then has to haul the horse around in an auto trailer.

A friend has reported another of those times when progress has outguessed itself. He has learned that the fine old red Prince Albert tobacco tin is going to be replaced by a squashy, slimy-feeling plastic pouch. Like all right-thinking men, my friend deplores this sacrifice of the real to the phony.

"I remember," he said almost in a wail, "as a child seeing my father, an inveterate hunter, trade a bright red Prince Albert tin to a tribal chief in the Indian territory for the exclusive hunting rights on his property — after having failed several times to buy the privilege for money.

". . . There are no longer any unsophisticated redskins around to trade with, but if there were, I dare say their reaction to a plastic tobacco pouch would be, 'Ugh!'"

You're darn right, it would. Those Indians know when they're getting gypped.

AS I think of the disappearance of the Prince Albert can, I realize more and more that an era has ended, an era when great commercial companies liked to provide their customers with more than the provender of trade. Prince Albert tobacco was as good as any and as abundant for the price, for instance, but in addition, PA gave you this wonderful metal cask.

If you were a boy, it was invaluable. It was perfect, for instance, for transporting tarantulas from their native hole in the ground to the top drawer of the teacher's desk. Tarantulas arrived whole and fearsome. You can imagine the general state of a tarantula who has been imprisoned in a hip-pocket plastic pouch for half a day.

The Prince Albert tin made a fine vault for those most precious of marbles, the aggies. They fit about right into it and could be kept separate from such plebeian marbles as crockies and steelies, which were normally kept in a one-pound sugar sack that had been modified by the addition of a drawstring at the mouth.

The Prince Albert tin was good for just about anything. If you ran onto some high-quality earthworms, you could drop them into it and carry them in your pocket. They wouldn't bother you at all, and the odor wouldn't be noticeable for a couple of days.

To many people, the Prince Albert tin has been a waterproof matchbox, a first-aid kit, or a secret receptacle for old olive pits.

THE Prince Albert tin was especially suited to hiding things. Many a young man in the old days entrusted to it all his treasure, his best marbles, his private half-dollar, the note from the girl in the next desk that he wouldn't have anybody see for the world, and perhaps his horned frog. All these he would bury in the Prince Albert tin. It always held up. If he was sneaking his dad's Camels to smoke, he probably hid them in a Prince Albert tin under the corner of the feed bin.

With the Prince Albert tin gone, the world is probably going to be a lot more candid and a lot less worthwhile.

A PROPER FIREPLACE

A FRIEND complained recently that his fireplace wouldn't burn wood unless the gas jet under the wood was lit. I told him his fireplace didn't draw, and he didn't know what that meant. It indicates the low estate into which the fireplace has fallen since it became merely a status symbol or, at best, a vestigial remnant of something that was good far away and long ago.

In the old days, it was well known that no man could build a proper fireplace who didn't have a little witchcraft in him. He had to have an instinct for where to locate the ledge in the back wall of the fireplace relative to the ledge in front so that a maximum of draft and a minimum of heat went up the flue.

A properly built fireplace would never belch smoke out into your room and would provide at least a little heat.

The modern fireplace setter usually has an automatic furnace and doesn't care about his fireplace, but the old-time fireplace owner cared about the heat, usually too much or too little.

THE old-time fireplace was a tool and not a decoration. To begin with, it was comparatively enormous, and it had no fire

screens. Protection to the floors against snapping embers was provided by whatever human flesh came in contact with them and by an enormous stone hearth.

The modern fireplace has a kind of basket arrangement into which you put such sticks as you wish to burn. The andirons in the old-time fireplaces had no back end to them. The fire was backed up by a great backlog, a log which usually required a couple of half-men to carry. It was placed in the back of the fireplace and smoldered there for two or three days while the smaller logs burned in front of it. Since most old houses had at least two fireplaces, the paterfamilias had to hop it to keep them supplied with wood.

Once started in the frosty fall, the fire was never allowed to die, though at night it was banked to save stoking chores. The ashes in the fireplace were raked up above the embers to preserve them live against the new day's fire.

About once a week you collected the ashes and put them in the ash hopper behind the smokehouse. Rain soaking down through the ashes would eventually emerge in the trough below as liquid lye, useful in making soap.

It was a hard life but cheap. Wood, water, and air then were free to everybody. Two of them aren't now, and the other is getting a little scarce.

SOME expert someday should bring out a book on fireplace cookery. It was all done in cast-iron utensils. The iron teakettle usually sat on a pad of coals at the side of the hearth. The frying pan might occupy another pad. The baking went on in an iron dutch oven heaped with coals. Cornbread baked this way had a cakelike quality, and no good crackling bread has been baked any other way.

In the great iron pot on the crane, beans or blackeyed peas would simmer and simmer until each bean became a thick puree in a hull.

This, of course, was living hard, but in those days we had a favorable balance of payments.

ASAFETIDA

THERE has been a lot of interest in asafetida lately. We are told that nobody now knows what it is or what to do with it.

A generation ago a lot of kids didn't know what to do with it either, but they wore it in small sachets hung around their necks by their mothers. It was supposed to ward off diseases. It warded off quite a bit of things. The theory was that asafetida smelled so bad that if the germs couldn't go somewhere else, they wished they could.

The kids who wore these bags all grew up loners. They felt all their lives that they were not wanted and that humanity generally was turning up its noses at them.

One old-timer dictionarist noted that asafetida has a "powerful and persistent alliaceous odor," which shows how bad it is.

ASAFETIDA, the substance, is a gum resin made of the sap of a plant called Ferula Asafetida. Actually, there are half a dozen such plants. They say the most popular for asafetida is called Ferula Fetida, which gives you a good idea of what it is since "fetid" means "stinking."

These plants grow in Asia in such places as Iran, Turkestan, and Afghanistan. They belong to the same general family as carrots, parsnips, parsley, caraway, and anise. Queen Anne's lace is in the family. Mostly, they have bushy leaves and a thick root.

The producers of asafetida whack the leaves off the root. While it is still growing, they cut the root off close to the ground. They then cover up the root with leaves and let it steam in its own juices, so to speak. After about a month, they cut a slice off it, and the thick juice bleeds out of the cut surfaces. This juice is then condensed into asafetida.

When it is processed, the wily Asians sell the stuff to some gullible sucker like the American Mother of the Year.

Evidently, the Russians by now have taken over just about all the production centers of asafetida, which leaves us smelling more like a rose than we usually do in diplomacy.

I HAVE had no personal experience with asafetida. My family leaned instead to the mustard plaster school of advanced family medicine. We preferred to hurt rather than stink.

Asafetida is not used much anymore, though the authorities say that it is a useful stimulant to the sympathetic nervous system, an excellent palliative for those who belch too much and are given to stomach gripe, and an effective drug for settling down those who shake with the screaming meemies. It is apparently just as effective at keeping people at a distance as the best of the modern men's colognes.

In India, they say, people esteem the drug as a seasoning for food.

As the Latin teacher used to remind us every day, there is no disputing about taste.

FLOUR-SACK PETTICOATS

THE TV was on, and one of those peerless commercial announcers was asking what was the world's most popular brand of underwear.

"Bewley's Best," shouted a Dallas old-timer immediately.

His companion, he says, at almost the same time, yelled, "Pride of Ardmore." He came to Dallas in the early 1920s from Malone down in Hill County and she came from a farm near San Angelo.

It would be interesting to trace why each had a different brand on their flour-sack drawers. It might indicate a trend in some poll.

"I remember," says the old-timer, "when a bunch of boys would peel off and dive in the blue hole on the creek, the ones wearing them would get quite a ribbing."

The old-timer and his companion must have been sophisticated and affluent. In our part of the country, good cotton cloth from flour sacks was deemed too valuable to waste on small boys. Small boys were not supposed to need any underwear. They were supposed to keep their nakedness covered, and if they did, who would know whether they had any underwear or not?

A small boy was supposed to sleep in his shirt, and he was supposed to get under the covers before anybody glimpsed his nether parts.

In some families, this shirttail practice lasted beyond the small boy stage.

EARLY in World War II we were always having some big guy come up with the two skivvy shirts and the two pairs of nainsook drawers he had been issued in his hand.

"What on earth are these for?" he would say.

We had a special Indoctrination Officer to explain to these recruits how to put on the drawers one leg at a time without getting them turned backward. He also explained that these had to be washed every day with a scrub brush on a concrete apron and that they must be snow-white when the captain inspected them.

This caused a great deal of embarrassment. Who, after all, could feel comfortable while somebody looked at his underwear?

We were a modest people in those days.

In our country, fine cloth like that from flour sacks was used mostly for ladies' lingerie. Most of the expansive petticoats which older women used to wear were made from flour sacks. This was a time when the consumer got his money's worth from a manufacturer. He not only got the flour but this fine cotton cloth, the like of which cannot now be purchased.

This cloth was soft and finely woven. As it aged, it became silky to the touch. From repeated washings the brand names would gradually fade into something almost ornamental. As a matter of fact, they paste such brand names all over cloth now and sell it to you new as sportswear.

A brand name on her underskirt never bothered a lady then. After all, if anybody ever glimpsed her underskirt, she was already undone, compromised, ruined. What difference could a brand name make?

If a lady's underskirt drooped too low, her daughter might say, "Mamma, your brand is showing." That is as far as it went.

WHEN it had served its time as a lady's petticoat, the flour-sack cloth could be boiled for an hour in an iron kettle in the backyard, washed thoroughly with lye soap, and then cut up into dish towels. Bewley's Best was almost an eternal cotton cloth. When holes came into it as a dishcloth, you cut out the good parts and put them in the ragbag. Nearly always, you had to patch something in those days, and nearly always the ragbag had something to patch it with.

People don't know how to do this anymore, of course. They think they have to be able to buy energy. They think they have to have steak. They think they have to have lower prices and higher wages. They even think people have to have underwear that was designed for the purpose.

THE OLD-FASHIONED DESK BLOTTER

THE decline of fine moral sentiment in America may very well date from the disappearance of the old-fashioned desk blotter.

We are not talking here about the modern desk pad with its handsome metal or leather corners and its vast expanse as sterile of expression as the modern executive's prose. Rather, we mean the old-fashioned large sheet of blotting paper which used to be on every desk in our West Texas country and which was used for blotting. Nosy small boys who learned to read script backward could find all kinds of trade and personal secrets on these blotters.

Mostly, they were given away and carried advertising for some firm or other, but nearly all of them carried some stirring motto or a bit of useful advice which would guide the recipient along the right path in life. A lot of these messages depended heavily on angel mothers, noble dogs, and the man who stands

foursquare; but some were more utilitarian.

As a matter of fact, some were downright self-serving. Our county attorney's desk blotter contained that quotation from Coke that said a man's home is his castle. It came from a company that printed legal forms. Mr. Clem Fisher, the blacksmith who ran the volunteer fire department and sometimes managed the town baseball team, had a desk blotter that read, "The smith a mighty man is he." Maybe you couldn't call it a desk pad. Mr. Fisher's desk was a shelf in the corner of the shop, and his desk pad was covered with several years of coal dust, as were his ledgers. He was handier with a sledge than a stub of a pencil and regretted the few moments he had to give to office management.

Mostly, though, the desk blotters exhorted one on to nobler living and sounder conduct.

Unfortunately, some were offensively frivolous. One carried some of the words of "Oh, don't send my boy to Harvard."

THE authors of these sound and beautiful sentiments were predictable. Edgar A. Guest was a much-quoted man: "It takes a heap of livin' in a house to make it home." James Whitcomb Riley was often represented with "I cannot say, and I will not say / That he is dead. He is just away." There was Benjamin Franklin and "A penny saved is a penny earned." Of course, everybody in West Texas in those days already knew that, but it was educational to know that Franklin said it and made it official. Anonymous was well represented with such wisdom as "A friend is one who knows your faults and doesn't give a damn."

Most of the authors were standard inspirationalists, but a few wrote high literature.

SIR Walter Scott was quoted more often than you would think, especially in those lines from *Marmion* which went, "Oh, what a tangled web we weave, / When first we practice to deceive." High-class blotter owners might display Browning's "Grow old along with me! / The best is yet to be," or Edwin Markham's line about drawing "a circle that shut me out."

The really profound motto was "Greater love hath no man than this, that a man lay down his life for his friends."

Yep, we have gone to pot and long hair since people quit living with these guides to the better life.

THE REAL FOUNTAIN PEN

THE modern ink pencil is another example of how the world is slipping into the slipshod. It has made people forget the real fountain pen, which was once a status symbol that had an air of stability and worth about it.

When, as a child, I used to visit my grandmother, I was sometimes permitted a glimpse of the bedroom of my youngest uncle. He was seldom home, being then at that stage of the early twenties when it was important for young men to horse around and see the girls at night. There on the starched white cover of his stand-table rested three objects, his dress-up watch with its twenty-four carat enameled gold hunting case, his Masonic pin, and his fountain pen.

These said a lot for the character of this young man. He had enough money to own a spare watch. The Masonic ring testified to his devotion to the solid institutions of the community, and the fountain pen showed that he had an open, progressive mind toward business. Obviously, he was a comer.

A man in those days showed off his fountain pen mentality by wearing the pen up there in the coat pocket where some people now unsanitarily stuff their handkerchiefs.

THE real fountain pen was a formidable-looking engine. Our former colleague, Francis Raffetto, owned one.

This pen was about the size of a good stick of kindling wood. It was marble in color, but not so much so that you couldn't tell that it was genuine imitation marble, not just some common ordinary agate.

When you witnessed the signing of some papers with this magnificent pen, you forgot the presence of human participants. You were conscious only of this giant pen writing away in words that were doubtless intended for the ages.

Those were the days when men liked to sign their names in India ink so that it would last as a testament until the Second Coming.

Raffetto's pen was a Schaeffer, but all the other pen companies were producing twelve-cylinder models like Parker's Scarlet Tanager.

A LOT has happened in later years to degrade the fountain pen. During World War II, Eversharp came out with a pen that was supposed not to leak when you went up in an airplane. A lot of good shirts were ruined as a result. Also, during that war somebody invented a pen that would write underwater.

It was a great sensation for a time until people discovered that it was unhandy to write underwater.

We have reached the ultimate in the modern, disposable dime ink pencil. It has no dignity about it and hardly any intrinsic worth. The ink from it fades rapidly; it will barely last longer than a modern bank account. And it is certainly no status symbol.

A man caught wearing a fountain pen these days would be ruined. Nobody would think he had a progressive, open attitude toward business or was a man of ideas. In these days of the computer, men who can write are in the way. The modern attitude toward business is the pushbutton approach.

WHEN THE MULE WAS GREAT

AN East Texas friend has sent me a clipping which says that the mule is now disappearing from the United States of America. You might notice that the United States of America is disappearing from the United States of America, too.

Back when the mule was great in America, food was so cheap that beer taverns gave the food away free. Even twenty years ago, so one restaurant owner told me, cabbage was so cheap that he just gave it away in the form of slaw or other salads. The American farmer was producing cheap food, apparently, and doing all right because he wasn't buying any high-priced farm machinery nor any Near Eastern fuel.

I have made a scientific graph of this, one line showing the number of mules and the other line showing the food supply. The two lines go off in all directions, and only when the mule line and the food line are together has America been happy.

My friend's newsclip says that there are so few mules now in this country that the Department of Agriculture has quit counting them. In other words, you use more stupidity on the point of the enumerators than you can find stupidity in the mules.

Anybody can see that the expenditure of more stupidity for less is a losing proposition.

THE mule seemed to bring out the best in the American worker, such as my East Texas friend. He didn't want to do it, but his dad said that he had better keep two shovelsful of gravel in the air all the time while loading their construction wagons. After all, you can't have a pair of hundred-dollar mules sitting around and waiting on a fifty-cent son.

The mule was perfect for this kind of work. In physique, the mule ran largely toward ears, which don't require nutrition. The mule, therefore, required little food, and it could be of the worst kind. He didn't demand a stable to shelter him from the weather. He was tough. He was tough to handle, too. There was an old axiom that you had better not ever try to begin to harness a mule from the rear. He had quick, sharp hooves.

Still, all that the mule required to perform nobly was a mule skinner of his own intellectual level. He would buck those shoulders into the collar and really pull. When you let him rest, however, you could look into those wicked little eyes and see that he already had a predetermined plan about how to handle you.

Occasionally, a mule would decide that he was tired of work and wanted to talk to the walking delegate, and he would brace all four feet forward and defy anybody to move him.

I KNOW a mule skinner who once was faced with a balky mule. I will not name names because the principle of confidentiality is involved, and it hits close to home. Lacking the usual fence post or two-by-four to argue, the mule skinner hauled off and delivered a mighty left hook to the mule's jaw.

The left hook dropped the mule to his knees, but it also broke the skinner's fist. The mule didn't have to work for three or four weeks.

You would just have to say that the mule won.

THE COW-MILKING BUSINESS

I HAVE mentioned before that "pshaw" was an expletive rarely used when a cow stepped in the milk bucket.

A lady from Stamford has now protested that I have mixed up "pshaw" with the old cow-milking exclamation, "saw."

"My dad seemed to use the word 'saw' several ways," she adds. "First, the word gently spoken to the cow informed her she was about to be milked. Secondly, if she failed to be in the proper position, he would repeat the word in more of a commanding tone as he touched her right hind leg, reminding her to move it back for milking.

"Third, if old Holy moved for some reason, the 'saw!' became a more forceful reminder that she had best be still."

The lady is right, of course. An indignant and loudly bawled "saw" with a healthy kick from a clodhopper boot was the punishment for a major infraction — unless the cow's owner was present, when the whole thing was overlooked.

I knew all this, but failed to remember it. I just don't like to remember milking a cow.

I SUPPOSE that cow-milking was the lowest employment that I have ever enjoyed. Milking demands finger muscles deeply rooted in the neck and shoulders. Most of those fancy-dan milkers who can flip a stream of milk here and there have thick necks and thin heads.

Cows come in all kinds. There are large, malicious cows. There are small, sneaky cows. Some cows can kind of coil their tails down from the top without being seen and use them to pop a fly off the ear of the milker, taking most of the ear as well. The man I milked for had one cow who could pop you with her tail while thrusting a foot at the milk pail.

When you lost a bucket of milk this way, it was never the cow's fault because she cost money, while a milker was pretty cheap.

This man had one cow who always decided at the gate that she wasn't going in that night. When this happened, you were supposed to wheedle her with a handful of oats instead of chasing her. Chasing her would have curdled her milk.

This man wouldn't let us use a milk-stool. The human damage would grow back.

I QUIT this job shortly after the farmer stopped my pay. He said I had let one of his cows go dry too soon. But I was ready. The outlook of thousands and thousands of cows ahead of you to be milked does not appeal to an average, imaginative, lazy man.

As I left the place, I remember I was scandalized at the idea that unwitting people let little kids get on this stuff.

Nowadays, I understand, there are great improvements in the milking business. They have machines now which neither say "saw" nor cultivate the cow. They just reach up there and take the milk. Furthermore, some scientist has about found out how to convert cottonseed cake into milk without passing it through a cow.

When this happens, the cow has had it. Let her go on and curdle.

TOOLS OF THE TRADE

WELL, the country has finally gone to the hot place in a handbasket. Here is a classified ad that appeared in the *Daily Oklahoman,* and it reads: "COWBOYS WANTED. Must have own saddles."

Anybody with any sense can tell America has had it.

As a boy years ago, I was occasionally privileged to get a glimpse of a real old-time cowboy. He would suddenly be on the railroad station platform after the noon passenger had departed, a lean man with sun-lines around his eyes and the look in his face of a resigned bitterness at what people had done to the country.

Already jobs were so far apart that he rode to them in the chair car instead of on a horse, and he got a job usually when there was something to do like breaking out horses that the local farm boys couldn't handle. Always on the platform beside him, though, was his saddle in gunnysacking. Often, it was the only luggage he had.

A cowboy without a saddle was a possibility on the order of a baseball player without feet.

THE saddle is a sample of something that was very important a generation or two ago in America. It was a Tool of the Trade.

This was a time when men took pride in owning the tools of their trade. It was the mark of a craftsman, and to speak frankly, a man who was willing to work with company tools didn't have much self-respect.

The idea that a company could have furnished proper tools for any job would have raised hoots and jeers. The welfare corporation had not arrived then, and it was well known that companies were skinflint and miserly, given probably to shorting on tools as they did on wages. That was the popular view of it.

Besides, a man's tools were an extension of the man. They were Thor's hammer and Arthur's Excalibur. Something in the temper of the blade of a barber's favorite razor was simpatico with his temperament. He could work better with it. A carpenter sensed a nuance of balance in his own hammer that fitted it to his hand.

Only in the last desperate straits would a man sell or pawn his tools.

THE old-time craftsman made one exception in his disdain of men without tools — the locomotive engineer. After all, there was a limit even to what a man of pride could be expected to do.

Anyhow, that's what the saddle meant to the cowboy. When cowboys without saddles hire out, that America is dead. Better to give the cowherds jeeps and call them hired hands.

THE ORIGINAL MOTEL

THE original motel was the wagonyard. Wherever it was, the local wagonyard was probably called the OK Wagonyard. It wasn't a chain, or anything like that. The name just signified that here was a safe place for a man's family and his movable valuables, which was usually all he had.

The wagonyard was usually a compound covering a city block with another block behind it of corrals. Around the compound were one-room cubicles with all the comforts of home. Around the walls were double-decked bunks. The guest was supposed to furnish his own bedding and usually preferred to. The cornshuck mattresses provided in some OK Wagonyards were full of ticks.

In the center of the room was a round-bellied coal stove with four potlids on its top, plenty of room to cook anything that a wagonyard family might want to eat except perhaps biscuits.

Few of these cubicles had any windows. They depended for light and ventilation on the front and only door. The door was usually shredded in certain places so that ventilation was no problem.

You could park your wagon in the compound and put your livestock in the back corrals free of charge.

The best thing about wagonyards was that they used little energy. A man had to light his cubicle with his own lantern.

A MR. Poteet ran the OK Wagonyard in our town when I was small. He was a genial, small man who was always tolerant of small boys but skeptical of parents who allowed little girls to become tomboys.

Mr. Poteet occupied a small office at the entrance to the wagonyard. It had two residential type windows but needn't have bothered. Neither window had been washed in forty years and each was covered with an interesting glaze of old sandstorms and water. Inside the office it was very dark, but that was all right. Mr. Poteet never kept records. You just went into the office and paid your dollar, and he put it in his pocket.

He would then walk out with a grand wave of his hand and say, "Make yourselves to home."

Except for the feedstore. This was in the back end of the office and was padlocked. From it he would sell oats, bran, and corn shorts by the hundred-pound sack to men who had folding money and by the bucket to visitors who dug up only coins.

For an impoverished family, Mr. Poteet always gave them lodging for taking over the control of the outfit when he went home for the day, except for coal and feed, of course.

A LOT of proper thinking people regarded the wagonyards as sin pots. Great-Aunt Martha, for instance, always deeply "suspicioned" that men swapped families and wives there and often drove off with the wrong woman and the wrong ten kids. The reason for this is hard to document.

Mostly the wagonyards served migrant families, but some ranches would send in for supplies men who would stay overnight, and there are accounts of some of these rakehells who would stay up until ten o'clock at night playing forty-two or pitch and guffawing in a way that disturbed decent people.

On the whole, though, you would have to say that less sin went on in the wagonyards than goes on now in motels.

SINNERS IN THEIR HENRY FORDS

OF late, the exhortations of the environmentalists have taken on a religious feeling. It is almost as if humanity is being excoriated for what it has done to God's green earth.

It is good to know that Great-Aunt Martha perceived all this fifty years ago. Aunt Martha perceived that the auto was an instrument of the devil as soon as she saw the first one. It was an instrument to lure the unwary down the primrose path to the quicksand down at Jim Bowhart's crossing.

"There he goes in his Henry Ford," Martha would shriek, her dark eyes afire with fury and her skinny, tall old body stiff with indignation. Any automobile was a Henry Ford to Aunt Martha, be it a Model T, a Stephens, a Chandler, or a Reo Flying Cloud.

"There he goes, a-sinnin' and a-singin'. Wicket! Wicket! The Lord will put down the wicket."

The automobile, she felt, was a sign of the coming end of the world, the Lord having made men mad with a desire to travel fifteen miles an hour.

AUNT Martha's pet sinner was one of the Whittaker boys who owned an early-day version of a sports car, a red Model T which was little more than a chassis with two bucket seats and a gas tank mounted on it. He liked to tool around the rutted country roads, stopping every two or three miles to fix a flat.

The sight of this young man with his goggles and his cap with the bill turned backwards was enough to send Aunt Martha into a jeremiad. She felt that his evil machine disturbed the livestock and kept the cattle from giving down their milk. He had also besmirched the reputation of many a young maiden by allowing her to sit in the bucket seats with her knees out of plumb.

"The Lord will provide for him," Aunt Martha would promise, with her customary gift for phrase and quotation. "The Lord will remember the prodigal calf. He will be divided between the sheep and the goats."

"Aw, Martha," Uncle John would protest, "he's just a kid."

"Out of the mouths of babes," she would remind him knowingly.

In memory, Great-Aunt Martha seems to have been a pretty good environmentalist. Certainly nothing in her house was ever thrown away to litter the countryside. Every piece of wrapping paper which came into the house was carefully smoothed and folded for future use. The semiweekly newspaper turned into matches to transfer fire from the stove to the coal-oil lamp. Old clothes and rags became quilts. Every piece of string was worked into a ball for future use.

"Waste not," Aunt Martha would say firmly, "and you will have it. A stitch in time is a penny saved."

She would be most gratified, no doubt, to find all her prophecies confirmed in our present smog-ridden world.

THE BURMA SHAVE ROAD

IT is not often that the subdued pages of the *Wall Street Journal* reek of tragedy as they did on July 8. There it was on page 22, the report that the Burma Shave signs with their roadside jingles are being systematically killed out.

"Five years ago," reported the *Journal,* "there were 7,000 sets of Burma Shave signs in 42 states. . . . Since last fall a two-man crew has been traveling the country uprooting the signs, and by next September there won't be any left."

Allan Odell, the president of the company, said that motorists hurrying along superhighways no longer have time to read signs.

"As a consequence," he said, "ours just aren't as effective as they used to be."

It's too bad. The Burma Shave signs were one of the few remaining relics of an America that was certainly slower than it is today but which seems in retrospect to have been emotionally richer, more comfortable, and happier.

And if the Burma Shave signs of recent years have seemed strained and not very funny, it may be because none of us feel very funny anymore.

IN the Burma Shave heyday, roads had time to wind around the countryside a lot and to dip down by streams that had not been poisoned by wastes and to skirt the sides of a pleasant hill instead of cutting a raw gash through it.

Unlike the superhighways which rise above the terrain in lordly domination, a Burma Shave road lived close to the land and the human beings it served. The green meadows came up to the edge of the narrow pavement. The cornfields grew tall right up to the fringe of

sunflowers in the borrow ditches. Men built their houses beside such roads so that they could sit on the front porch and enjoy the company of the drummers and the peculiar city people who went roaring by at the breakneck speed of forty miles an hour.

A journey by auto then was a trip, not a speed run. By the time a man reached his destination, he had an exact knowledge of the condition of crops all over the area. He had probably borrowed some water a time or two along the way and had talked with the country's inhabitants. He had the news.

♪ *On a long and dusty drive to some far distant place like Wichita Falls, the Burma Shave signs were entertainment.*

THE modern advertising of billboard and TV sometimes has a faintly sinister feel. It smells of subliminal influences and consumer motivation. Burma Shave was never that. The little signs were amiable greetings. They aimed merely to entertain people and remind them of a brand name. Whether they sold merchandise I don't know. They were as old-fashioned as the Boyce Motometer.

If Burma Shave sticks with outdoor advertising, it will have to come up with something different.

It will need a sign that a motorist can glimpse, one that will cause the motorist, after driving five miles down the road, to say, "What was that?"

He will then whip his car across the dividing parkway and speed back down the road to find out.

This is Progress.

LARIAT COUNTRY

The feel of the place still comes back, not a memory exactly but an emotional tone, a feel, the echo of a lost happiness and a lost contentment.

LARIAT COUNTRY

AN OFFICIAL WHISTLE

A FRIEND has taken exception to a recent newspaper cartoon showing Dallas as a whistle-stop, as the passenger trains disappear.

The phrase, says my friend, cuts him to the quick after all these years. It is the kind of invidious term that should never be used.

"Even to this day," he says, "many of us who emigrated from a small town to the big city wince a little to hear our hometown referred to as Just a Whistle-Stop (Elevation 512)."

I, of course, wouldn't know about this because Lariat, the metropolis of Precinct 1 out in West Texas, was not any whistle-stop, by dog. It was just a whistle. As the afternoon passenger approached from the south, the engineer would let loose a long screech. The man in the mail car would manipulate his mechanical grabber and snatch the mail sack from the right-of-way crane. He would then heave the Lariat mail sack into the nearby cotton field. That was all for the day.

And that was good. After all that excitement, we had had about all we could take of the Santa Fe Railroad for one day.

LARIAT, however, was not just an ordinary whistle. It was an official whistle. At the spot where our depot was going to be built someday was a six-foot, 2×8 stanchion set up on the right-of-way. It was painted red and was always beautifully kept by the section gang. At the top of this red post was a white circle, and in the circle was a large "W" to remind the engineer to do his duty while passing through this, the pride of the plains.

I have always thought they put up this marker to remind the engineer about Mrs. Porter's cow, Old Spotty, a huge beast of uncertain Holstein strain who liked to graze on the right-of-way with her rear end turned toward approaching locomotives. Old Spotty had been known to hold up important local freight, like a crate of oranges bound for Clovis.

At the time, the Santa Fe had a standard price of fifty dollars for every cow which its trains hit, but it did not like to hit one because of the oratory that always broke out over three counties about the calloused railway barons.

The railroad apparently especially dreaded Old Spotty, because Mrs. Porter had a constant suit on file against them for scaring Old Spotty and curdling her milk.

IF Lariat had been referred to in those days as a whistle-stop, we might have resented it. We could resent almost anything if there was a point to it.

Nobody seemed to mind being just a whistle, though. After all, there were advantages in having the train not stop. The news butch might have got off the train and sold a pear and taken money out of the town. Some of the drummers with their checked vests and fancy cigars might have corrupted our youth to the point of getting them out of the cotton fields.

It was a good thing to see the evil world of rounders go whistling by our town.

THE MAN WHO RAN LARIAT WEATHER

THE weather lately somehow reminded me of The Judge. He was a fat, peppery, red-faced old man who wheezed as he talked and would occasionally rear back with a big breath and blow like a whale.

The Judge was in charge of the weather out in the Lariat country in the early days. He did not merely record the weather, though it was his job to read the rain gauge once or twice a year when it was necessary. The Judge ran the weather in the Lariat country.

He liked to go out late at night after everybody was asleep, about 9:00 P.M., and study the moon. He would then forecast the weather for the next day, and he would usually say it was going to be dry. He was 98 percent

right, too, because 98 percent of the time it didn't rain.

Nothing disgusted the Judge so much as a stretch of cloudy, rainy days.

"You take a long spell of rainy weather that covers up the moon," he said. "How you gonna tell whether it's gonna rain or not?"

When he had to read the rain gauge, he always added a tenth of an inch to replace that soaked up by the dust in the gauge. Anyhow, it helped the land prospectors.

OF course, the Judge was hopelessly unscientific. He believed, for instance, that a ring around the moon meant rain the next day. All we intelligent, scientific people chuckle behind our hands at this idea. We all know that it won't work unless there is a star in the circle. One star means rain in one day, two stars, in two, etc.

If you don't see any stars and it still rains, it means that you'd better see your eye doctor.

The Judge had certain other ideas that won't hold water. He held that for every day of thunder in February, there would be a killing frost in April. Obviously, this is sheer superstition. There is no way that a killing frost in April can cause thunder the previous February.

However, the Judge kept the records. He had the only weather records in town, and he was a man who believed books ought to balance. If the thunders in February didn't match the killing frosts in April, he reran the records until he found the error.

The Judge had other ideas that are said to have some scientific basis, such as red sun at night, sailor's delight.

He believed that it would be dry when the horns of the new moon turned up. Anybody can see the logic of this. The moon catches the water.

PEOPLE laugh at the Judge's ideas these days, but when the Judge brought in spring, he brought in spring. He didn't fiddle around with it the way the modern industry has done for three days.

Matter of fact, I kept books on him once, and he was fully as accurate as the Cardui almanac. I would hate to see the modern government or TV weatherman match himself against the Cardui almanac.

And I feel a little as the Judge did. If it's going to stay cloudy and cold, how can we tell whether tomorrow will be cold?

Probably the best advice is:

Hold onto your overcoats, boys. The North will rise again.

A HAMMERING ARTIST

HERE is a handout which says that an Iowa house-building company is now using an automatic nail-driver instead of a hammer.

Sorry to throw water on this new invention, but the automatic nail-driver was in operation out in the Lariat country forty years ago. Its name was P. V. Kemp, known far and wide throughout the precinct as Peevy.

Most people place a nail, tap it in place, and then start to drive it, but not Peevy. He more or less tossed the nail at the spot where he wanted it and drove it home with one powerful blow of the hammer. When his hammer went wham-wham-wham, it meant that Peevy had driven three nails.

People liked buildings that Peevy had nailed together because often, before he could stop himself, he had put six nails in a joint that ordinarily got only two.

The quality of his work was beyond cavil. Many of the timbers he once nailed together have long since rotted and blown away, but the nails are still firmly in place. Peevy, now retired, told me this not three years ago.

THERE are union carpenters, nonunion carpenters, and even master carpenters. Peevy prided himself on being a genuine jackleg carpenter. Furthermore, he was a specialist. He did no contracting himself, because he couldn't have afforded the quantity of nails that he used up. And he would not deign to touch a saw or a square. He was a hammering artist pure and simple.

The town's contractors usually did not call on Peevy until a building was all but ready to go up and the lumber had all been cut. For one thing, if a board hadn't been cut, it was likely to be nailed forever in place before Peevy's hammer could be stopped. Also, Peevy was a prima donna. He looked on men who used the saw and plane as inferior types, mere caddies furnishing the material for his hammer. This did not cause strikes. It caused fisticuffs.

As a result, Peevy often had nothing to do except wander around town and explain how a nail, properly, ought to be driven.

But he always wore his carpenter's apron and carried a couple of nails between his lips and had his hammer at the ready in the little carrying slot on the leg of his overalls.

I WOULD like to see Peevy as he was in his prime matched against this new nail-driving machine. I don't think it would turn out like John Henry's contest with the railroad-laying machine.

But there are undeniable advantages to a mechanical nail-driver. As the experts say, mechanization creates jobs. I notice in this picture that it takes two men to operate the mechanical nail-driver instead of the one who operates a hammer. Also, this machine undoubtedly requires a maintenance crew of four or five. It has thus created at least four jobs that never existed before.

I hope that the men who operate it hew close to Peevy's artistic philosophy.

The main thing wrong with most people, he said, is that they want to save on nails.

AN OPEN MIND ALREADY MADE UP

THE only man I've ever known who was never wrong was Throckmorton Jenkins, who lived in a half dugout and farmed 320 rich acres in the Lariat country.

He was a tall, enormous, square-looking man. His great, square hands, his great, square face, and his clodhopper-shod feet made him look as rudely made as a Karloff Frankenstein monster. His demeanor was always grave. He was never known to laugh or make jokes. His eyes were always thoughtful.

Asked his opinion about anything from the President of the United States to the bog where the water drained into Main Street during a rain, he had one invariable reply:

"Well, I been thinking about it."

Like Miniver Cheevy, he thought and thought and thought about everything.

HE had never finished grade school, but what he had learned he knew. He could still parse a sentence and decline a verb. He was expert at figuring the area of an odd patch of ground or the angle that a rafter had to be cut, and he was much admired for his ability to estimate the probable weight of an animal.

Throck never got caught in any of the quarrels which shook our town. He was just thinking about it all during the schism at the Baptist church, when the members siding with their resident minister threw the dissidents out of the church house. He refused to take sides in the argument over whether the young high school coach and the girl English teacher ought to be fired because they were so brazen as to have a date and go to the movie in Clovis, traveling the whole ten miles together without a chaperone.

Pressed for an opinion on these serious matters, Throck always replied gravely, "You got to consider the pros and cons."

All except once. The druggist once tried to make conversation by saying, "Throck, what do you think of the World Series this year?"

"World what?" he exclaimed.

Nobody knows yet whether he was a very wise man or a very timid one. He was never adequately tested.

THROCK was not a fence-straddler, really. He was known to believe strongly that school should be turned out two weeks at cotton-picking time so that the kids could be put in the fields and be made to do something useful for a change. He was against tobacco in any form and the use of strong drink, whether it be whiskey or Coca-Cola.

Once the county judge decided to make votes in an election by proposing that the county put caliche on the town streets. When he found out the country districts were going to snow him under, he switched sides. Throck was disgusted.

"If they's anything I can't stand," he said, "it's a man that can't make up his mind."

A town wit summed him up pretty well. "Throck," he said, "has an open mind that has already been made up."

PLEASANT W. CARTER

IT says here in a news story that more people were hard at work in the United States in January than in any January before, and it is a dismal statistic. What on earth do these people think they are doing?

This snare certainly never caught Pleasant W. Carter, a thin, neat man who was in his forties in the Lariat country thirty years ago. Pleas was not lazy. As a matter of fact, he was a good workman when he chose to engage in something. He had nothing against work; he just didn't see any point in it when it wasn't necessary.

Pleas held that the whole point of a man's working was to accumulate enough money so that he could afford to "lay off" for awhile.

He made a life style out of laying off and enjoying the sensation of being alive, and he probably was right.

HE lived with his mother on the edge of town in a five-room bungalow which Pleas had built himself. It sat on an acre of ground in the middle of a thicket of fruit trees and berry vines and in front of a huge garden. They were always canning and preserving; and when the wild, sour plums were ripening, Pleas would

make one of his overnight outings to the sandhills "to get away from it all" and come back with enough plums for jelly for five families.

When he needed money, he worked, and he never lacked for work. He was very fast at heading maize and kafir with the big hooked knife that was used in those days of manual harvesting. He was a good rough carpenter. He was a concrete man. He understood handling the scales at the elevator and keeping the scale records.

When he had accumulated $200 or $300, however, he was ready to quit work and enjoy it. He wasn't mean about it. If the local contractor suddenly needed a hand, he could call on Pleas, but Pleas was always apologetic about breaking his layoffs.

"Jim was in a tight," he would explain, "and I just had to help him out."

His wants were simple: enough Prince Albert tobacco for a pipe or two a day, a cup of coffee in the morning, a few shotgun shells, and the neat work clothes and well-kept rough shoes that he wore.

He lived, I think, a happy and full life simply by not wanting.

IN the winter, when other men were scraping the ice rime from their beards and battling the snowdrifts, you would find Pleas seated before a cherry-red base burner in the little house reading the *Saturday Evening Post*.

The little house faced away from the town. In the summer, you would find Pleas sitting on an old daybed on the front porch, where the morning-glory vines climbed along twine supports, and looking out over broad fields and pastures toward the rim of the horizon and toward the towering, icy white cumuli sailing like great ships across an azure sky.

In time, his mother died, and Pleas lived alone in the little house. Then, he died, and everybody went to the funeral.

That was years ago. The little house is gone now. The fruit trees are dead stumps, and sand drifts cover the ground where the garden grew.

But the great clouds still sail across the sky, just as they will when you and I are gone.

UNCLE CHARLIE'S LIGHTNING TALE

T HAT was a pretty spectacular lightning storm in Dallas Sunday morning, but any old-timer who settled early on the high plains could have told you about dozens that were worse. Some of them could also have told you that there is nothing dangerous about lightning if you know how to handle it.

Our Great-Uncle Charlie was one of those. In handling lightning, he said, the thing to do is keep your eyes open and stand ready to dodge. Men get killed by lightning, he argued, only through fool carelessness in letting it slip up on them. In his opinion, it was best during an electrical storm to stand with your back toward something so that it could not get at you from behind.

He had a narrow escape during one severe storm.

He had been riding the fence in the south pasture and had not knocked off and turned the horse homeward until dark.

H E had ridden only half the five miles home when one of those fancy plains electrical storms rolled in over him. Lightning popped, crackled, and fried the air. As it reached a

crescendo, half a dozen bolts of chain lightning were ripping the black heavens at the same time. Thunder was jarring the earth. Little balls of light glowed on the horns of some of the cattle.

Uncle Charlie was riding along zigzagging his horse so that the lightning couldn't get a good bead on him when a sixth sense told him to duck. He did instantly, down on the side of the horse, Indian fashion.

Almost at the same moment, there was a tremendous boom, and a ball of yellow fire, blue at the edges, glowed in the air right where his head had been, glowed for a moment and then faded.

All the air around smelled blue, Uncle Charlie said.

For a moment, he had thoughts of getting down and hiding under the horse, but after one stunned moment, the horse had his own ideas. He set off in a wild run for the corral. Uncle Charlie almost had to pull leather to stay on during that ride, and him at the mercy of the lightning because he couldn't watch it and handle the horse.

Luckily, the lightning had shot its wad in that one big bolt, and he wasn't bothered again.

L IGHTNING, along with snakebites and madstones, was one of the favorite topics of talk when people used to pass evenings by amusing themselves. The women turned white when Uncle Charlie told his story in all harrowing detail, and the men listened to him respectfully.

Unfortunately, along came the superheterodyne radio with its six dials, and everybody had to stay absolutely quiet during the evening while the operator tried to tune in something.

The fine art of lightning conversation began its decline.

BROTHER SHULTER AND THE LORD

THE new preacher just shouldn't have asked Brother Shulter to deliver the Thanksgiving prayer at the Baptist church out in West Texas. An older preacher would have known better.

Brother Shulter was a big elderly German who was the pillar of the church, but he was undependable in his approach to prayer. This happened forty years ago during a depression drought year. Wheat had gone down to fifteen cents a bushel. The kafir and the milo maize had withered on the stalk and had produced no more than rags of fodder. The people were broke and were living on cowpeas and parched wheat.

"We thank thee, oh Lord. We realize we do not deserve all the things we have been given," prayed Brother Shulter that morning. "But it is just about all we can take."

The new preacher got a little upset because the audience produced such a chorus of "Amen."

EXPERIENCED preachers did not call on Brother Shulter to lead a prayer. He was probably the most religious of men in the church. He probably furnished more money to the church than any other member. He was strict, law-abiding, courteous, and generous to his fellows, and known to be a man of his word. He also would patch the shingles on the church on his own.

It was simply that he had a personal acquaintanceship with God, and he believed in being as relentlessly honest with God as he was with his fellowman. He believed in letting God know how things really were down here on earth occasionally.

Usually, they weren't very good. Brother Shulter was never much miffed about this. He believed that God expected people to help themselves and to lend a helping hand now and then.

The inscrutable ways of the Almighty did puzzle him at times.

"We realize, oh Lord, that you are the source of all blessings," he once said in an anguished prayer that he was allowed to utter, "and here I am in the same shape I was last year."

One of the things that bothered preachers about him was that the congregation, when it bent over the pews, didn't seem to be moved exactly by a spirit of reverence.

AN experienced preacher soon found out about Brother Shulter and put his talents to work in fields other than prayer. He could always be depended upon to pass the collection plate, tonelessly humming "Praise God from whom all blessings flow" as he went about the work. He was the automatic chairman of the building committee and always had to raise the money for the church Boy Scout troop. He was a powerful, gnarled old man and, if somebody died, he was always present to dig the grave and to find something for the widow and orphans to do.

He just didn't go for humbug in his praying. "We ask thy forgiveness for all our fellowmen," he said once in a prayer, "including the sinners at the Great Plains elevator."

He seemed to have got along with the Lord very well in his way and died loved and respected.

AN EXTREMIST IN PLAINS COUNTRY

AN extremist, as everybody knows, is anybody who disagrees with you. Back in the 1920s, from a Texas point of view, the country was in the hands of extremists. The Republicans were in power in Washington.

We had one such extremist in our small town in West Texas. He was the postmaster, J. Carl Macklin, a short, square man with a great belly and a massive, jowlish face. He had come from some place east like Chicago and started a store which specialized in blue jeans, work shoes, and longhandled underwear. In time, as the town's only Republican, he had inherited the post office and the good-natured scorn of all right-thinking people.

For one thing, he persisted in wearing a derby, which was a kind of an affront to the masculinity of a Stetson-hatted town.

People liked Jay. He was a generous man, friendly if a little reticent, but it was impossible for the men of the community not to make him the butt of every kind of joke.

After all, it was ridiculous to have a Republican out there on the plains, and an extremist in a derby hat at that.

NOBODY was cruel or mean to Jay. He was just the natural target of all the ribbing that anybody could think up. After the Santa Fe passenger had delivered the mail, he would do the normal thing of closing the little doors at the stamp window while he sorted it.

The other men of the town would pound on the shelf outside the window and make loud jocular remarks about men who loafed on government time. He was a part of the town crowd while somehow being apart from it. In the afternoons, when the town men gathered at the croquet court for two or three hours of sport, he would be jeered because he had to kneel on one knee to see the ball. His belly was so big that he couldn't make a shot otherwise.

He heard a lot of snide remarks about the physical characteristics of Republicans.

Jay took all this quietly, peacefully. He had sad blue eyes that could have lighted with resentment, but they never did.

He merely looked a little sadder and more reflective as the years went by.

THEN there came a Christmas day during the Harding administration. Santa Fe Train 21 had just left the mail for the day, and when it was sorted, the men of the town swarmed into the small lobby. They called on Jay to come out. Nobody was going behind those walls because it was against the law and would get you in trouble with Uncle Sam.

When Jay came out, somebody grabbed the derby from his head. Somebody else, with a hoot, kicked it out the door into the street. Then the county judge produced the largest and most expensive white Stetson that could be bought and put it on Jay's head.

"Merry Christmas," everybody shouted. Jay's placid face broke into a slow grin.

And he wore the hat the rest of his life, even when it became as old and as sweaty and dusty as the hat of a rancher.

Proving, maybe, that Christmas gifts do something.

UNCLE PRESS'S INSOMNIA

AT the coffee table the other day one of our fellow workmen remarked that he had read somewhere that the weasel is an unusually sound sleeper and that you can even pick a weasel up by the tail and jiggle him up and down for several minutes without waking him.

As a gentlemanly sort, I naturally did not contradict this, though it seems to me that animal identification is not one of the stronger human talents now. Half the population of the county nowadays thinks it is seeing a weasel when it is only seeing a loan shark. This sleeping animal may very well have been a weasel, but it sounds an awful lot like Uncle Press.

Uncle Press was a distant relative for whom the bugle never blew and the alarm clock never rang. In experimenting at waking him up, some of the family tried such things as shooting off a ten-gauge shotgun outside the window and rolling him out of bed. Once they even stripped his bed of cover during a Panhandle blizzard. Uncle Press turned blue, and his teeth began to chatter but he slept on.

In his own mind, however, Uncle Press was the nervous, restless type who had trouble sleeping always. He seldom appeared at the breakfast table in the morning without some story of pitching and tossing around all night.

ALL this was the more ridiculous because Uncle Press slept very audibly. His snore began with something like a horse's whicker, shifted into the sound of high-pressure steam, mixed in a whistle or two here and there, and ended usually in a horrible choking rasp. At times, he would mix in some doleful moans. It was a very rhythmic, powerful snore, and after fifteen or twenty minutes, the walls of the house would begin to hum in resonance.

The others of the family would become a community of desperation all dedicated to the task of silencing the snore until they could go to sleep. Ordinarily, Uncle Press was impervious to sound or force. Ice water did not faze him. You could slap and pound and yell until you tired out. If you did manage to wake him, he was always hurt.

"I wish you wouldn't wake me up, Jim, just when I finally managed to catch a little old catnap," he would complain angrily. "I'll have a devil of a time ever getting my eyes shut again."

One night some of his husky nephews laid hand on Uncle Press and toted him out and left him in the radish bed for the rest of the night. He finally appeared the next morning with the story that he had hardly slept a wink all night. He had wandered around all night in search of sleep and had weeded half the garden before he finally relaxed and got some rest.

Probably the family would have made him sleep in the barn, but the West Texan of that day held that his horses had to get their rest. A man could make out as best he could.

UNCLE Press complained that when he did occasionally get a little sleep, once every two or three weeks or so, he had such horrible nightmares that he ended the night exhausted. I don't think he was being a fraud. Most men who discover a weakness in themselves wish themselves into the opposite state. The thing that a man is proudest of may turn out, in a searching examination, to be the thing he lacks.

Maybe the weasel can outsleep Uncle Press, but the chances are that the weasel knows he is asleep.

UNCLE BEEMAN'S BEST STORY

SUNDAY afternoon may be TV football time now, but fifty years ago it was family visiting time, a time when all the menfolk dragged out their best stories and paraded them again before an audience.

Uncle Tip's story was about the time he had told off a railroad division superintendent and thus lost a good sixty-dollar-a-month job on the section gang. Uncle Charlie usually told about the time when a whole mess of snakes fell into his wagon bed from an overhanging tree limb. Probably the best story was Uncle Beeman's account of how he broke an outlaw horse over in New Mexico.

Uncle Beeman's way of telling it made the difference. There wasn't much suspense in the story.

Even if you hadn't already known the outcome, you knew somehow that Uncle Beeman was going to break that horse.

HE talked in a long drawl, accenting a word occasionally with a small period of silence after it. When he worked up to a crisis in the tale, he had a way of stopping and rolling himself a Bull Durham cigarette, leaving you on edge to see whether he was going to change the story and improve it any.

He seldom did. It started when he was warned that he was risking his life in riding this horse.

"Never was a horse that couldn't be rode and never was a rider that couldn't be throwed," Uncle Beeman had said nonchalantly.

Four men had roped the horse and eared it down while Uncle Beeman checked the cinches himself. Any horseman with regard for his life would attend to the cinches personally. When Uncle Beeman had got into the saddle, the four men let go, and the horse rose up and went yonder.

It took all of fifteen minutes to describe the animal's bucking techniques. It sunfished. It tried to crush Uncle Beeman against the corral fence. Finally, it tried to fall over backward on him, but Uncle Beeman was on to that.

He quit the saddle temporarily, but while the horse was down, Uncle Beeman jumped back on and fetched the creature a blow between the ears with the handle of his quirt.

AFTER that the horse seemed to lose its spirit. It bucked halfheartedly for awhile, but a great cheer went up from all fourteen people at the corral as they realized that the outlaw had met his match.

Finally, the horse stood head down, quivering, in a corner of the corral, and there in the saddle, Uncle Beeman took out the makings and calmly rolled himself a Bull Durham cigarette.

He lit it, too. He always lit the cigarette at the end of the story.

AUNT HECK

WE once knew a farm woman out in West Texas who was named Hecate and always wished she had been named Dorothy. All of her life she wore on her face an expression of patient pain.

She had reason. All over half the county when she was older, she was known as Aunt Heck, and boisterous boys, when they were out of her hearing and couldn't offend her, used to concoct imaginary conversations with her that always ended with a protest, "Aw, Heck."

Aunt Heck was the victim of a father who had been overeducated for his vocation of handling a sodbuster. He had not only graduated from high school but had attended one of those small academies in the Tennessee or Kentucky mountains which believed that a man was not fit to face the world without a good dose of *Bulfinch's Mythology*.

Evidently, he fell in love with the myth of Hecate. It is a fair assumption that the woman who wanted to be called Dorothy didn't. She probably in her gentle way hated Hecate.

Some people still think they are god, but most of us, like Aunt Heck, know we are not and had rather be called Dorothy.

IT did not matter to her that Hecate was the daughter of a Titan and a sprite. The Titans, of course, were the barbarous forefathers of the Greek gods, six boys and six girls of them. There are no sprites left except maybe in Playboy clubs, and they didn't last there very long.

It did not matter to Aunt Heck that Hecate was a pet of Zeus, himself the grandson of Titans, until in the inner-family killing, he established himself as lord of creation. Hecate was given authority over heaven and hell, the earth and the sea. She thus overlapped on Selene, the moon goddess who gave birth to fifty daughters and two sons, the huntress

Artemis, and Demeter, the goddess of crops. This was all right.

But Hecate was the undoubted goddess of magic, ghosts, and witchcraft. On the first of a month, people used to gather at a crossroads and offer up sacrifices of black puppies, black lambs, and honey to her. Sometimes she would appear at the crossroads surrounded by ghosts and hellhounds.

In her later years, she was represented as a three-headed person with three bodies standing back to back so that she could guard the crossroads.

Nobody has yet explained what she did about that fork of the crossroads where she wasn't looking. The Greeks always left a way out for themselves.

WE have no evidence that the woman who wanted to be called Dorothy ever knew of the divine origin of her name, or cared.

Papa probably forgot to instruct her in *Bulfinch's Mythology*.

She lived a blameless life, a little more careworn than most farm women. In the spring, she worried about the nesting turkeys and whether they would be caught in a fatal cold rain. She always turned up with more than her share of food at the church dinners. So far as I know, she was always kind to black puppies and black lambs.

She died eventually, worn out as most of the old-timers were at the end of seventy years or more of hard work.

When they were trying to get her obituary together, a brash young reporter whom I know asked the family, "Does anybody know how to spell Aunt Heck's real name?"

Nobody did.

A MAN NAMED PETE

A MAN named Pete died in a midwestern prison not long ago. I knew him well, and my people had known his people before either of us was born.

All his life Pete stole things. Mostly he stole nothing of any great value, but it was enough that he was educated in reform school and made a career out of prison. The odd thing was that he came from a normal enough family. The other children made themselves into respectable housewives, truckers, and steam engineers.

Pete himself was a bright, affectionate, appealing small boy, a sturdy, square youngster whose laughing, black-Irish face was lightly dusted with freckles. Later on, during his short vacations between prison terms, he used to come calling on his friends; and he was accepted, not merely because a decent person in those days hadn't the heart to turn away a black sheep but because there was something pleasant, entertaining, and ingratiating about Pete.

He was impulsively generous. He was a tireless entertainer of children. When he was visiting, he managed always to take on and discharge all the small chores that had been accumulating for months.

And then the restlessness would possess him, and he would disappear. Nothing would be missing from your house, but the neighbor's saddle would be gone.

IT seems clear now that Pete was a kleptomaniac, but in those stern and prepsychiatric days, he was a thief.

He wasn't even a very good thief. He inevitably stole the thing that would lead to his undoing. His first known theft was in grade school where he took one of those pencil cases that used to be made out of empty rifle cartridges. The significant thing was that this was the only cartridge in the whole township that had been decorated with enameled flowers. His guilt was evident.

In the vacation between graduating from reform school to the pen, he did a really desperate thing. He stole a car. Naturally, it was an unusually fancy Ford that belonged to a deputy sheriff and was known everywhere. He didn't even get out of town.

During his prison years, he made himself into a really fine mechanic. He could qualify for extra pay at nearly any garage. During his last job, however, the proprietor noticed that the place had unaccountably run short of cotter pins. They found three nail kegs full in Pete's room. Typically, he did not try to explain. He didn't know himself why he had taken them. He grinned ruefully and obediently went back to jail.

It was as if he didn't want to succeed in stealing.

PETE never got along with his dad, and maybe that was it. He admired the old man, but his dad was one of those stern, morose people incapable of emotion except in a backhanded, critical way. It seemed to friends sometimes that Pete committed many of his outrageous acts out of bravado, to make the old man look at him, and the old man always angrily did what he could to get Pete out of trouble.

They say that when Pete was last arrested, he sighed rather contentedly. After forty years, prison had become his home.

I am sure nobody claimed his body when he died. His only relatives were nephews and nieces who would have been embarrassed by him. All the other people were dead. His old man died years ago fitfully worrying about Pete, and I wonder if Pete died crying out, "Papa."

In that unaccountable way that only human beings can manage, the two between them lost the only world they ever wanted.

UNCLE SETHEL AND THE SNEAKY RATTLER

A NATURE note has arrived in the mail. It says: "Rattlesnakes will not attack a man unprovoked and will very often crawl away rather than chance a human encounter."

This will be received with some skepticism in the Lariat country. It is well known that rattlesnakes are pretty good citizens and keep down the number of homesteaders and other varmints on the rangeland. We only quibble about a "man unprovoked." Suppose the man is provoked. Will the rattlesnake attack him?

When I was growing up in West Texas, there were vicious rattlesnakes and other rattlesnakes that had been domesticated.

I remember once when Uncle Sethel came running from the north quarter to escape a rattlesnake. All he had done was strike the snake's hindparts while digging a posthole. According to Uncle Sethel, the snake then rose up and made an insulting noise with its tongue and took after him.

He arrived home white-faced several minutes later at a high lope with the news that a rattlesnake was chasing him. All the men got out their hoglegs and went out to shoot the snake. You didn't get much chance at target practice after the rustlers were cleared out. They couldn't find any snake or any track of one.

Somebody remarked that it seemed unlikely that a rattlesnake would race a grown man across the prairie for a mile.

"You boys better watch where you put down your feet," said Uncle Sethel. "This is a sneaky snake."

WHEN I was a West Texas brat and a Boy Scout, we used to go camping by pack mule or chuck wagon. We would get to some dry lake bed near a windmill and char some potatoes and burn some meat.

Then we would bed down for the night by throwing our bedrolls on the ground and lining them up north to south so that the magnetic forces of the earth would not disturb our sleep. Then we would take a lariat or two and make a ring around the bedrolls.

It is well known that rattlesnakes will not crawl over a lariat, but we weren't too convinced of this. The thing that a rattlesnake won't crawl over is a horsehair lariat, and ours were only good Manila hemp.

We were not bothered by the story that rattlesnakes are particularly belligerent. They aren't. But everybody knew in the plains country that rattlesnakes like to crawl into bed with people.

After all, I had a great aunt who had to kick a big rattler off her bed in the morning for years before she could dress. She would have thrown him out except somebody might have seen her in her bloomers.

THOUGH we had a rope circle around our bedrolls, few of us slept very good on these Scout nights out. Probably, it was because we hadn't precisely aligned our bedrolls with the north-south magnetic poles.

Truth to tell, we never did discover a rattlesnake in our midst. It may be because we used burros, and a burro can kill a snake with a cuff of the hoof.

Still, we didn't find any dead snakes.

Maybe, as Uncle Sethel said, they're sneaky.

TRAVELING LIGHT

YOU take these airline passengers whose baggage keeps getting missent around the United States. Maybe some disaffected employees do it on purpose, and maybe their right hand doesn't know what their left hand is doing. Anyhow, the basic fault is with the passengers and their foolish notion that clothes are to carry instead of to wear.

I learned this from Great-Uncle Caleb. Uncle Caleb was my dad's uncle, and he used to visit us nearly every winter on the farm, arriving without notice in such a way that it would touch off a two-day family celebration. Uncle Caleb was a rare man in those days because he was retired. Late in his life, somebody had discovered that a small hot puddle on his farm contained curative medicines good for rheumatism, hydrophobia, senile behavior, and the digestive system.

As a result, Uncle Caleb had a guaranteed princely income each month of twenty dollars, which he used to visit various nephews and nieces.

You couldn't call Uncle Caleb a

freeloader. He would work like a dog on the farm all winter but only on condition that he not be paid. As an independent man of means, he explained, he did not wish to be in the position of a mere wage earner.

WHEN Uncle Caleb arrived unexpectedly at our place, usually just after the cattle had all been fed, he was a walking bundle.

He always wore his overalls over his good blue serge suit, thereby protecting the suit from cinders and other threats in the smoking car. He always wore his three shirts, one over the other. Because of this, he had to wear the collars open, so he always carried his fine, hand-knit necktie carefully folded in the left hip pocket of the overalls. His two other pairs of socks were kept in the left front pocket of his overalls; he kept the right-hand front pocket empty so that he could put his hand into it while standing and look dignified. Uncle Caleb naturally wore his shoes on his feet. If he had thought he needed another pair, he would have thrown them away cavalierly and bought another pair out of the savings which he kept banked in a secret pocket of the blue serge coat.

This was just about all of Uncle Caleb's rig. He had only one pair of long underwear. He held that anybody who bought more was foolish or sissy because it wasn't going to get that cold.

He carried only one thing in his hand, a small leather case containing his meerschaum pipe. He did not particularly prize the pipe but feared that the fine purple plush lining of the case might get damaged.

WATCHING Uncle Caleb unpack on a first night was a fascinating experience for a small boy because as each layer came off, new marvels were exposed. Out of an old-fashioned, knee-high wool sock, upheld by a genuine supporter, might come one of those little ladders with a performing acrobat on top. Once he extracted a small wooden horse from the void between the seat of his overalls and that of his blue serge church suit.

He carried a beautiful small Bible in the inside coat pocket of the blue serge suit, three fishhooks in the bib pocket of the overalls beneath the turnip-sized gold watch which he often used to correct the sun, a buckeye in the serge pockets for luck, and a pocketknife which could be extended to become a dirk.

As he often said, he had everything about him that a man could want.

"Always travel light," Uncle Caleb once remarked, as he extracted a pocket anvil from the carpenter's rule pocket on the leg of his overalls. He used it to brad together a break in his blue serge suit belt.

UNCLE JOHN'S KINGDOM

ANY old-timer who got up in that cold and rain Wednesday morning knew in an instant that this was the kind of day to be spent sitting on the front porch and thinking about fixing some fences sooner or later.

A cold, rainy fall day used to be appreciated back in the days when people were running stock or growing crops. It was a gift from the Lord. It was one of the few times a man could take off with a good conscience from the eternal round of trying to catch up on things you were behind on. Even then the Calvinistic conscience would not be stilled entirely. A man felt better if he worried a little about some fences that needed to be fixed; but he didn't have to do anything.

The old-timers whiled away this benison of idleness in various ways. Some caught up on their file of the *Semi-Weekly Farm News* and got mad reading about the IWWs. Some pasted patches of paper on the front gatepost and practiced with the .22 rifle. Some sharpened their pocketknives, which was the proper thing to do always if you couldn't think of anything else.

But nearly everybody worried a little about some fences that needed to be fixed. They didn't want to waste the day entirely.

WHEN I was a boy, the best place to be on a cold, rainy fall day was Uncle John's harness room.

It was the one floored room in the barn, a big barn with a wide hallway running down the middle toward the stables in the rear. The harness room opened off this hall. It was Uncle John's den, his spiritual home, his refuge from the continual lecturing of his wife. He was safe here. Aunt Martha would never have dared to invade the barn. This was Uncle John's kingdom, just as the house, to which she reluctantly admitted him for meals and sleep, was her domain. In Aunt Martha's eyes, this was right and proper and ordained by the Baptist church.

The harness room was full of wonderful smells, the smell of harness oil and saddle soap, creosote and horse sweat. It contained the lifetime plunder of an old man, such things as discarded currycombs, dehorning clippers, used cinch buckles, used pieces of rock salt, and old surcingles.

It also contained the bottle of whiskey which Aunt Martha always said Uncle John didn't drink.

ON a cold, rainy day, Uncle John invariably grew fidgety and found that he had a lot of harness repairing to do. He was widely known for the care he gave his harness.

Kids were welcome to go with him. Uncle John would rig a swing out of a rope plowline in the big hall to keep, as he said, the kids out of his way in the harness room. He would work while the rain roared on the sheet-iron roof and the water cascaded from the eaves. Normally a shy, taciturn man, he would grow louder as the day passed. Eventually he would sing a few verses from "Amazing Grace."

On a cold, rainy day the feel of the place still comes back, not a memory exactly but an emotional tone, a feel, the echo of a lost happiness and a lost contentment.

AUNT MARTHA AND "THAT MAN"

FOR forty years Great-Aunt Martha seldom called him anything except "That Man," a term delivered with a twist of distaste on her face.

A small rail of a woman, she harried him as a terrier might a mastiff, her bright, nervous eyes glinting with pleasure as she saw a verbal gig sink home. On the occasional times that she was able to stir Uncle John into an angry roar, she hurried meekly into a chair in the corner, opened her Bible, and studiously pretended to read, thus becoming visible proof of the kind of saintliness that was here being mistreated.

This always made Uncle John madder still, but not for long. He was a big, placid man who was accumulating the false-fat of middle age. He liked to laugh. To Great-Aunt Martha a finger which had touched a playing card had somehow become stained with sin that could never be removed, but Uncle John liked to sneak off and play pitch with the boys and boom out exultantly, "High, low, jick, jack, and the game," when he was winning.

Aunt Martha was a literal believer in the Bible, but Uncle John professed to be puzzled by some of it, such as that story about the lion and the lamb lying down together.

"It sounds all right for the lions," Uncle John would say, "but you going to convert any lambs to that?"

"Blasphemer! Blasphemer!" Aunt Martha would moan softly, running for her Bible, but you sensed in her a sort of pride at his wickedness.

AUNT Martha and Uncle John had divided up the world between them. The house was her domain, to be defiled neither by man nor pipe nor dog. Even in rainy weather when he couldn't work the farm, Uncle John spent little time there. His kingdom was the barn, and the harness room there was fitted out with such creature comforts as his burned and battered pipe and an old solitaire deck. If you were a visiting younger relative on a rainy day, he might sit there taking an occasional swallow from a large bottle of Dr. Funston's Fistula Remedy and talk admiringly of his wife's talent for bedeviling a man into exasperation.

"There is no finer woman than your aunt," he would begin, "but . . ."

FOR forty years they lived thus. Every noon during the spring plowing season they had the same argument because he didn't rush from the dinner table back to the fields. Aunt Martha held that any idle minute gave Satan a chance to get in his dirty work, and Uncle John, who liked to lie down on the boards of the front gallery and snooze awhile after eating, resented her lack of concern for the livestock.

"Martha, you'll wear the horses out," he would complain.

Through forty years and six children and death, disaster, good times and hard — mostly a little hard — they lived secretly proud of one another but apparently unwilling to allow the world a glimpse of any affection. That would have been unseemly behavior.

Uncle John died one spring of a cold that turned suddenly into pneumonia, and Aunt Martha, choking to keep down the great well of her grief, observed, with that twist of her face, that he had brought it on himself.

"He always did change his union suits too soon," she said.

UNCLE ED'S EPIC

WHEN I knew him in the old days out in the Lariat country, Uncle Ed Wingate was already old. He had not only made the Alaskan gold rush but had written a manuscript about it with this title page: "HOW I MINED FOR GOLD IN ALASKA UNSUCCESSFULLY. An Authentic Account Told in the Exact Words of the Narrator."

I don't exactly understand how he did it, because I never have really understood gold, much less mining for it, but Uncle Ed and his companions swarmed in on treasure trove from the land side. They had to cross a series of icy mountain ranges, each of which took some lives. They carried their subsistence on their backs.

Uncle Ed disposed of this episode very crisply. "The reader could never imagine the hardships we went through," he wrote, thus transporting the reader from Dawson to Fairbanks, in a hurry.

Although Uncle Ed's account never got published, no friend of his ever read this passage without nodding a head sagely.

"How true!" the friend would say.

UNCLE Ed's manuscript is typical of most of those turned out by people who "have a real story to tell." Sensible human beings unfortunately want to get to the point in writing, and slithering along over icy mountain ranges is not the point.

The professional writer takes a different approach. He does not want to get to the point. It would cut his revenue. He is bemused by every penguin, if they have them up there, into long pages of description. Every mountain that he crosses becomes twice as high, and there are three times as many ranges to cross. He describes the sensation of a man dying of thirst in all this snow. (By the way, how did they manage that?) He throws in some dialogue to show the rough camaraderie of the miners, especially the roughness.

The professional especially spends pages and pages on the painted ladies whom Uncle Ed disposed of with, "The reader cannot imagine the depravity of these hussies." Anyhow, this was the way Uncle Ed felt about it in his later years.

Mostly Uncle Ed's account was like a diary: "Mar. 5. Ate breakfast. Broke camp. Jones cannot travel. The reader will never believe this."

BY any reasonable guess, Uncle Ed on his odyssey traveled four or five times as far as Ulysses, but in seventy-six cramped, handwritten pages, Uncle Ed managed to preserve the whole epic for posterity.

Homer was able to make a good fat book out of Ulysses, throwing in strange whirlpools, one-eyed giants, and song and dance girls in the islands against whom you had to lash yourself to the mast. Homer didn't exactly describe any beautiful women in detail. He didn't have to. He had already set up the situation.

Homer got this great big book out of a tinhorn adventure while Uncle Ed got nothing. But, of course, Homer wasn't Ulysses.

GRANDPA PEARSON AT EIGHTY-PLUS

I HAVE never seen any point in a human being's getting older. Recently, I have reread Cicero and Charles Lamb on the matter, and they don't make a very good case. They flourish a lot of rhetoric.

Grandpa Pearson begrudged the years also. Grandpa was eighty years old plus and lived on a farm two miles south of our town in West Texas. Late on summer afternoons, he would take his place in a thronelike chair on his shaded front porch, and glaring straight ahead through near sightless eyes, he would rule over the prairie.

Occasionally, he would call out, "Evvy, bring me a toddy."

Evalina was his youngest, the one who had stayed home to take care of him. She was a pretty old maid of twenty-five, dark haired and with a patient, quiet face across which dark shadows occasionally passed.

To anybody, aged ten to seventy, who would stop a moment at the front gate, Grandpa Pearson would shout out advice on any subject they were worried about along with long slabs of his reminiscences.

Grandpa Pearson took a very dim view of getting old.

"ALL I ever got out of it is that people wait on me hand and foot now," he said. "But nobody ever does anything the way I say. And if I rear up too quick to raise hell, I always pull a hamstring. Be damned if I know why nobody can mix a toddy that I can taste anymore.

"If it was left up to me, I'd just as soon put in another crop of kafir and milo and maybe about twenty acres of Sudan grass. You have to watch that Sudan. You can lose your unmentionables.

"While a man is growing a crop, he never sees anything but the rear end of two horses, but that's more than I see now. At least, something sometimes happened up there."

Grandpa Pearson always said that if he had his life to live over again, he would live a more rakehell life.

"When I was young," he said, "I wasted a lot of time saving for my old age. Old age and money don't have anything in common."

GRANDPA Pearson's life changed radically one day. A long bowlegged man with a sardonic squint and a deprecatory chuckle just showed up and married Evalina. It turned out that they had been courting for awhile, not behind Grandpa's back but twenty-five feet beyond his limited eyesight.

Grandpa was not mad. He just wondered. He pointed out that this Pres, Evalina's man, had been for several years an agent for the cattlemen's association. "Been all over at least forty counties," said Grandpa. "Seen all them strange people."

He was going to run the Pearson farm, and Grandpa had to admit that Pres was a good one. He would keep an eye on the Sudan grass. Also, said Grandpa, Evalina had taken on a new and vigorous interest in life and could even mix a good toddy.

If Pres wanted to spend the rest of his life facing the rear ends of two horses, that was his business.

SEPARATING THE GEESE FROM THE GOATS

GREAT-AUNT Martha died too soon to relish the present discomforts of the world, and relish them she would have.

She preached all her life that the world was going to the hot place in a handbasket, and she took grim pleasure in seeing her worst forebodings come true.

Even in her day she detected in the world deadly and primeval sins. People were buying things on credit at the store. The ten-year-old Langston girl was openly wheeling about the neighborhood on a *boy's* bicycle. The preachers were delivering perfunctory one-hour sermons, and the congregation hardly contributed one "amen" every five minutes.

"Oh, Lord, forgive them all," Aunt Martha would exclaim, correctly aligning her influence alongside that of the Deity.

It was her theory that it all started with Original Sin. She was a labored reader at best and never could explain what Original Sin was. When asked about it, she would shout, "It's Original Sin, that's what," and her lips would curl in triumph and her black eyes would gleam with satisfaction at having thus outwitted Satan and his earthly questioners.

Original sin, in her view, was likely to extend to canned salmon, Post Toasties and other store foods not properly prepared at home, and also to novels like "Survey of Eagle's Nest."

THE Youth Rebellion of our times would not have surprised Aunt Martha. "As the twig is bent, so the child is spoiled," she liked to say.

Nor would the race troubles or the prevalence of murder have astonished her. It was in the Scriptures, according to Aunt Martha, that in the last days there would be wars and other rumors and the son would turn against his father and the lion would sit down on the lamb.

The end of the world, or the Last Trump as she called it, was always frightfully imminent to Aunt Martha. She expected it at any moment of the day and was ready instantly to get the chickens under shelter. At times, she grieved that it did not come at the instant when the Lord could have caught Seph Trimble red-handed when he was short-weighting her on some pullets that she was selling.

She always comforted herself with the thought that she and the others pure of heart would have their day at the Last Trump. They would be gathered to the bosom of the Lord while various merchants would be gathered to a bosom she had rather not mention.

"At the Last Trump," Aunt Martha would assert firmly, "the geese will separate from the goats."

THE current financial crisis would not have bothered her at all. She had no use for banks or business. Money, she said, is the root of everything.

The prevalence of murder would not have impressed her because murder was prevalent all through her frontier existence. A pistol was not necessarily bad, but the presence of one ordinarily indicated a gambling man, and a gambler was the tool of Satan.

Aunt Martha lived seventy-eight years expecting at each moment the Last Trump and didn't understand the years very well, but she lived a life of very simple piety.

I think she is undoubtedly among the geese.

SPOKEN LIKE A MAN

THE MALE ANIMAL

Any thoughtful man, as he looks down at the shavings the barber has been carefully trimming away, is bound to think, "Well, there's six more inches I'll never get back."

THE MALE ANIMAL

THE AVERAGE AMERICAN MALE

AN outfit called the Family Economics Bureau of the Northwestern National Life Insurance Company has just issued a "study" of the normal American male, the conclusions of which I resent.

After all, I am just as average as the next man, maybe less so.

The normal American male, says this report, has backaches all the time. He drinks 3.7 gallons of alcohol every year. (Evidently, some of them drink most of it at once.) He wears glasses and may very well use false teeth or a bridge, wears a 10D shoe, and detests buttermilk. He may have received a plaque for something in the last year.

If you do not grade out very good on this, don't worry, for my mind which cuts through such things like a scalpel has spotted the fallacy in all this business. The report says the average man drowns if he falls out of a boat accidentally.

If they're going to figure in all the people who drowned, the statistics are obviously not normal.

I DO not grade out very high on the scale myself, and I consider myself fully as good as any other average man, except in math.

For instance, I do not have backaches. It has been years since I felt anything from down there.

I am supposed to wear glasses, but generally I forget and leave them at home. Instead of false teeth, I have an elaborate system of fillings firmly anchored by a few veins here and there of the old original grinders. I have not received a plaque for anything in the last year, though I deserved several, and my shoe size is a secret between me and the luggage company which custom-tailors my shoes.

I fall out of the boat regularly, mostly from having left my eyeglasses at home, and I have not drowned yet. I feel safe in saying that it wouldn't happen to a man more than once or twice in his lifetime.

The trouble with such studies is that they are made by polling American males who say they are normal but are afraid to confess the things that really plague them.

A DEEP study into the secret life of the normal American male would produce some standards for judging his normality that would be a great deal more valid.

The normal American male, for instance, is likely to come wide awake in his own bed in the dark of 3:00 A.M. and wonder what the devil he is doing there and how it all happened. At such times, he is likely to brood on what might go wrong next.

The average American male is behind on his lawn-mowing, and his checkbook is always $2.27 out of balance, except that it is $2.27 to his credit one month and $2.27 to his loss the next. The average American male has a dog with psychic problems that he doesn't know how to handle and an automobile with problems that the mechanics swear are psychic.

He is a man who is merely trying to hold on as best he can, and he is barely able to do it.

RULES FOR RAISING HAIR

A CLOSE student of the local scene wants to know why most of the bareheaded drivers of sports cars around here are shiny bald.

He thinks it is part of the drive toward protective coloration, that these characters instinctively seek something which will blend them into their environment inconspicuously. If you have 5/20 vision in one eye and will look when the sun isn't shining on the bald spots, you can see that this is wrong.

When you ask why most sports car drivers are bald, you might as well ask why most men who eat steaks are bald. Or who gig frogs. Or who beat their wives or don't beat their wives.

Or who do anything except peddle Alberto V05, or whatever that stuff is.

You ought not be surprised if most men are bald. After all, this is the Century of the Common Man.

We uncommon men who are long and thick of hair and sparse and thin of limb are now often referred to as Upright Tarantulas.

A S a onetime winner of a prize for intensive hair-raising on small areas, I have often been asked to help out the victims of baldness. There is no help.

The best thing to do is get a skinned place on the bald spot and get some sympathy.

For the man who still has his hair, however, I have drawn up some standard operating procedures. They might help him to keep it. First of all, if you have hair, do not be in a hurry to get some water on it. The healthy animal body secretes rare oils which help to protect the hair follicle. Consider the wise dog. He wets his coat only for fun and dodges baths whenever he can.

It is possibly true that dogs have a tendency to stink, but how many bald dogs have you ever seen?

H AIR, like fine cookery, is ruined by an excess of cleanliness. History proves that widespread baldness came in when lye got easy to get and soap got cheap. There is not one single instance on record where the Indians complained about the poor quality of scalps.

The second rule, if you have hair, is do not be in a hurry to get a haircut. It might not grow back.

If you have to have a haircut, get some good, responsible barber like my old friend, Toledo Kemendo, the Shakespearean expert. He knows how to cut hair and still leave a starter crop.

AGAINST THE RAZOR'S EDGE

WHENEVER one of these guys comes on the TV commercial telling how he got sixty-two shaves out of some fancy new kind of razor blade, you have to wonder which the man likes best, his razor blade or his face.

As an expert who has tried about every razor and every blade, it is my opinion that the man who shaves more than once with one blade edge is nuts. His sense of values must be as dull as his razor; he is too obtuse to deserve the Affluent Society. He is converting one of the day's pleasantest and most useful ceremonials, the morning shave, into a painful necessity.

Sure, you can scrape your face thirty times with any blade if you want to. The Indians shaved all their lives with only one clam shell; they were willing just to pull their whiskers out by the roots.

You have to decide whether you're going to save skin or pennies, and the man who is going to save on razor blades has a long way to go to make his fortune.

SOMEWHERE between the ages of fifteen and twenty, every man begins a period when he is going to have to shave every day of his life. He can either enjoy it or delude himself that he is going to save money on it.

Most of the TV presentation on shaving is wholly haywire. The average TV shaver shown looking at himself in the mirror has a toothy grin, as if he had just sold somebody the last half-spoiled egg on the shelf. In bitter truth, the average shaver, just awakened, who looks at himself in a mirror is aghast. He is undeniably dismal. Sacks that look like they were carrying mercury hang down from his eyes. His hair stands on end like the beehive hairdos that the girls have been wearing, but without any of the charm. Wrinkles hang across his face like ill-fitted draperies on a window. He can reach his hand up and flick them around.

This is where the value of a good shave comes in, the unbelievable alchemy of a lot of hot water, soap, towels, even the good cans of aerosol lather, though they are hardly a replacement for plain old shaving soap and a luxuriantly bristled shaving brush.

And for crissakes, a new blade. You can yank your beard out if you want to or chop it out like weeds out of cotton. I like for a beard to melt against the razor's edge.

THERE is a ritual to a good shave: copious sloshing of hot water, lots of soap and lather, and the accumulation of a slight mist on the mirror. Any good shaver will sing during the ritual. Nothing cheerful, of course. Most of us have found out that a good, well-rendered, gloomy song will produce a happy day.

It is best to pick out a gloomy tune and begin it in a hopeless and toneless baritone, such as "Birmingham jail, lord, Birmingham jail . . ." By the time you are in the shower where the tile walls can turn you into a cappella, you can sing that "her beauty was sold for a rich man's gold . . . she's a bird in a gilded cage."

You'll come out a different man. The sacks will be gone from your eyes and the wrinkles from your face, and you will be fit to face eternity again.

People who like to use a razor blade thirty times can get a huge supply of once used blades at our house at 90 percent off.

ADVANCED IDEAS ABOUT MEN'S SHOES

THE office critic came by the other day and said, "When are you going to get another pair of shoes?" Ordinarily, nobody pays any attention to him because he is a fop given to wearing knitted shawls over his head when the air conditioning is turned high.

In this instance, however, he had a point. Although barely more than five years old, the shoes I have been wearing lately have a slightly worn look. The threads show where one seam has pulled loose from the sole. They have white marks over them where I have waded in mud, and the lace of one is broken. I have replaced it with some beeswaxed small stuff from the boat which is darn sure not going to break.

The thing that most people don't realize about this pair of shoes is that they are perfect for the rainy weather we have been having, because each has a hole in the bottom. All you have to do is lift your foot, and the water will drain out.

It is odd that in these thousands of years, shoemakers have never solved the drainage problem they created.

IN fact, most shoemakers do not know how to make a man's shoe. The drainage problem is typical. Most men's waterproof shoes are so low-cut that a man is likely to step too deep into a puddle while wondering how in the world to play Sir Walter Raleigh to one of those pretty girls in plastic rain boots.

When this happens, all that a man can do usually is pretend that he is really energetic and jump high in the air and make hydraulic pressure squirt some of the water from under his feet when he lands. Hydraulic pressure has never been as good at this as drainage.

A man's shoe ought to be made with vents in the sole equipped with one-way valves which will let trapped water escape but prevent any from entering. Common sense says, also, that men's shoes ought to come equipped with strings tapered from the middle so they will break at the ends and can be used by adding a new tip.

Men's shoes also ought to be reduced in size, so that a man who wears a Size 14 can find a Size 10 that fits him and quit looking sheepish.

SO far, I have got small support for my advanced ideas about men's shoes, mainly because men are getting as vain as women. The town is full of businessmen in thick-soled, highly polished shoes, so tight that one single atomic bomb jar would bust every stitch in them. It is this kind of false economy that has put the country in the shape it is in today.

These men think they are fooling somebody about their personal hygiene, but those of us in the know smile behind our hands. "Bet his feet haven't been drained in four days," we tell each other.

I used to walk around in rainy weather hearing squirting sounds inside my shoes, but no more.

The average thirty-foot boat is drained better than a man's shoe.

THE VIOLENT STAGE OF BOY

A LEADING toy designer has been trying to get the toy-makers to stop making toy guns because they tend to lead to violence.

It was certainly true in my day. In the frequent fights between rival cowboys in which I took part, it was a standard tactic to whip out the old cap pistol and yell as swiftly as possible "Pow! Gotcha," thus establishing claim to the fastest draw. Shoot first and ask questions afterward was our motto. When two fighters powed at the same time, it nearly always led to violence, though the toy guns were discarded as less reliable than a fist or a stick.

At a certain age of boy, though, almost anything tends to violence. It raises the question of whether we ought not stop manufacturing boys.

If a manufacturer came up with a toy Dove of Peace, there would be some fights over it.

A S we got older, we discarded the toy pistol for a side arm which can best be called a hand catapult, since its ancient name is out of favor in these days of equal rights. It was not a slingshot. Two strips of rubber were rigged to a forked stick, and a small firing pouch was tied to the other ends. Used like a bow, this instrument would heave a rock true and hard.

Since there was no question of who got off the first shot with this weapon, it did not ordinarily lead to violence in itself. The supply of rocks on the high plains was not limitless, though. Every boy gradually amassed a collection of properly sized and shaped rocks, retrieving each rock after its use. He came to know every hue and indentation of his rocks.

To find one of your prized rocks in the collection of another led to violence swift and sure.

Another activity in those days which tended toward violence was a game called pop-the-whip. The boy caught on the end always resented it.

S OMEHOW, I do not believe this toy designer will succeed in his crusade, laudable though it is. Every boy goes through a Roy Rogers stage, and many girls do, too. Lacking a toy gun, a boy with his imagination can convert almost anything into one, a crooked stick, an old piece of pipe, or a properly shaped bottle.

I am not arguing for this. It is just the nature of boys. They live violently, and what the answer to them is no adult has yet found out.

Some men never get over the violent stage of boy. They remain violent all their lives. But most finally mature, which is a word for saying that they have got so old that it hurts when they get hit, and come out for less violence all the way around.

THE MAN WHO THINKS HE HAS EVERYTHING

E VERYBODY knows about that problem of what to give a man who has everything, but a Dallas woman has come up with a tougher problem.

"What," she asked the other day, "do you buy for a man who thinks he has everything?"

This is a delicate question. This state of mind is a beatific thing that comes only once or twice in the life of a man and ought not be disturbed.

Time and the world will take care of it fairly fast. It is a time in a man's existence when he wants nothing that belongs to another man. He is satisfied with his own undeniable great gifts, his obvious good looks and way with the women, and his own hilarious sense of humor.

It was that time of life for Muley Hawkins, an old friend of mine, when he decided he would like to be postmaster. When he went to see the congressman about it, he was equipped with nothing except a handshake and the announcement that he wanted the job.

"You ask to be postmaster," said the congressman helplessly, with a vague wave of his hand toward Muley, "and you have nothing else to lay before me?"

Said Muley stoutly: "What else do you need?"

I am unusually fortunate in being able to attain this state of mind two or three times a month. Then, I have to help the youngster with his homework.

APPARENTLY women never experience this sense of intense well-being and extraordinary talents that comes to every man at least once in his life.

Stuart McGregor, a wise man and the editor of the *Texas Almanac,* told me once of the time that he moved, undismayed, from the small town of Coleman to the University of Texas. He went equipped with just as much confidence as a man from Coleman, Texas, ought to have.

He was late registering, and he came in the door late to Miss Roberta Lavendar's Latin class, so that he was framed there in a kind of spotlight.

"Do you know any Latin?" she asked.

McGregor drew himself up to the tip of his stocky frame.

"I was valedictorian at Coleman High School," he announced.

This was undoubtedly the high point in Mr. McGregor's self-esteem. In the years since, Mr. McGregor has always been too modest about one of the best and most exact minds that most of us have ever seen operate.

There was a time in my own life when I was absolutely irresistible to women. There were just a bunch of them around too dumb to know it.

WHEN a man thinks he has everything, there is nothing that you can give him. At this stage of his existence, he is prepared to admit that Winston Churchill, say, has certain abilities that he does not possess. Churchill's abilities, however, will seem a small thing in comparison to his own talents at handling a road-building caterpillar.

It is best just to leave a man alone when he thinks this way. He really does have everything.

THE FINE, UNCLUTTERED YEARS

A MAN has finally come right out and said that you ought not to despair if you have reached middle age. The best years are ahead, he says.

It is high time that somebody came to this conclusion. The fine, uncluttered years truly are ahead for the middle-aged man. These are the years when his hair becomes automatically detachable, and he can finally get at that case of dandruff and scrub it off.

When he wants to have his teeth fixed, he can just leave them with the dentist. No more of that sitting around in a dentist's chair. The man beyond middle age no longer has to chase women, mainly because they don't feel that they have to run.

Obviously, these are the beautiful years, free of the ugly clutter of steaks, girls, and important tennis matches that mar the picture of youth.

THE life of the older man is intrinsically superior to that of the youth because it is more efficient. For instance, when a man of sixty breathes, he just uses less air than a brat of twenty. There is less pollution.

Or, take the problem of food. The man beyond middle age does not have to waste a lot of money on sirloin strips, potatoes au gratin, and big green salads decked out with imported Roquefort. A bowl of Post Toasties is about all that he ever wants.

The aging man does not have to spend his money on fancy weskits, derby hats, and brass embroidered sock supporters. He isn't going anywhere. And he is usually thankful that he isn't. It would keep him from getting in bed at nine o'clock. If he didn't get in bed at nine o'clock, he might not get up for one of the main events of his day — his morning bowl of Post Toasties.

This is the life, boy, as you easily see. You don't have to climb any mountain peaks just to shoot a bighorn. You don't have to get up on water skis and get pitched in the drink and then laugh about it. Just coast on through this golden existence of the golden years.

You don't even have to work like the dickens to write a good book or found a new company or win an election. Some youngster is doing it.

MOST of us who have reached middle age have discovered that you don't have to read to keep up with the new books. Today's sensational new novelist is very like the sensation of forty years ago. You don't even have to reread Shakespeare. You remember him.

Some people carry this too far. A friend of ours was telling us about an eighty-five-year-old man who has quit reading newspapers. "I've already read it before," he said. Plainly the man is misguided. Today's newspaper comes to you hot from the press full of all kinds of goodies. And anyhow, how are some of us going to make a living?

It all adds up, though, to proof that the golden years are truly the golden years.

And like every man who has grown older, I say to the devil with it. I liked steaks, pretty girls, climbing a mountain peak if I wanted to, discovering a new author, and dandruff. And actually, you didn't have to go to the dentist too often.

PROGRESS

IT is hard for a wise, sensitive, tolerant, broad-gauged, maturely handsome man in the prime years of human existence to take the brashness and the supreme self-confidence of youngsters of twenty to thirty years. They are always going around chinning themselves in public or otherwise calling attention to activities you quit five or ten years ago as frivolous and painful besides.

It is best to be philosophical about all this. After all, progress goes on. In prehistory, when man was a lake dweller or lived in caves, the young males picked up clubs and drove the old males out of the herd. Now they allow you to stay around to show how useless you are.

MR. MCGREGOR AND THE PLAYBOY BUNNIES

I HAVE just received an invitation to become a Dallas charter member of the Playboy Club, which is the name for those night spots where pretty girls dressed up as bunnies attend the male members.

This is a very exclusive invitation. It says here in the letter that I was invited only after an acceptance committee recommended me. The letter is signed by a genuine printed logotype of the signature of Mr. Hugh M. Hefner, the man who thought up this particular bunny run, and it was rushed to me by third-class mail.

As it points out, there are many advantages to being a club-type Playboy besides the bunnies, and it costs only twenty-five dollars to try. For one thing, closed-circuit TV shows you around the club as you enter, and you get to hang up your special nameplate in the foyer. For another, you can get a sirloin steak plate for the price of a drink.

It happens that I don't like for people to charge as much for a drink as they do for a steak.

ALSO, TV has nothing to gain from the impression of my face, closed-circuit or not, and though I do not have a personal nameplate, it is becoming obvious that my name is on an addressograph plate which is hung too many places already.

Mainly, though, this invitation just came too late. All the bunnies run nowadays when they see me. They think I am Mr. McGregor. When I travel out into the Lariat country, I am still allowed on the benches at the exclusive Pete's Recreation Club; but I am not allowed at the tables because I might accidentally punch out somebody's eye with a cue, thus ruining the felt tip on the end of it and causing untold damage of seven or eight dollars. Like Mr. Yeats's old man, a great many of us have ceased to talk so splendidly about love and politics these days, which is to say that we have discovered good taste.

Twenty years ago I would have been flattered at being named officially a Playboy. Nowadays, however, it is no good being a Playboy unless you are also a Justice of the Supreme Court, climb Mount Everest, or write Robert Frost.

Custom these days requires that a Playboy have something else to do in his spare time.

ACTUALLY, the Playboy Club is probably a wonderful organization for the young fellow aged twenty-five to thirty.

The trouble is that whenever I go to a place like this to enjoy myself, I always run into a bunch of old duffers whom I knew in college. They are kicking up their heels and chasing bunnies and paying steak prices for bourbon and branch water. The spectacle is all too silly.

The spectacle of ancients carousing like this spoils the evening for the rest of us. You wonder why they ever came to the club in the first place. They ought to know better.

GIRL CONTROL

A GREAT deal of very deep learning is contained in press handouts which never get printed. Here, for example, is a handout which says: "The male fiddler crab has one very large claw which is used to signal females."

At first glance, this seems to be one of the better anatomical specializations that evolution has produced. It also explains why so many of us who have stubby claws do so poorly at attracting females. Evidently, when the fiddler crab spots a shapely girl fiddler crab, he merely makes a beckoning motion with his giant claw, and that is all there is to it.

Those of us who do not have giant claws do not fare so well. We crook a finger at a neighboring girl, and she runs off to tell her father right after he has bought a fresh supply of shotgun shells.

You have to face it. Some guys can attract the girls by waving a giant claw and others have to wave a twenty dollar bill.

APPARENTLY, girl control is a thing built into some men and has nothing to do with how they look or their muscular build. A boy named Preacher Conroe had it out in the Lariat country when we were all growing up. Actually, his name was Howard, but he was called Preacher because he always knew the Sunday school lesson.

On the face of it, Howard did not have a giant claw. He was long and gangling, talked through his nose, and wore thick glasses. Also, he had big feet and always walked with his toes turned in because, being an intellectual, he had decided that this would cure his flat feet.

Furthermore, Preacher did not like girls. He said they made him sweat.

All this meant nothing with the girls, particularly Saribeth Tompkins, a pretty but determined girl. She would always be waiting around the front gate to talk to him when he walked by the Tompkins house, and if he tried to sneak back through the alley, she would run around the house and meet him.

"Why, Howard," she would say, "imagine meeting you here."

ONE day she caught him alone on a stretch of prairie near town and chased him down. Preacher did his best, while trying to keep his toes pointed inward, but he wasn't a very good runner. Saribeth caught him, knocked him down from the back, and pinioned his arms to the ground.

"Howard," she asked solemnly, "why are you always chasing me?"

He gave up after that. He and Saribeth dated. She watched over him through high school. She watched over him through Abilene Christian College. He really did become a preacher, and they got married.

She often tells people now what a rakehell he was and how she barely saved him from perdition.

OPEN THE GATE

APPARENTLY, the gate was invented by the time Adam and Eve were kicked out of the Garden of Eden. It had to have been, else what could have kept them from going back? I have a picture in mind of what happened when they set up the first gate outside. Adam is waving Eve to the rear. "I came first," he says.

"Yes, dear," says Eve. "Open the gate."

He opens it and she steps through ahead of him. This has been going on a long time.

THE PLIGHT OF THE MALE ANIMAL

THE Book of Knowledge has just put out a bunch of newspaper paragraphs to show how much it knows, and one of them reads: "It is the male ostrich that incubates the eggs, not the female . . . a number of females may lay their eggs in one nest for a single male to incubate."

Maybe this is startling stuff to the editors of the Book of Knowledge, but it is pretty old hat to any man of worldly experience. It typifies the universal plight of the male animal. He goes through life highly pleased with himself, thinking he has six or seven slick chicks on the string. In the end, he finds out that they have teamed up against him and that all he had was squatter's rights.

It is the male animal's vanity that he can handle any number of females that gets him into trouble. He quickly finds out that they've all handled him.

THE principle of male gullibility runs throughout the animal kingdom, though the female wiles used to work on his vanity sometimes hide the principle.

Look at the average chicken yard, for instance. On any given day the hens are always busy working up an egg while the rooster struts around and preens himself like a congressman just reelected. You would think the rooster lived a life of idleness and ease.

But who is it that has to get out of bed every morning, summer and winter, to take care of the crowing? Not the hens. They sleep late. Lacking a pillow to cover up their ears, they use their wings.

Quite likely, the rooster has to get his own breakfast.

In the same way, the female lion busybodies around hunting food for her brats while the old man sits back and takes it easy. This is merely the female lion's way of demonstrating to the world, however, that her husband is incompetent to deal with any problem.

Actually, the mournful look on any male lion's face will tell you who does the worrying for that family.

A few animals like the tiger who know what they want, a nice fat goat maybe, manage to beat the rap on this business.

THE male tiger is more of a traveling man type than the lion. Most of the time he spends away from the family covering the territory. As a result, the female is left to feed the young ones. This is not as hard as it sounds, because a tiger will eat anything when hungry.

Out in West Texas, the centipede has things worked out pretty well, also, because the male and female centipedes do not live together. They scare each other.

The tiger and the centipede probably symbolize the higher aspirations of the human male who has spent a little too much time on the nest. When things have been especially boring, he would like to be a tiger and get out of town for the week and get into some new kind of trouble. When things are really desperate, he wouldn't mind being a centipede.

But generally he remains an ostrich. He is stuck with the confounded nest and the job while the girls all go off to play bridge.

THE SEASONED HOUSEHOLDER

The seasoned householder refuses to worry about a leak in the house when he can foresee a much larger leak in his pocketbook.

THE SEASONED HOUSEHOLDER

THE SEASONED HOUSEHOLDER

ONE of the benefits of being a householder is that something is always happening to keep your mind off frivolous amusements. Last week, the shrubs were burning up in the drought. With the rains came a leak in the roof.

When a leak shows up in his roof, the new householder betrays his amateur status. He becomes agitated. He gets mad at the builder for using the inferior materials in his house. Actually, it is not the fault of the builder but of the materials. Or the new householder blames the previous owner for not taking sufficient care of the house.

The seasoned householder, however, accepts the inevitable. He realizes that the breaks run about eight to five against him in owning a house.

The seasoned householder refuses to worry about a leak in the house when he can foresee a much larger leak in his pocketbook.

THIS was the way it was at our house when, after the recent rains, a tape over a joint of Sheetrock began to pouch suspiciously. The paint was faintly discolored.

Recognizing a leak is one thing, however; proving it is another. You hunt up the ladder and patch it up where it is coming apart. You ascend to the roof at risk of life and limb, scooting along it to avoid falling off. You do not look for the leak at the point where it shows up in the ceiling, for a leak in one part of the house usually shows up at the opposite end. It follows its way across the house through some mysterious system of conduits.

After you have examined the roof inch by inch for two hours, you usually make the discovery that we did. The roof is sounder than a dollar. It doesn't have any leaks.

You go back down to take a look at that baggy tape. Maybe water hasn't caused it. Maybe it is a wood tumor. You poke a finger gently against the tape, and it breaks. A small spurt of water spits gypsum on your face.

Since water is there, the conclusion is obvious. If the roof is sound, the leak has to be in either the foundation or the walls.

YOU can go over the foundation inch by inch if you want to. Possibly somewhere some water along it has built up enough back pressure to spill over into the attic. You can look for chinks in the brick. Usually, you will discover that there isn't a hole anywhere in your house.

You can then do one of two things. We have tried them both. You can go over the house inch by inch, pounding everything lightly with a hammer. If you do this, you are bound to hit whatever it is that is causing the leak, and you might accidentally fix it.

Or you can call in an expert and let him fix the house while you try to patch up the bank account.

A MODERN FOOLPROOF APPLIANCE

AS any sensible person knows, one of the marks of a good householder is an adequate tool kit. Naturally, I don't have any.

It was with some rejoicing, therefore, that we acquired an electric sander the other day just before starting to paint a room. Sanding the woodwork for new enamel by hand is a long and tiresome process. With an electric sander, you just press the button and go zuut-t-t. If it turns out you were wrong, you just rip the piece of wood off and replace it with a new one.

I explained all this to the family.

"Stand back out of danger," I ordered firmly, "while I sand this door."

It was all a little premature, however. The electric cord on the sander was only six feet long, which doesn't give you much range on a door.

I checked the instruction leaflet, and it said that I ought to have an extension cord of sixteen-gauge, three-way cable, and this made sense. Whenever you buy a modern foolproof appliance, you always need something else to make it work. Furthermore, said the leaflet, since I had two-hole electric outlets, I needed an adapter plug to drain off the excess electricity used by this vigorous three-tine instrument.

THE adapter was easy to find. It turned out to be a kind of plug fitting the wall fixture, with an extra wire to allow the excess electricity to drip out without overloading the motor.

Sixteen-gauge, three-way cable was harder. I tried department stores. I tried electric stores. Everybody was out. I finally tried the jovial gentleman at the neighborhood C&S Hardware store, and he said he thought it quite possible that nobody made three-way, sixteen-gauge cable.

He tried a sister store by telephone, and they told him they had once had some.

"Well, why don't they ever leave me any?" groused the jovial gentleman.

This was just before we discovered, in the back of one of his shelves, a huge drum of three-way, sixteen-gauge cable.

"Nobody ever tells me anything," grumbled the salesman, whacking off twenty-five feet of it.

Finding the three-way fittings was something else, but we made it; and I went home to put everything together.

The operation was complicated. In moving everything for the painting, we had somewhere buried all the screwdrivers.

A KITCHEN paring knife works pretty good for this, but you have to be careful to get each wire of the three-way cable connected to the right terminals. If you got the ground cable, for instance, connected to the positive one, it would just feed electricity back into the circuit, and pretty soon it would be dripping out all over the sander. I know this much.

When I had assembled everything, the junior mechanic of the household said reassuringly, "I bet it don't work." It did, though. True, it sands backward; but it works.

Of course, you can't just let electricity drip out of the adapter onto the floor. It would ruin the varnish. You have to buy another thirty feet of wire and tap it off to a water pipe.

And by this time, the wife has sanded about half the woodwork by hand.

HOW TO BAKE A CHERRY PIE

A S usual, my conversation the other night was brilliant. The talk was about food, and I had managed to get it steered around to me and Escoffier.

"Anybody can bake a pie," I said.

"Why don't you?" asked some inconsiderate joker.

"I am supposed to stay out of the kitchen."

As you may guess, I baked one. Some people insist on confusing sparkling talk with promises. And if I've said it once, I've said it a hundred times. Anybody can bake a pie. The only thing you have to do is alter the quantities in most standard recipes.

Take the cherry chiffon pie which I whipped into shape in the seventh round. The recipe for the crust calls for one cup of flour, an eighth of

a teaspoon of salt, a third of a cup of shortening, and ice water.

If you want to know where the ingredients are for the pie filling, that will come later. After all, patience is the secret of all fine cookery.

H AVING got your pie crust stuff together, here's the way you do it:

You mix the flour and salt together and then dump in the shortening. You cut the shortening into the flour. You do this by taking two knives and going chop-chop rapidly back and forth. After about three minutes of this, you knock the side out of the crock. Dump the whole thing in the garbage pail and start over.

This time don't chop-chop so enthusiastically. After a bit the shortening and flour will combine into something that looks like grains of rice, though why it wants to is a mystery. This is the time for the ice water. Do not just throw in a glass of ice water. The dough just vanishes.

Throw the whole thing out and start over.

This time put in the ice water with a medicine dropper. Ha, dough, b'gad! Gather it all up in a little ball and put it on the rolling board. Roll from the center outward. You will soon see that it does not spread like pie crust. It grows like an octopus, shooting off arms this way and that. This is a sign of not enough water, I finally discovered.

Throw the whole thing in the garbage and start over. Also, the accumulation of stuff around now will itself foul up anything you try. Stow all the ingredients back in their proper places. Wash all dishes. Hose down the kitchen floor and try to pretend that you're thinking of baking a pie for the first time.

Then ease up on it again. Eventually you will get a pie crust, even if you have to throw it in the pan. As I've said, it's easy. Anybody can do it.

AS I have said, though, you will find that the recipe has been altered to something remotely resembling the facts. Here are the ingredients I used to produce a delicious single pie shell: fifty pounds of flour, two one-pound cartons of salt, seven drops of ice water, and a case of shortening. (I actually had half a gallon of shortening left over, but it has flour in it.)

In finishing the pie, plan to start with five gallons of cherries.

THE ONLY CIVILIZED HUMAN BEING

LET'S face it. The person who has the most reason to be thankful this Thanksgiving Day is the modern American house cat.

You may find that hard to stomach along with the other intake awaiting you this day, but the fact is inescapable. Time was when the house cat had to live hard like human beings. But today you'll notice that while you have to eat turkey, the family cat is dining on sirloin properly prechopped into acceptable chunks so that the cat will not flip its tail at it and walk away. True, this may be warmed-over steak, but what steak lover ever gave away willingly a good medium-rare morsel?

When you settle down to watch the game on TV, you'll probably find the family cat all settled down in your favorite easy chair. You'll have to move over into a corner and watch the game from the TV end zone. Very few people like to watch TV from the end zone, but the family will point out that the cat looks so fetching there, daring you with her soft eyes to displace her.

The house cat has undoubtedly become the main beneficiary of the affluent society.

ON the whole, the cat may really have earned it. The house cat is fast becoming the only civilized human being.

Man is returning to the wilds. Equipped with his portable liquor cabinet, his catalytic tent stove, and his portable electric generator, man ventures forth fearlessly into the wilderness to rough it and to kill his deer at the feeding lots. The cat is not this stupid. He prefers the life of central heating and tediously cooked foods. The average cat wouldn't touch venison. He won't hunt. Why should he be satisfied with a scrawny sparrow when he can have delicately cooked chunks of pheasant breast? Why eat a steelhead minnow when you can get chunks of lobster in drawn butter?

When you come to think of it, why indeed?

The cat is becoming the only reliable epicure left in our country. We had a cat once which dearly loved fresh green beans if they were cooked with enough chestnuts. She liked Niblets whole grain corn cooked in butter but would raise Sam Hill if offered anything else.

Her relentless demands on me were what caused me to become a great chef.

True, the cat has not yet acquired a good sense of wine, but neither have our people.

MORE and more, the cat seems to be becoming the mainstay of the American home. The youngsters have to get away to the dance or the football game. The lady has a club meeting, and the husband gets home late. But if the family hearth were lit, you would find the house cat lying before it, dreaming with open eyes about primeval times and dinosaurs when meat was bigger.

A cat does not like to leave the home. Most of the good cat fights I've seen recently occurred with a sliding glass door between the combatants.

The house cat should be offering up especial thanks today. Probably he or she won't, being busy with deciding what chair somebody might want to sit in.

WHEN THE ICE STORM COMETH

IT takes a little winter weather like this to bring home the lesson of that fable about the ant and the grasshopper, especially if the ice storm catches you by surprise and you open the pantry door and find nothing there to eat.

At such a moment you are likely to remember that the grasshopper also frittered away the golden harvest days playing gin rummy and watching TV when he was told to go to the grocery store. In contrast, the busy, industrious ant toiled back and forth between home and the supermarket, storing up bacon and eggs against the day when the ice storm cometh.

It makes you wonder how the grasshopper made out. Did he really starve to death, or did he too have for breakfast the extra supply of Fritos jalapeño bean dip that somehow got stored away in the pantry?

Admittedly, this may seem like free advertising, but the way the dip tastes when you're out of cream, it isn't.

FOR a moment, when I first opened the pantry door and looked in on nothing, it was with a feeling of facing cold, privation, and private famine. In this case, the nothing was absolute — not just some patent dry cereal.

Thus faced with disaster, a man's mind is likely to give way a little. Your first impulse is to run to the window and look at the neighbors' houses and wonder which one of them is a lousy ant.

This is the way to madness. If a man gives way to his animal instincts under these circumstances, the very fabric of society will crumble.

It is best to make up your mind that the ant is no gourmet, anyhow, and make the best of what you've got. A half-cup of Lea & Perrins sauce heated to a lively simmer will give you quite a lift. Dog food is perfectly edible. You don't have to eat it like a dog. It was served in cans to people during the war. You can make a perfectly good bread out of corn shorts. Just take them away from the horses.

We made out on bean dip until we finally got the car to mush, and I made the lone, dangerous trek to the grocery store. Arriving well-wrapped in sheepskin coat with my snowshoes over my shoulder, I beat my leather mittens together and whispered to the clerk, "Any word about the folks in Whitehorse?"

"Nope, but the Yukon is frozen over," he replied casually. "Feller came by awhile ago and said pass the word to people going over the pass."

AS far as drama is concerned, he stole my line.

As a result of the storm, however, I have introduced certain reforms at our house, which I recommend to others:

Don't give that bone to the dog. Bury it yourself. A lot of good soup meat goes out on those bones, and can be reclaimed.

Beef up the quality of the food in the survival kit in your car trunk. Some of it now makes you wonder whether you survived. A little lobster Newburg would help.

Find some good ant and stick close.

If you can afford one, buy one of those Saint Bernards with a cask on his neck.

EXERCISING THE MASTER

MANY a man has found his life governed by a dog who has decided the master needs more exercise.

We have such a dog in our house, a kind of dachshund type with feisty terrier characteristics. Out of all the household, she has picked me out as the one person who, in the old Army phrase, is unphysically fit, and she has a twenty-four-hour training schedule which I am supposed to meet, mostly running.

Usually, I have just got settled in a chair after a hard day's work and am waiting to see Perry Mason get his comeuppance, which he will one of these days, when I feel a determined nudging at the shins. Here is the dog mouthing the rubber mouse which is the signal of the chase.

I usually try to get out of this strenuous exertion by grabbing the mouse, throwing it somewhere, and ordering "fetch."

Our dog knows "fetch" well enough, but when ordered to do so during a period which she has designated for exercise, she wags her tail and cocks her eyes and tries to pretend that if she only knew what the word meant, she would do it. You make a rush for the rubber mouse, and the chase is on.

IF you do not fall into this trap and just stay in your chair, you find a dog sooner or later in back of you shoving with the forehead and brandishing the rubber mouse with a glint in her eyes that says, "What's the matter, fatso? Do you want to sit here and lard up and die of a heart attack?"

It always ends in a chase, preferably in the backyard from my point of view. You chase and chase, watching out for the low tree limbs and the stray pyracantha shoots, while the dog demonstrates for you what a superior physical person ought to be able to do. Our dog has some traits that resemble poor sorry professional basketball players. She likes to demonstrate how agile and tricky she is in comparison with the chaser. She is a showboat.

A great many of these clever moves are obviously demonstrations of how I ought to perform the maneuver.

I have interpreted it as an attempt to shame me into some kind of movement — and I naturally resist any kind of movement.

OUR dog is not particularly interested in running under a leash because I am obviously then exercising her. She likes to direct the exercising at me.

There is no mistaking it. She is taking care of my health whether I like it or not. She does not work at this with any other member of the family because she believes, apparently, that their health is sound enough. When I seem to be winded, she is always willing to stop a minute but not close enough for me to get that rubber mouse and burn it.

She works hard at the job, apparently. Usually, when I get inside to a chair, she collapses on the floor for an hour.

FORGING FEARLESSLY AHEAD IN THE RED

AS announced a few weeks ago, our household went on a Spartan expense account promptly at 12:01 A.M. this New Year's Day.

It is pleasing to report that our program to eliminate wasteful spending is proceeding apace even if the world today is stacked against the man who wishes to practice the old-fashioned virtue of thrift. We have had to work out a few snarls in the program. Anybody who wishes to follow our example would do well to see that he is well set up to practice thrift before he starts.

At our house, for instance, I ventured the opinion that a great deal of money was being wasted on detergents that could be invested in new fishing lures.

"Put in less detergent and more shirts," I told the person who is the real head of our household.

"What shirts?" she retorted.

As a result, I had to go downtown and buy six shirts before we could save anything on the price of laundering them. This is the kind of thing you run into if you start out on thrift without planning. Thrift takes a certain amount of wise investment.

A FEW other plans for saving have backfired. For one thing, I had the idea that if you separated the eggs and cooked the yolks one day and saved the whites for the next, you would cut the egg bill in half. Our family has a tremendous egg bill, three or four eggs a week per person sometimes.

It turned out, though, that most modern eggs come with the yellow and the white mixed. The modern egg is a packaged deal.

When you break it into a hot pan, the yellow spreads out through the white like a starfish. You cannot separate it into compartments. Furthermore, it is not practical to save half an egg. You would be better advised to practice thrift somewhere else, such as punching only one small hole in the pepper can.

There is, by the way, a vast waste in eggshells. Here you are throwing the only solid part of an egg into the wastebasket, but I have worked out no answer as yet, except to use the eggshells to improve a pot of coffee. However, you have to cook an awful lot of coffee to eliminate waste in eggshells this way. If anybody has a solution, I would like to know it.

If enough people will get behind us, we will all force the supermarkets to stock shell-less eggs.

ON the whole, our first New Year's Day of thrift was discouraging, but it was at least a start. The income tax people's little booklet had just arrived, a chilling reminder that Uncle Sam as usual is looking askance at bargain-price income tax payments. And this bright new day of a new year had hardly begun when the doorbell rang. It was the paper boy wanting his monthly fee.

At this rate, how can you hope to save money?

And there was the matter of the new practice casting plug which I was demonstrating for the younger fisherman of the family. It went through a window pane. I am pretty sure that the insurance policy protects window panes against acts of God, like practice plugs, but I may be seven dollars in the red instead of forty-three cents ahead.

Still, our household is forging fearlessly

ahead in the red, taking care of the pennies and letting the dollars take care of themselves. We don't have any dollars anyway.

WHEN FINGERS ARE ALL THIMBLES

THE Family Economics Bureau of the Northwestern National Life Insurance Company says home sewing is an "in" thing again. It says even men are making their own clothes. I am not one of the men, however. I do not make my own clothes. They just look like it.

If truth were known, men always have done a lot of sewing. Their wives are just ashamed to admit it. Many a man, when his pants pockets have developed a hole at the bottom, has taken the family sewing machine and run a straight seam across the pocket above the hole. When a new hole develops, he runs a seam higher up. This goes on until the bottom of the shortened pocket reaches the mouth of the pocket, and then a crisis develops.

I, myself, take complete credit for solving the loose button problem. When a button comes unsewed, I sew it back with fishing line instead of thread.

Yank too hard on this button, and the fabric pulls out, ending all silly problems about replacing buttons.

STILL, most of us male sewers are not exactly easy in the craft. Our fingers are all thimbles. We are willing to risk a button or an inside ravel, but we stop short of critical jobs like the seats of pants.

Awhile back I tried to make some curtains for our outboard cruiser, which is known either as the *Outward Bound* or the *Reluctant Dragon* because of its engine habits. We had attempted to dye some old curtains blue, and they had turned into a really unique fabric, something between a purple and a macabre red.

I hemmed the things up on all sides and down the middle.

A friend looked at them and said, "I didn't think there were supposed to be flounces in them."

"I didn't either," I admitted.

You can't do much about a flounce that just develops naturally. You don't know what to do to take it out. It seemed that the fabric also had gathered itself so that a number of small pockets had been sewed into each curtain.

The pockets would have been useful storage places, but the curtain had also shrunk somehow by a third.

THE Family Economics Bureau says some men have been making their own sports coats, and I believe it. I think I have seen some lately on the streets of Dallas.

I doubt that these people will supplant the tailor or the ready-made garment, however. They think of everything. I recently bought a new suit, and when I put an ink pencil in the lapel pocket, I discovered the pocket already had a hole in it through which the pen could drop down behind the coat lining.

I was slightly annoyed until I found that the maker had left a seam unsewn at the bottom of the coat through which I could extract the ink pencil.

You can't beat these old foxes at their own business.

THE BUILT-IN CARDINAL

ONE advantage of living in Dallas is that an astonishing number of houses come with a built-in cardinal. As a home appliance, this red bird beats a fireplace all hollow and may be more fun than a walkie-talkie.

For one thing, if you are lucky enough to hear the first clear cardinal call of a season, you know in that instant spring has begun.

The days may have been lengthening. The air may have begun getting balmier, with the frequent sharp setbacks so familiar in Dallas, but nothing will have seemed to change much. Then, on arising, you may have stepped out to the back slab in the early hours to look at the weather and test the intent of the wind, and suddenly out of the black dark will come the brilliant "cheer, cheer, cheer" of an unseen cardinal.

It gladdens the heart. In an instant, you realize that you haven't heard this call since the autumn and that YOUR bird is back and that winter is as dead as the sparrow moltings.

The cardinal's call is the undeniable beginning of spring just as the final, grudging leafing of the mimosas is its guarantee.

THE cardinal merits every ounce of the affection which the human race lavishes on him. He isn't merely beautiful; he is a kind of civilized bird.

Those of us who are not scientists are perhaps entitled to read some human traits into the birds we watch in spring. The mockingbird, for instance, is a loud-mouthed bully, an exuberant bird which thoughtlessly prates whatever he hears. Some of us expect most of them to be saying, "Vote for ———," before the year is over. The lark walks like and presents the belly of a plutocrat; it should wear dollar marks.

The grackle seems perpetually "turned on." Its fan-tailed flight is beautiful, but on the ground it seems always confused and uncertain. The crow is a raffish intellectual, so much more intelligent than its fellows that it can afford them an occasional sardonic kindness.

And the poor, timid hummingbird is an evanescent flash of the essence of rainbows so short that it is like an ache in the heart.

THE cardinal is none of these. He is a good householder and a good neighbor. He is expensively sleek but not fat. He is properly prudent about such hazards of life as cats. He has settled himself a summer neighborhood and stays there. It is not true, for instance, that ours is a Kentucky cardinal. He is an 8500 block Rolling Lane cardinal, where he has lived in summers for years. I know him thoroughly, and from the cock of his head when he looks at me from the power line, I think he is acquainted with me.

He is our whole block's best neighbor.

And he so gladly sings.

THE PYRACANTHA BATTLE

ONE of the great boons of gardening is the privilege of tying up pyracantha in the spring. Since the old-time leech doctors disappeared, pyracantha is the only thing that really bleeds you in the spring and drains you of the many miasmas of winter.

After this bout, some of your friends may ask you when you got back from the wars.

They refer to the damage on your face and hands. Actually, any war veteran would have more sense than to tackle pyracantha. Pyracantha is not a malicious plant; it simply is rebellious and ornery. Also, it pretends to be a clinging vine, but along each seductive clinger are a whole lot of spurs such as you find on fighting roosters.

While pretending to be clinging, the pyracantha waves its new stalks in such a way as to take out half your lobe.

It is not, like the wisteria, a strangling vine, but it has its own idea about where the knife points will be.

FOR the last thirty years, I have been forcing pyracantha to do my will, up to a certain point. As a last resort, I take up the pruning clippers and cut off all the branches heading out where I don't want them to. It works pretty good except that once one of the runners, while I was pruning, grew up my pants leg, and we had to have a surgeon to get it loose.

A young woman of my acquaintance has objected that the pyracantha ought to be allowed to grow wild and free — like the poets. She has never been hemmed in as I was once when attempting to clip a pyracantha hedge. After a half-day's work, I discovered that this hedge had hemmed me in and was seeking to destroy me, or at least put the spurs to me. I did not flinch. I waved the electric hedge shears at the mass, and it faded away.

Of course, I could have whipped this pyracantha single-handed, but my hands were less cut up as a result.

I MUST say that I like pyracantha. It merely fights a battle with its human protagonists. It never calls on human help to whip a sorry kind of pest or a weather condition. It apparently can whip these all.

I have begun to like plants that want to live. Pyracantha is only one. A live oak will take root and grow and grow where you've lost two or three Chinese elms. You can't kill ligustrum. Holly of any kind, in Dallas, took up an old residence here. Nobody has to spray this stuff, and nobody really has to pay any attention to it.

The pyracantha and I are going to get along all right. It never asked any help, and it sure hasn't given me any.

NEVER TRUST NATURE

RECENTLY, I came across a nature hint that states: "It is safe to hold a queen bee in your hand as the queen bees use their stings only on other queen bees."

This is one of the most valuable bits of information I have ever been given — up to a point. Questions cry out for answers, however. How does the queen bee I am holding in my hand know I am not a queen bee? I am so regarded in certain circles. A more pertinent question is how do I know that the bee I am holding in my hand is a queen bee?

All this points up something I have argued for a long time. Never trust nature. Nature is fickle and unpredictable and you seldom discover it until you have a hot hand.

Never trust nature farther than the distance to the nearest pruning clippers.

I RAN into this problem only the other day. I had gone out in the backyard to do my exercising, which I do every day when I can remember it. Everybody ought to do this, and it is simple. You ought to stay in shape. Go out in the backyard and plant your feet firmly. Settle yourself. Then, breathe. Do not do this suddenly because you might tear loose a muscle. Take it slow and easy.

I had been working vigorously at this four or five minutes. I had breathed at least five times when I suddenly discovered that a nearby wisteria bush was winding a shoot around my leg. Naturally, I was amused because the wisteria had mistaken my leg for another kind of oak. I started unwinding it, but as I did, it wound itself around my arm. Then, I found it was settling around my neck, and I called the young man of our household. He rushed out with the pruning clippers, and I polished off the wisteria.

"It goes to show you," I said, "that man can easily triumph over nature."

"Yeah," he said, "but what's that that is cramping up your ear?"

We got rid of that tendril, too, and we got out of the backyard. But, I'll tell you, that escape was narrow.

A FEW days ago I took some people to the boat. It was infested with buzzing, flying things. I folded up an old newspaper and started batting, against the protests of my wife and all others present.

"Do not anger these wasps," they said. "They will sting."

"It's just a bunch of old dirt daubers," I said, flailing away. And the evidence supported me. There were dirt dauber nests all over the boat. This lasted until one sat down in the middle of my forehead, and sure enough, it was a wasp.

Fortunately, I have one of the thickest heads in existence. It didn't hurt much.

But don't trust nature, queen bee or not.

THE SPORT OF BACKYARD LIVING

I T says here in a current news story that backyard living has become the American way of life, a statement which is considerably less than the unadulterated truth. As a matter of fact, it is a pretty good sample of the adulterated truth.

You might be tempted to believe that it was started by some man selling backyards.

There was a time a few years ago, before universal air conditioning, when backyard living seemed to be about the American way of life. It was the only place an American could breathe in the summertime anyway. In the summertime the American way of life now is in front of the air-conditioning vent. The average American likes to grow his mint patch now on the top of a tall frosted glass. Instead of charcoal-grilled steak, he eats cold salmon. If he has to go to the backyard to change the lawn sprinkler, he may very well swoon.

People who just loved to garden before air conditioning have now become learned connoisseurs of Johnson grass.

A lot of people have eliminated the backyard altogether and moved to apartments where they can look out the window at greenery that doesn't represent their own fertilizer money.

T HERE was a time when I pursued the sport of backyard living, and it had its moments. There were moments of high comedy on the patio when a june bug got up the pants leg of one of the guests. There were high dramatic moments at the barbecue grill when the host's fingers came off on the fork along with the wieners.

There was even an evening when a party of

ten sat silent, transfixed, for five hours facing a wandering Great Dane who had appeared out of nowhere and was squatted glaring, waiting for somebody to make a move.

It turned out that none of these could compete with air conditioning, and it is safe to say definitely that backyard living was not the thing that killed baseball. It was all very well to go out into the backyard and make a brave show out of enjoying something you had to do anyway, but the backyard was the place where you met nature face-to-face in the form of poison ivy, fire ants, and black spot on the roses.

The swimming pool threatened for a time to revive backyard living, but it is basically a device for allowing young males and young females to show off their physiques — an innocent pleasure which has seemed to intrigue them for several generations.

IF you have to enjoy backyard living, you don't have to endure the backyard to do it. Stay inside and cool off.

If you want to grill a steak over charcoal, for instance, put the steak on before you start your evening shower. Go on and dress and enjoy the air conditioning. The steak doesn't need six people watching it to cook. You may have to turn it over a couple of times.

An ingenious man can even get rid of this chore. One way is to find a patrol of Boy Scouts. Most of them are somewhat behind on their good turns, and if you offer them one good turn for each time the steak is turned, it will never char.

Matter of fact, we have had as many as five Boy Scouts turning the steak at once.

THE BIRD REBELLION

MAYBE I'm overly sensitive, but birds of Dallas have seemed unusually insulting here lately.

I first noticed this on a recent dawn on our back slab. At this time of the morning, I always walk outside to take a look at the sky and see if, by good luck, it won't be too wet to plow. We have a red oak at the edge of the slab, with one low limb about head-high. It should have been pruned long ago, but we are reluctant to saw it off because of all the fertilizer that has been invested in it over the years.

As I stood there in the half-dark beside the limb, I began to have the uncanny feeling that I was not alone. I turned toward the limb and there, not two feet from my head, sat an enormous jay silently glaring at me.

When I glared back, he simply settled himself as if to say he had no intention of moving. I went back to the house considerably shaken.

After all, it does something to a man's psyche to be stared down by birds.

WE also have a sparrow that keeps trying to shove me away from the corner of the yard where the pyracantha berries are ripening.

And on Saturday I was on my way afoot to a nearby bus stop. Roosting on a fireplug along my route was a crow. He did not make a motion to fly as I walked by him. Instead, he glared at me and began to cuss me out. He had a kind of northern accent, and I couldn't make out what he was saying, but the tone of his cawing made his meaning plain, so plain that the small boy who was selling roses from a bucket nearby went into stitches.

With great dignity, I ignored the uproar and walked on by.

Nobody likes to have something like this done to him right before the eyes of the local rose industry.

NOBODY knows what is making these birds so unruly. Maybe they're all on their way home from Chicago and are looking for some authority that they can demonstrate against. We don't have any authority at our house, however. It is run on permissiveness.

Maybe the birds are finally rebelling at their lot in this land of plenty. The bird sees the affluent getting the hog jowls and caviar while he gets a can of worms. Maybe the government ought to start a program if they can think up a good one. Or maybe the birds have just been spending too much time around college campuses.

I am unable, meantime, to decide whether to purchase the good will of the birds with limitless free sunflower seed or pacify them with a shotgun. It is a national problem, and there is no easy answer.

FEAR, ANGER, AND THE EMPTY HOUSE

A FEW things exist in life so powerful that they can shatter the composure to which the ordinary human male manages to pretend before the universe. Among these are fear, anger, and the empty house.

When the family announces that it is going visiting for a week and leaving him a bachelor, the average householder is likely to think, "Good. We will have some peace and quiet around here. Get some reading done." This is because the human mind comes equipped with little traps to fool itself.

When he walks into the empty house that first night, a man's sense of values changes. It sounds awfully quiet. Matter of fact, it sounds darn suspicious. Something must have stopped, or may be about to blow up. It requires a hurried check of all the appliances, most of which are broken down, of course, and not about to blow up.

After this, the first thing a man does is turn up the TV loud, not because he is going to watch it but to have some voices around. This peace and quiet is just about all that he can take.

What the average man really wants is some peace and quiet with a lot of noise around.

A FTER a time, average householder settles down under a reading lamp with the new book he was going to finish, but he can't read. He can't concentrate because there is nothing to concentrate against. Where is the piano that he used to have to tune out of his ears? Where are the questions from which he used to have to struggle back to the argument of the book?

Without the struggle, there is no inner drive to read. Furthermore, he becomes aware that quiet is interrupting him. Quiet is not nothing. Quiet is a big black cat lurking somewhere there in the dimness of the corners of the room, making his presence always felt.

After a few days, the average householder works out something to kill time. If he owns a dog or a cat, he may go out into the yard and chase it inside the house and lock it in, just to have some life around. Maybe he starts watering everything.

At any rate, more reading is probably done on fewer words in empty houses than in any other place.

ALL American men cook now, of course. As a matter of fact, they are all chefs of originality. At least, the stuff that comes off their barbecue grills doesn't look like the ordinary food that used to come off barbecue grills. However, if you are batching, there seems small point in preparing eggs Benedict for one person.

This is when you begin to wonder about John Montagu, the fourth Earl of Sandwich, who two hundred years ago first threw a slab of meat between two slices of buttered bread and made a meal of it. Was he benefactor or curse? Apparently, he did not invent the sandwich because of an empty house but so that he would not have to interrupt his gambling to eat. One old story says that he spent twenty-four hours at the gaming tables without any refreshment except some slices of cold beef between slices of toast. But he has kept a lot of us empty-house people alive.

After awhile, sandwiches get pretty tasteless. I recommend goose liver. You don't have to be enthusiastic about chewing it.

SQUEEZING OUT THE LYRIC SPIRIT

AN East Texas woman was having her say about daylight saving time recently. "It has ruined the flowers this year," she complained.

I share her feelings, not only about daylight saving time but about air conditioning, and I was thinking about it on a recent morning while standing on our backyard slab as the sun came up. Suddenly, there came one of those moments when the city disappeared and the world came through. The distant traffic noise died. Blessedly, there wasn't a jet plane overhead. It was too early, apparently, for the several childish voices who at any given moment are imitating Tarzan.

And suddenly it was autumn, and the feel of old and distant autumns came flooding back, the kind men used to treasure. The still air had an edge of chill in it. There were a few browning leaves in the oak. From a distant tree, a jay jeered at a cat. Here, behind the high board fence, the world men had always known existed again, fifty by eighty feet of it.

And I would have missed the moment completely if I hadn't fled air conditioning.

In his infinite ingenuity, man is perverting the natural world, and soon he will live in a delusion.

ONLY future researchers will know, probably, how much of our present growing insanity is due to the time dislocations brought on by air conditioning. A perfectly respectable man, for instance, wakes in the middle of a July night and suddenly rushes outside to knock the snow off the Japanese yew so that the branches won't be broken. He knows as soon as he opens the door that his behavior is crazy.

As for the presumptuousness of a mere man using daylight saving time to move a star like Betelgeuse an hour backward or an hour forward in heaven, this is sheer lunacy. It is enough to unsettle minds as firm as mine, and mine is awfully firm.

In our country, man does not know autumn now by the great and old things, the turn of a leaf, the unsettled behavior of the birds, or the shift of the stars in their places above his head. Maybe he knows it because the kids go back to school. Maybe he knows it when his wife changes her clothes. But maybe, also, he becomes aware of it when someone says, "Oh, my, the State Fair again."

A measure of how far we have dehumanized ourselves along with earth is the fact that people don't talk anymore. They arrange meaningful dialogues.

MAN, in his centuries-old job of taking a perfectly wonderful world and turning it inside out, may lose most by squeezing out of himself the lyric spirit. He will not kill poetry, because poetry is everything he doesn't understand; but the lyric vein, like the whooping crane, will not grow under crowded conditions.

In a hundred years, man will probably read no more odes about autumn smoke.

Instead, the poetic description of autumn will probably begin: "The signs of air pollution were evident."

THE CAREFREE BOATMAN

Boating, to most men who have recently discovered it, isn't a sport. It certainly isn't a craft. You wouldn't say on a sandbar that it is full of pleasurable thrills. Boating, to the average unseamanlike stiff, is a pure escape device.

THE CAREFREE BOATMAN

A GOOD BUY

OUR friends nowadays have a favorite opening gambit with which they put me at a disadvantage in a conversation. "I see you have bought a boat," they say.

This boat is fairly hard to miss as it sits out there in the middle of the driveway. A few people have missed seeing the house during the time it has been there, and we are thinking of putting up a sign saying, "Residence in Rear."

It is not exactly true that I bought a boat. I, more or less, fell into it. I was the victim of the awful pulling power of a *Dallas News* want ad. Valentine Marine out there on Harry Hines Boulevard had advertised an interesting boat.

I have long been an armchair and boating show boating expert. I went out and looked at the boat and, in my most expert voice, made Mr. Valentine an offer which was ridiculous, and he took me up.

It is amazing how difficult it is to back out of an offer made in an expert voice, and Mr. Valentine did not act as if he thought it was ridiculous.

LATER on, one of my friends, an old boatman who like Ivory naturally floats, was telling me that I had made a good buy.

"It is the wrong way to buy a boat," I said, in my most expert manner. "I'll be lucky not to get a hull with dry rot."

My friend looked at me coldly. "This is an aluminum hull," he said.

As time for the lake trials approached, I got more and more jittery. People kept saying not to worry. Respect your boat but don't fear it, etc.

"They will send out an expert boatman to show you how," they said.

"They" did. Some time after the boat was running around the lake it seemed a little sluggish. "I wonder if I put in that drain plug," said the expert boatman. He hadn't. When he pulled up the deck hatch, there was a sizable part of the lake inside the boat. It was an unnerving experience, but apparently meant nothing.

He put in the drain plug, and we continued on. Apparently, they are building boats better these days. They work just as well with the lake inside as outside.

Later on, when we had got the boat back on the trailer, we waited quite awhile for it to drain so that TP&L would be sure to have enough water to operate the power plant that day.

WE had to land the boat at a miniature concrete mole. The lake was rough and the wind was on the beam. Like all old Navy characters, I have had to do a little shiphandling. I knew what to do. Go in hot like a destroyer. Back down with engines full, and let the wind drift you into the landing.

The Navy is different, however. There you have a helmsman to tell what to do and to raise hell with if anything happens. I quickly discovered that in this do-it-yourself type of landing, the engine does not necessarily take reverse gear. That expert boatman really has strong leg muscles, and we got off without even scratching my beautiful hull.

My boating friends are after me now to get the boat in the water, but after that experience, I'm not too anxious. I'm pretty sure that water is going to wear off some of the paint.

HOW TO DOCK A BOAT

THE man who runs the Little Mineral Boat Dock at Lake Texoma has threatened to tell the papers about how I almost tore off one side of his fueling dock recently. This piece is written to head off false rumors that are bound to crop up.

It is true that my handsome, low-income Lone Star boat did come in contact with the Little Mineral dock and that a deaf man living across the lake on the Oklahoma shores did hear for the first time in twenty years.

Actually, it was not my fault, though. Some slipshod workman had put the dock six feet too far to the west, and I did not notice it until too late. If the dock had been properly placed, I would have made a perfect landing.

Anyhow, there never was any danger. The danger came after the boat was tied up. We had aboard a couple of friends, Gordon Brown and his wife, Mary Alice. In rushing to get ashore after we were docked, they both reached the edge of the boat at the same time and might have swamped us.

They got off the boat so fast that five minutes later they were having trouble breathing.

I HAVE since read all the instruction books on how to handle outboard boats, and in no manual is there any instruction about what to do when a dock is placed six feet too far to the west. This is a grave omission and might cause a less quick-witted person than I am some trouble. He might miss the dock altogether.

The problem was complicated by our boon companion, John King. He had been standing on the edge of the dock beckoning me in with his fingers when he suddenly turned and ran like a scared rabbit and hid behind the gas pump. In running, he stepped on his finger and later pretended that he had bruised it in fending off my boat.

Naturally, I handled the problem as I handle all problems. I met it head on.

Ours is a sophisticated set, however, and any compliments that I got for my presence of mind were plenty lukewarm.

WHEN I finally got ashore and had lectured the junior navigator of the family about doing everything easily and taking no chances, I walked over to Gordon. He was checking a filling in his upper left jaw.

"The dental profession must owe you a debt of gratitude," he said.

This is the Brown style, of course. He does not like to go around peddling a bunch of sentimental compliments.

At this point, King wanted to know whether everybody didn't want some coffee off his boat where the water hadn't been spilled. For some reason, everybody did.

The professional at the dock looked a little puzzled about the whole thing, but I wasn't puzzled. I knew exactly what I was doing.

I just didn't know how not to do it.

A NIGHT ON THE LAKE

WHEN planning to spend the night in a small boat, it is best to be an expert like I am, or you can get into bad trouble.

I recently took a couple of youngsters up for a night on our boat, which we are currently calling the *Anon* because that way you don't have to go to the trouble of painting a name on it. We arrived just as a blow set in. Fishermen, each carrying about a bushel of sand bass, were hurrying in to cover. The lake was getting rough.

The Little Mineral marina folks had taken note of my recent criticism that their dock was located six feet too far west for me to do good docking and had relocated it. As a result, I was able to hit it head on instead of just glancing against it.

"An expert does not tempt the fury of the deep," I told the boys. "We will tie up here for the night. I will now cook supper."

Fate controls the lives of mariners. I have never started to sea in a storm in my life that the cook didn't serve meatballs and spaghetti, thereby ridding everybody of the need for food. It turned out that the food aboard was a can of meatballs and spaghetti.

If I hadn't been an expert, I would have got sick cooking it. The boys assured me they had never seen a better meal prepared on a pitching boat, and that was all that was necessary since their hunger was satisfied. The stuff is good for fish.

THE *Anon* has bunks for two people. The boys took the bunks, and I settled down on an air mattress in the cockpit. Very shortly I learned where the guy got the idea for that song, "Jounced in the cradle of the deep."

I must have slept or looked the other way, for suddenly I was awake with a large bare foot in the middle of my face, and one of the boys saying, "What is happening?"

What was happening was that it was about 2:00 A.M. Some boatman, evidently inflamed by the stories of bushel catches of sand bass, had landed and was irritated because there was nobody around to sell him gas. He had his wife ashore to handle the lines and was bellowing at her through a bullhorn.

"Go wake the so-and-so up," he ordered her in Captain Bligh fashion.

This was when I witnessed mutiny. She swarmed back aboard in four or five places and hit him, probably with a marlin spike.

You are supposed to rush to the assistance of somebody with mutiny aboard, but how do you do it with a bare foot in your face?

DAWN in these latitudes does not come at 2:30. It does not come at 3:00, or 3:30, or 4:00, or 4:30 either. These are false dawns, even if you jump up and try to pretend they are going to work.

Dawn finally came in a kind of exhausted way, and everybody was awake.

"Stand back," I told the boys. "On a pitching boat, an expert must handle this. I will now cook the eggs."

I was holding the stove on the counter with one hand and anchoring the water pitcher with the other and reaching for the spatula with the third hand when the carton of eggs slid off and hit the cabin deck. I salvaged four eggs from it. If I hadn't been an expert, I would have lost the whole dozen.

We finally got out of there and anchored in a quiet cove off a lee shore. It was 7:30 A.M. by then. The boys assured me they had never spent a more restful night.

They then crept into the cabin and went to sleep.

ADVICE FOR PROSPECTIVE BOAT BUYERS

A TEXOMA marina man has suggested that there is room now for a learned treatise by an expert such as I am for the prospective boat buyer.

There is indeed. Ignorance about boats in this country is almost as widespread as boats. A man the other day had the nerve to advertise for sale a cruiser "with kitchen." Such ignorance! Everybody knows that a kitchen on a boat is called a head.

The first thing for the ignorant greenhorn to learn is that boats generally are divided into port and starboard. This is important because ordinarily when you are trying to land the boat portside to, you will land on the starboard. This is called the International Rule of the Road. Boats usually have a pointed end and a blunt end. You determine port and starboard by standing in the boat faced toward the pointed end and thrusting out your arms. Your left arm will be pointing to port, your right to starboard.

Do this before you fall overboard because afterward your starboard may be pointing to port.

You will find also that boats generally run better if the pointed end is directed forward except in a high wind. Some then run better with the flat end ahead.

BOATS are made of various materials, none of them strong enough. When picking a material, it is best to pick one that is waterproof. It may be more expensive to begin with, but it will save you money in the long run.

Generally speaking, boats of less than three hundred feet in length do not come equipped with private swimming pools; so if your new boat is forming a swimming pool, this is not good. If you need patching material, chewing gum is best because the average boatman naturally mixes a huge batch of it in an emergency.

Boats are equipped with a number of things. They all have freeboard, which is a lie. You pay for every inch of it. They also have a thing called gunwales, pronounced gunnels, until you make your first rough landing or two. Some old-fashioned boats have a fire extinguisher and an oar, but the Coast Guard Auxiliary is always surprised when they find these.

Some boats have lights which work, but more have lights that don't.

Nearly every boat is equipped with a yachtsman's hat, which is a great relief.

THERE are other things that the beginner should learn right off. If his motor does not work, for instance, there is something wrong. However, the beginner should not let himself be bothered by the indecipherable talk of old salts.

He is likely to see the master of a small paddling canoe running toward the dock in his yachting hat and bellowing, "All hands fall in on the No. 1 athwartship passageway."

Generally, a rope on a boat is not a rope. It is a line. People do not hurry. They bear a hand. In an emergency, however, it is perfectly all right to yell, "Hurry up and hand me that lousy rope."

FOURTH OF JULY AT THE LAKE

OUR compatriot and sometime companion, Wick Fowler, has a stylish ketch named the Princess on Grapevine Lake which will almost sail itself. This is fortunate as the owner is somewhat absentminded.

On the afternoon of the Fourth of July, Fowler and I and John King and Buck Marryat set sail on the Princess. Grapevine Lake has probably never seen such a collection of sailors. At least, they acted like they hadn't. Marryat immediately began striding back and forth as far as he could on the foredeck, shouting commands in a Captain Bligh voice. King turned on his radio. Fowler busied himself with trying to see that some of the sails didn't blow overboard, and I sat very still hoping that my weighty thoughts would not affect the trim of the boat.

She practically sailed herself as usual. Soon we had time to notice that a bunch of skiers and swimmers were splashing the water around and wasting it. We criticized this. There was barely enough water for us boats as it was.

Then we noticed that the Corps of Engineers had put the dam too near the end of the lake. There was hardly room enough for a boatman to turn. We criticized this and decided to write our congressman and get him to do something.

AFTER this we turned our attention to such routine but required tasks as the inspection of girls in bathing suits in other boats. Marryat lost the bailing sponge overboard, and in recovering it we were forced by wind and water to inspect one boat a second time.

At about this time, King decided to brag on his radio. He pointed out that he could put it in his vest pocket and that he had bought it at a bargain at a discount house sale.

"Just listen to that volume," he said.

It turned out that it was Fowler's larger radio playing.

"Fowler," said King, "at times you are something of a something."

An ad company friend came up in a speedboat and then roared off somewhere. Pretty soon, he came back and roared off in a different direction. After a bit, he was back again speeding away in the direction he had originally taken. Restless fellow. Always looking for new accounts.

People began to ease up alongside and ask, "Are you out of beer?"

Fowler, an experienced hand, always answered, "Yes."

Apparently, it wasn't their intention to offer us one.

THEN we noticed it, a crowd collected around a small cove on the opposite shore. They were drawn up in ranks around the small natural amphitheater like the crowd at a country baptism except that these were clad in the bright colors of beach clothing.

We wove over in that direction. Divers were working. Boats were circling the cove. A little eight-year-old boy was somewhere beneath the surface, and too late, too late, a man found him and carried him toward the resuscitator.

Casually, he had gone into the water. Casually, he was dead. It takes very little to ruin an afternoon. We headed for the slip, and the Princess steered herself. I know. I steered her.

TOWED HOME

ONE of the more disgusting pleasures of boating is getting towed back disabled to the dock.

This first happened to me several weeks ago, but the experience starts out about the same every time. You pull away from the dock for a day on the water, and there are few things finer than a summer morning on a boat. The water is a sparkling sapphire. There is a cool breeze off the lake, and the sunbeams dance brightly on the distant tree leaves and cliffs.

You have just opened the picnic basket and got started on the day-long banquet of sandwiches when the boat stops dead in the water. A boat which had been racing you passes and its wake upsets the iced tea.

After a bit, a fellow boatman will come by and say, "Are you in trouble?"

The first time this happened to me, I replied, "Don't worry. We are in no danger. This is a waterproof boat."

Since then I have learned better and am glad to get a tow.

You might not think it, but nine times out of ten when your boat won't run, it is the engine.

IF this should ever happen to you, you should first check to see whether the engine is running. If it is not, there is a regular checklist to run through on an outboard motor.

You should check the fuel supply and be sure that your fattest guest is not sitting on the fuel line. You should check the electrical system. If you take a piece of metal in your hands and lay it across the battery poles, you can feel it if the battery is all right. Maybe you ought to pull off the engine shroud and look at the spark plugs. When you have done all this, you will find out that there is nothing wrong with your engine. It just isn't running.

You will be tempted to sit back with another sandwich at that point and try to find out what is wrong with your thinking on this engine. This is pointless. The outboard motor was invented by a man with a left-handed brain who did his thinking in Swedish dialect. It is beyond the capabilities of the average brilliant human brain. For instance, it is built backward but runs forward.

It is best to accept a tow back to the harbor and call the local outboard mechanic.

Do not brag about the waterproof qualities of your boat. When you get ashore, people will be asking you to explain it for months.

IN recent weeks, I have been towed home so often that people no longer stand around the dock, clamping their jaws tight while they watch me try to heave a line without getting it wound around my leg. Just the other day, though, I set a record. I got towed home by a sailboat.

This was the small ketch owned by Wick Fowler. It draws about a foot of water when moored and three feet when Mr. Fowler is in it.

"I would like to have a picture of this," said the attendant at the Little Mineral dock when the sailboat came hauling me in.

Later, I offered to pay Fowler for the wind he had used up, but he seemed rather contemptuous.

"I could have done it with the jib," he said.

BAYARD'S BOAT

OFTEN when enjoying the thrills of pleasure boating, such as trying to get my twenty-three-foot Lone Star off a sandbar, I find my mind going back to Bayard Fitch, who was the founder of boatbuilding in the Lariat country.

But for a lack of water, he might have been as famous as Alden or the other yacht designers.

Bayard was a thin, bony man, a bachelor who made his living by running the broom factory and doing odd-job carpentry. He was friendly enough but secretive and reflective. He spent more time in the shop-factory that occupied one room of his two-room shanty than he did among people.

Nobody knows why he built a boat. If he had built it when Running Water Draw was at the flood, he could have floated down it past the caprock into the Brazos and drifted on to Africa; but he built it toward the tag end of a dry summer. The nearest water was a creek up at Hereford, and if you had put Bayard's boat in it, it would have acted as a bridge rather than a boat.

At any rate, Bayard called in some people one day and unveiled what was undeniably a boat, even though it was a little dusty.

PROBABLY he unveiled the craft before other people because he needed a lot of help in heaving it on a truck. Bayard's boat was really built, by golly. It was a kind of johnboat with rounded, stubby ends. The sides were of 2×12s mortised together, and the bottom was tongued and grooved oak planking.

If there had been any rocks at all on the high plains, Bayard's boat would certainly not have been in any danger from the rocks.

The sea trials for the boat took place in the galvanized stock tank belonging to Mr. Crow about half a mile down the road. When put into the tank, the boat was as dry as an unirrigated cotton field. However, there was hardly a foot of space between either end of the boat and the edge of the tank. It was hard to judge speed and maneuverability.

Some of us later hauled the boat out and tried it in one of those big pond tanks at a ranch windmill, but all that the boat did was settle down until its bottom was in the mud of the tank.

Nothing leaked, though. This was obviously a sound craft. We hauled it back to Bayard's yard where, on late afternoons when the shade was right, he would sit in it with such of the town youngsters as were pleased to gather.

MOST of us laughed a little at Bayard then. Now, when you still haven't got off the sandbar, you wonder.

Boating, to most men who have recently discovered it, isn't a sport. It certainly isn't a craft. You wouldn't say on a sandbar that it is full of pleasurable thrills. Boating, to the average unseamanlike stiff, is a pure escape device, as it must have been to Bayard.

There are moments at night when you have finally got anchored, or think you have, which are so different in quality from the workaday world that the spinning earth slows down and you can watch the wheel of the stars in the northern sky and hear the cicada beyond the water's edge.

They are fine, worthwhile moments, but the boat is merely a device for attaining them. It didn't create them. Bayard was the first of a new breed.

CLEANING THE BOAT

IT is said that six hundred years ago some English soldiers were chasing Robert the Bruce with the idea of chopping off his head.

He hid in a cave and went to sleep. He was awakened later by the Englishmen arguing outside his cave. Some wanted to search it, but others pointed out that there was no need to. No one could have entered the cave, said these bright, intelligent ones, because a spider web covered the entrance.

It is further said that Robert the Bruce, in gratitude to the spider for saving his life, forbade his subjects to harm a spider thereafter.

Ordinarily, I would not believe this. Robert the Bruce never forbade anybody to harm anything; as a matter of fact, he egged it on. Nevertheless, anybody with any military experience knows that the people who get commendations are, like this spider, people who generally did nothing. This lends the tale authenticity.

However, I have reason to believe that this spider wasn't hiding Robert the Bruce, that it really believed that it had captured him.

I HAVE become convinced of this while cleaning up the boat at Little Mineral Dock for the coming season. There is probably nothing filthier than a boat which has been left alone for six months, unless it is the kitchen of a first-class restaurant. Dirt is everywhere. When you unscrew the cap of the iodine bottle, you even find dirt in the bottom of it.

Dirt daubers have been everywhere, too. These winged insects apparently do not believe flying is here to stay and are always trying to root themselves on sea power.

But the spiders are the real enigma. They are everywhere, too. They especially like to construct webs tying the wheel to the forward bulkhead, covering over the engine, or leading into the carburetor. They web over only controls of one kind or another. I tell you these people have something in mind.

For a time, I kept this boat at a buoy two hundred yards offshore. Every week we cleared out the spiders and next week they were back.

Furthermore, and significantly enough, they were always putting webs on the wheel and engine. They had something in mind, and it wasn't the good of the human race.

CLEANING a boat is naturally conducive to philosophy. After you've scrubbed hard for about ten minutes, you are glad to give over thirty to philosophy. How, I have often wondered while somebody else was scrubbing, did these spiders get two hundred yards across water?

True, I have watched them swing back and forth at the end of a web strand like an Italian boatswain's mate showing off on a swinging rope, but you can't swing two hundred yards. Some spiders can walk on water, but why would they walk across a heavy chop for two hundred yards when they could build a web anywhere ashore?

One logical explanation of how they got aboard may raise goose pimples. They might have come there from outer space.

TEACHING A CITY DOG TO SWIM

A SCANDALOUS situation has recently come to this writer's attention. It seems that many city-bred dogs do not know how to swim. The modern dog owner apparently will teach swimming to his child, for whom he paid far less than for his dog. Why does he not protect his larger investment?

The modern city dog prefers to have his water penned up inside his plastic bowl. He looks on water that roams around by itself as something wild and possibly dangerous. Take your dog to the lake, and the chances are that he will suddenly look upon the small waves lapping toward him as an enemy on the attack. He will begin to bark at them wildly. If his owner is present, the dog presently will trot

virtuously up to him as if demonstrating how he has held off this great threat to hearth and home. He will then retreat cautiously behind the owner's legs.

If the owner is not present, the dog will begin looking for a tree to hide behind as soon as he discovers that he isn't frightening the waves off.

OBVIOUSLY, the situation is dangerous. You ought to acquaint your dog with water. After all, it might rain in Dallas sometime within the next few years, perhaps in your dog's lifetime. How would he stand the shock?

It used to be thought that dogs swam naturally. You taught a pup to swim by tossing him out in the water and letting him find his way back. Do not try this with the modern dog. It may damage the modern dog's psyche permanently and knock something out of his pedigree. Do not attempt to accustom the dog to water by showering it at him, either. This will merely scare him, and he will run off into the underbrush.

The best thing to do is pick the dog up, all the while muttering soothing words to indicate that you would never do him a dirty trick. Hoist him up on your shoulders so that he will be dry and wade out in water up to your armpits. Sit the dog gently on the water and leave him there while you show him how to paddle back to land.

Something about sitting on the water gives a dog confidence to swim. As long as you are in the water with him, he knows that it isn't dangerous and there is no point in staying in there with you. He will swim like an otter to the shore.

ONCE ashore he will race up the beach, pausing at the picnic basket to shake himself and sprinkle down the food. He will disappear for awhile, but don't worry. He will be back. For the next few days, you may catch him eyeing you speculatively as if wondering whether you are really worth all the trust he is putting in you, but you will have the satisfaction of knowing that you taught him to swim.

It is best not to expect him to gambol in the water as old-fashioned dogs did in the days before water bowls. The modern dog is a reasoning animal. He will never see the point of swimming anywhere where he can be taken by a human being in a canoe.

FISHERMAN'S RECORD

AS a fisherman, I hold one world's record. I have crammed the use of the largest number of artificial lures into the smallest number of caught fish that anyone has ever heard of.

In catching one small fish, I normally use two kinds of Hawaiian wigglers, six different-colored slabs, two kinds of jitterbugs, five varieties of crippled shad, a rappallo, four different colors of plastic worms, one old bloody bandage from a cut thumb, a bucktail spoon, a silver spoon, and, finally, a live minnow or worm. Sometimes the worm works.

You wear the ends of your fingers out tying on new lures, and when you put the bloody ends of your fingers into the water to cool them off, some bass nibble at them but won't bite.

I have had bass surface along the boat and leer at me while I was fishing.

All this has just about convinced me that all those pretty lures were designed to catch a fisherman at the sporting goods store and not a fish in the lake.

I TESTED my luck again recently with two friends. We headed out of Little Mineral in my wonderful, shabby 23-foot cruiser which is known now around the lake as HMS *Reluctant* because of the way the engine works.

The fishermen around the boathouse told us that people out on the lake were shoveling in the white bass with scoops.

This should have tipped us off. We had brought along every other kind of lure, but we hadn't brought a scoop.

At the time, though, we thought nothing of it. We took off for the white bass foaming at the mouth. As the day wore on, the foam on our mouths dried into a white alkaline substance. My two companions performed frequent lure-changing drills. I didn't bother. I knew what I was going to catch beforehand. Fish just prefer not to associate with me.

In a whole day of fishing, we did not alter the ecology by one fin. It wasn't just us. We asked around to find out whether other boats had caught any fish. One weeping lady finally held up one small sand bass.

It was bound to have been my fault. My friends are infallible, great fishermen. They told me so.

I HAVE speculated a great deal about the aversion that fish feel toward lures I put in the water. Someone told me the other day that if you count the fish you have caught, you will never catch another that day. That may be my failing.

But considering the fish I catch, how do you help counting them? Suppose you have only one fish. If you turn your eyes away and rigorously avoid counting him, something keeps reminding you that you have one fish. You know you have one fish. That ends the fishing for you that day.

To be fair, the rule ought to apply only after you have caught enough fish to lie about.

A SUCCESSFUL FISHING TRIP

IT is the season of the fisherman now on our lakes. We were reminded of it during the weekend when we steered the *Outward Bound,* our outboard cruiser, out on Texoma and headed beyond the far limits of civilization two miles away.

The air was cold. The wind was blustery, and whitecaps chopped up the water. The boat rolled and pitched in all this. Gone were all the bright young exhibitionists on skis with their confident air that everybody was admiring them. The beaches, dun with the color of fall, were barren of the usual picnickers. We could see no scuba buoys.

But the fishermen were still there, mostly two men in a tiny boat bobbing on the waves. Bundled up, heavily capped, they sat concentrating on their lines with that stare that the world has interpreted as philosophical but is actually pure irritation.

A fisherman will do anything to catch a fish or just to think of catching a fish.

BACK in the days when I made weekly trips to the lake, two elderly fishermen always used to be fishing off a sand spit near Little Mineral Marina where we dock.

They were there at all times of the day and in all kinds of weather, silent, motionless, watching their lines. They were there in rain or sunshine, sleet or snow. On an early January morning when a storm had coated the hills, trees, and boathouses with ice, I got a first cup of coffee and glanced toward a sandspit, and there they were as always, silent, bent, watching their lines. A friend of mine once got lost in his boat in a fog at night and finally came upon them at two o'clock in the morning, still fishing in the fog. They kindly showed him and his boat, compass and all, back to his mooring.

They were there for years, as much a part of the landscape as the oaks and willows, and suddenly they were gone.

I asked about them, and a man said one of the old-timers had died. His partner didn't have the heart to come back.

The world can hardly afford to lose fixtures like this.

MY partner on this last trip was a fellow newspaperman who claims to be a fisherman. It wasn't a day for fishing, but he caught a couple to prove that they couldn't skunk him. We beached in a remote cove, cooked a hearty dinner, told a bunch of lies, and went to bed in a warm cabin.

In the early light next morning, he was fishing and I was downing a cup of coffee when we heard a snort. There on the opposite hill, framed in all the autumn colors, was a sleek, pretty young buck deer. He watched a minute and glided along the hillside like a full-color, evanescent shadow. It was a moment which made you catch your breath.

And it probably proved that there is no such thing as an unsuccessful fishing trip.

ANYBODY CAN SING UNDERWATER

A handout has reached me which says that frogs are able to sing underwater because they normally sing with their mouths and their nostrils closed. This, it seems to me, misses the whole point of the frog. Anybody can sing underwater. The remarkable thing about the frog is that he can sing on dry land.

ANYBODY CAN SING UNDERWATER

A SENSE OF HUMOR

IT says here that a man named Jim Atkins has registered in Washington as a lobbyist for humor. He wants to promote a greater national sense of humor, but I don't know about that. It might be dangerous.

If people start laughing at things that happen in Washington, D.C., for instance, it might be the end of our form of government.

Also, there is evidence that humor in the United States is already so widespread as to get out of hand at times. We are talking here of things like the solid rubber chocolate bar, itch powder, and the imitation tarantula that is planted in people's beds. It could be that humor, like the atom bomb, is safest when limited to a few hands.

Furthermore, there are more good tellers of jokes than there are good jokes.

The country is amply equipped with us humorists. It mainly lacks people with sense enough to laugh when we perform.

ASK any American you meet whether he has a sense of humor, and he will tell you that he does have one, a rich and deep sense of humor tempered by shrewdness and sagacity. He knows that he is a very funny man; he just can't get other people to see it.

After he has told a joke, he often has to interrupt his own hearty laughter to explain the point to his listeners. While he is saying, "Get it? It's a joke," humor withers on the vine.

In time, he may learn some professional techniques for overcoming this. He starts out by saying, "Hey, listen, everybody. I'm going to tell a joke." Or he may say, "A real funny thing happened the other day." This points out to his listeners that what he is saying is uproarious and that they'd better pretend to get the point even if they don't. It will nearly always result in some polite heh heh's.

Of course, congressmen have the best trick of all. A member of Congress can get proofs of his speech in the *Congressional Record* and merely stick in "(laughter)" at the places where the fools were too stupid to laugh.

It always has been hard to find a listener who can understand a jokester's point of view.

YEARS ago out in the Lariat country one of the town loafers loosened the saddle girth on a horse belonging to an old-timer named Perkins. When Mr. Perkins started to mount, the saddle turned with him, throwing him under the horse. The frightened horse started bucking and stepped on Mr. Perkins's hand. The horse tore up the saddle and knocked down the fence at the wagonyard, turning six head of mules loose on the town.

While the jokester was rolling on the ground with laughter, Perkins teed off and knocked the wadding out of him.

"The trouble with Perk," said the wagster, "is that he don't have any sense of humor."

Hardly anyone does except you and me.

PATENTING THE LEVER

ON some mornings, especially fine spring mornings, ideas flow like a freshet. A man can hardly keep them from springing into his mind, one after the other.

Mostly, these are wasted because they are brilliant suggestions about how somebody else can improve his work or his moral character, and the people are too stubborn to accept them.

But on the way to town the other morning, I sprouted one idea that is going to make my fortune. Do you know that nobody has ever patented the lever? In other words, it has never been officially discovered. Here it has been lying around for thousands of years and people have been using it without ever realizing what a gold mine they had hold of. This, friend, is over.

I have already drawn an engineering diagram of the machine, and I will have a patent on it as soon as I can build a working model. This may take several months. Obviously, I can't take some machinist in on the project, because he might steal the idea; and it is hard to construct a working model when you can't handle a file.

Heck, I can make a fortune out of this off the royalties of the crowbar makers alone.

AS soon as I get the patent, city councils, highway departments, earth-moving machinery people, and others who use the lever without any right to do it had better watch out. I am generally regarded as a nice guy when I don't have anything to bargain with; but when I get the upper hand, I am ruthless.

There is no point in arguing with me at this stage. It is useless to argue that people have always used the lever. They certainly didn't have my permission. And if some advertising outfit can take some common English words like "Band-Aid" and trademark them, I am entitled to the lever. I thought of it first. True, the Egyptians were using the lever five thousand years ago, but the Egyptians have always been slovenly about patent affairs. Look at Nasser. They've had pyramids for more than five thousand years and haven't patented one yet.

As soon as my patent comes through, you will see a big promotional campaign quoting experts. Archimedes, for instance, said that if he had a lever long enough and a fulcrum strong enough he could single-handedly move the world.

Hardly any other firm nowadays would be able to furnish a testimonial from an expert with as many years behind him as Archimedes.

SOME people may get upset about that phrase about moving the world, but we intend to assure the President personally that we won't build any levers that long. This is a patriotic outfit.

But Archimedes did bring up a point there. I may also patent the fulcrum. We could then sell the two inventions in pairs at a discount, or possibly we will just take royalties on thousands of other firms that use them.

When I get rid of the heavy intellectual burden of working this out and collect my money, I may start to work on inventing the wedge.

CALIBRATING HAILSTONES

THE weather reporters are just going to have to get a great deal more specific in their description of hailstones. Over the weekend we were promised hail ranging from marble size to golf ball size. We didn't get either, but that doesn't solve the ethical and scientific problem of how the weather reporters present it.

What do they mean by this? How do they calibrate the size of hail? Hail ranges at the present time from buckshot and peas, as far as I can tell, to baseballs. Some people have claimed to have seen hail the size of grapefruit, but if somebody claims to have seen basketball hail, this is another John Fitzhugh practical joke.

Weather reporters are going to have to calibrate the size of hail more than they have. This may be difficult because most weather reporters can't even use a twelve-inch ruler very well.

But let us get down to cases. What does a reporter mean when he says that hail fell which was pea-sized? Does he mean little green young peas or just ordinary canned peas or maybe chick peas? They are very different. His slack use of the size of peas might lead an insurance company to deny all hail claims lodged against it on account of the size of the hail was not specific.

Another fashionable description of hail is baseball-sized. Are the weather reporters referring to the live or the dead ball? This controversy has taken up enough time already in sport without having to transfer it to the weather forecasting people.

There is almost no baseball-sized hail, and when there is one, the seams are in the wrong place.

THE most prevalent kind of hail, according to the weather reporters, is marble-sized hail. Anybody who has ever played marbles for keeps, and most of us can recognize a weather forecaster or two as people who always lost, knows that this description is no good.

Does the weather reporter mean that the hail was as big as gophers? This was the tiniest kind of clamarble. It could be bought cheap, maybe a hundred for a dime. Did he mean they were as big as crockies, which varied in size but were cheap? Did the weather forecaster mean that the hail was as big as aggies, glassies, clear eyes, or cat's eyes, all roughly the same size but different in value? Nobody would risk one of those marbles in a game for keeps against an insufficient number of gophers.

Also, does the weather reporter mean that the ball was as big as steelies? An occasional steelie was three inches in diameter if the owner happened to be so fortunate as to have a father with a tractor that used ball bearings of that size.

The only standard size of hail seems to be golf balls.

HOWEVER, the people who ordinarily get hit by hail don't know anything about golf balls, and the people who know the size of golf balls think that hail should only hit the caddy, not them. You don't have any common denominator on measurement.

I don't know any remedy to suggest. This is a problem for the people who spend their time trying to describe hailstones. Hailstones tend to grow in size in reports as the square of the distance. If I were a weatherman on TV, I would always say, "Hailstones of infinitesimal size or larger will fall on the city tonight." This is scientifically accurate.

Failing that, maybe every telecaster ought to own a bag of many marbles and hold the one up that shows what is going to fall.

Let's get accurate, boys.

A NEW ART FORM

ONE thing wrong with TV is that it keeps breaking into the programs to show some commercials and interrupting the commercials to throw in a dab of program now and then. Since neither bears much resemblance to the fact, the viewer is confused about which fantasy he is seeing.

TV should get away from this crude style of photoplay and run the two together into an artistic whole. Here is this private eye named Harry O, for instance. He is always getting hit over the head with something. At the moment he is on a murder case. He is trying to track down a mad doctor in L.A. who is experimenting with transplanting human heads.

Harry O returns to his apartment late one night, and sure enough, somebody waiting inside bends a heavy crowbar over his head.

He comes to several hours later in the company of a young woman, one of several who are always dropping by to bandage his head. Harry holds his head in his hands and moans.

"Where is the aspirin?" he asks as he staggers toward the bathroom. "I always use Bayer's because it doesn't upset my stummick."

"Take Doan's Little Liver Pills, too," *she advises.*

THE scene now shifts to Wet Gulch, Arizona, where the rustlers and the sheepmen are fighting a range war to decide who controls the cattlemen. John Wayne rides in. He is tracking down a man who once cheated his grandfather in a horseshoe-pitching contest.

He stops at the Greasy Spoon Cafe and meets the town belle. A waitress. With his instinctive courtesy, the Duke takes off his hat and bows low.

"Beg your pardon, ma'am," he says, "but your panty hose is wrinkled."

She slaps his face, though she knows she is in the wrong. He takes the slap as a sign of her stupid gentility and rides off. He avenges his grandfather by shooting one of the crook's horseshoes in midair just as it is about to make a ringer, and he settles the range war by putting the cattlemen in charge of both the rustlers and sheepherders.

Meanwhile, the belle has bought herself some of those panty hose in that round-topped container. She is pretty standoffish with the Duke when he returns, but he notices her panty hose, and they get married.

The whole thing ends in a grand finale with all the settlers hopping around in a round dance and singing in chorus, "If you believe in peanut butter, clap your hands."

This technique could be profitably applied to TV athletics. We see a linebacker make a hard tackle. He gets up and spits out three teeth. "Even Colgate can't guarantee no cavities," he comments.

YOU could make something fine out of that old Indian chief who goes around weeping at the sight of a beer can on the landscape, especially an empty one. We show him before a cooking fire. He holds a large peeled stick in his hand. He sprays the stick with some stuff from a spray can and winds a strip of dough around it.

He holds the dough over the fire for a few minutes and it slips off into the flames.

"Ugh!" he says. "Always use Pam. Grub won't stick."

You get the idea by now. It's a whole new art form.

A MOVIE WITH EVERYTHING

PEOPLE say that the most supercolossal film ever shown at our movie houses was *The Bible.* True, the *New Yorker* magazine did imply that a person might learn more just by reading the book, but the *New Yorker* is not very good on supercolossal matters. It is better at micrometric nit-picking.

At any rate, the question is moot because I have come up with a better supercolossal idea. I am in the process of writing a screenplay adapting the *Encyclopedia Britannica* to the movies.

Let this stand as fair warning to competitive writers and other plagiarists that this subject belongs to me. I thought of it first. The idea hit me like a ton of books the other day when I was dreading having to look up something. I forget what the something was because it became no longer important. When you latch onto a great idea like making a movie out of the *Britannica,* you have to strike while the iron is hot. A week is none too long to spend on a subject of this magnitude.

"Here," I remember thinking, with my unusual infallible insight, "is a book that, as a movie, would be bound to have everything."

IT should be obvious to anybody, after some genius has thought of it, that the *Britannica* is the material for the most colossal supercolossal spectacle ever staged here or abroad. It has a giant cast including nearly everybody who has ever been heard of in the human race. The action of the book takes place in virtually every scene on the globe, and if you go easy on things like thermodynamics, there is plenty of action. As a book, it is weak on dialogue, but anybody can furnish that.

As a movie, the *Encyclopedia Britannica* would be the only device by which you could link together the Taj Mahal, giant pandas, Stonehenge, and Salome carrying the head of John the Baptist. The only other way to do it would be to have an imaginative director, and we're not going to have one. We are going to underplay the whole subject as far as our fifty-million-dollar budget will allow.

At the moment, I lean to allowing Alfred Hitchcock to direct the show, because even when you have read some of the paragraphs in the *Britannica,* you still don't know how they came out.

There would be a part in the play for everybody in show business, from aardvarks to zygote, though the casting might take a little time.

LUCKILY, I am superbly equipped to turn the *Britannica* into celluloid, for I have spent much of my spare time for thirty years in a scholarly project to find the missing item in it.

I started out in a hit-and-miss fashion, thinking up subject after subject, but they all turned out to be in the index. Now, though, I am following a process of deductive reasoning. All you have to do, obviously, is to list every subject included in the book and eliminate these from consideration. The subject not listed is bound to be the missing one.

Scholarly work of this kind seldom pays. It will be good through the movie to make pocket money.

ENTERTAINMENT ON A FOREIGN STATION

PROBABLY the weather Thursday had something to do with it. That raw, dank thirty-degree weather was not unlike Dutch Harbor on a balmy spring day.

At the barbecue joint I ran into a fellow savior of Dutch Harbor back during the real war, and the talk finally got around to how a warrant carpenter named Froman of the U.S. Navy once ran an American eagle as a ringer into a cockfighting pit and thereby lost a fortune.

Froman was typical of the cosmopolitan collection of old Navy men and converted civilians at Dutch Harbor during the days when my barbecue companion and I held the place together. He was a fine fellow, an able professional, and a good storyteller.

In the days of the Old Navy, Froman spent much of his time on the Philippine Station. There is nothing that a sailor on a dull foreign station will not do to improve the shining hour, and Froman and his mates after awhile were improving it by betting on the local cockfights.

They also began acquiring, fighting, and betting on cocks of their own.

THEY didn't fare too well, especially against one champion fighting cock. Matter of fact, they lost their T-shirts.

That was when somebody came up with the idea of importing the eagle. At this distance, how they got the eagle is a little hazy, but there is nothing that the American sailor cannot do once a project of this kind is set in motion. A battleship's crew, for instance, possesses unlimited resources for carrying out such a mission without ever bothering the busy naval officers who are burdened down with guarding the nation. This is the kind of mission a man can carry out on his own.

At any rate, said Froman, they got their eagle. They dyed him black and equipped him as well as they could with comb and wattles. They got together all the money they could lay hands on and bet it against the champion. On the appointed day they produced their eagle at the fighting ring.

That is the story as Froman told it. Probably there were the usual protests at ringside, but what sporting man is going to bar a foreign breed of fighting bird merely because he looks peculiar?

THE fight was short. The eagle ruffled his wing feathers. The fighting cock launched himself in the air and made a swipe at the eagle. With great dignity and in some puzzlement, the eagle drew back his head and stared. The cock made another pass. Again the eagle rather snootily withdrew his head.

Then, with one swipe of his talons he reached out and beheaded the fighting cock. He then began eating him.

"When he started eating," recalled Froman, "that's when the fight began."

That's when he lost a fortune, too. People started grabbing money on all sides.

Maybe this happened and maybe Froman made it up. A man will do anything at times for a little entertainment on a foreign station.

THE PYTHAGOREAN CONSPIRACY

POLYCRATES was the pirate-ruler of Samos about five hundred years before Christ. He ruled the seas around Greece and made a nice profit by allying himself with whatever invader was coming into the area and then selling out the invader to the other side.

On this sunny, chill morning he was restless. The Persians were not invading. The Egyptians were quiet. He had nobody to betray.

He called in his commander in chief.

"What do you hear about old Pythagoras since I chased him off to that island over there by Italy?" asked Polycrates. "What do your stool pigeons say?"

"They say, sire, that he has just sacrificed a hecatomb."

"Killed a hundred head of oxen?" shouted Polycrates. "What kind of lunacy is this? Everybody sympathizes with the plight of the farmer, but this is the wrong way to get the price of beef up. Instead of killing them, why didn't he just give them to somebody in need, like me?"

"They say, sire, that he was celebrating."

"Celebrating what?"

"They say he was celebrating because he has proved that the square of the hypotenuse of a right triangle is equal to the sum of the squares of the other two sides."

"What is a hypotenuse?" demanded Polycrates.

"I DOUBT that any human being except Pythagoras will ever understand what a hypotenuse is, sire, but as I get it, if you have a crossroads, it's a shortcut between one road and the other."

"The man is obviously haywire," said Polycrates. "I can add as well as the next man, especially in money, and a shortcut is just not as long as going around the corners. Still, the man is up to something. He was always an agitator, and now I won't be able to sleep tonight for worrying about what he is doing.

"I knew he was a wrong one when he went over in Palestine and got along with both the Arabs and the Jews. There is something shifty about a man like that."

"Only Pythagoras and Henry Kissinger can do it," agreed the commander in chief.

"If I had time," said Polycrates, "I would go over there and straighten that character out. But there may be a war around here pretty quick, and I may get a chance to sell somebody out for a big pile of boodle. I tell you, Cominch, never let sentiment interfere with business."

"A wise attitude, sire."

Thus passed the only chance to wipe out the Pythagorean Theorem in the beginning and save most of the human race from much tenth grade anguish.

POLYCRATES never got a chance to do it. The Persians soon buttered him up and invited him ashore to a banquet in his honor and killed him. As a high school student, I attempted to demolish the theorem and discovered that nearly all math teachers are biased in favor of Pythagoras. There seems to be an international conspiracy in back of the theorem.

As a result, generation upon generation of college freshmen have lived in anguish because of things like sines, cosines, and tangents. The average freshman has a hard enough time getting a date, much less understanding Pythagoras.

The man just didn't have any common sense.

THE GIFT OF TOTAL RECALL

I AM one of those rare people with the gift of total recall. The only trouble is that it has to be jogged up quite a bit.

This explains the panic that came over me when I recently awakened at 3:00 A.M. and realized that I could not remember who wrote Edmond Rostand. One moment I was sound asleep, and the next I found myself lying there wondering, "Who on earth wrote Edmond Rostand?" I knew his name as well as my own, but I just couldn't think of it.

I could remember all the other pertinent things. I could remember the professor saying that this was one of the great plays. He was a thin-lipped man with a sardonic grin, and if he said something was great, you had better believe it until the semester exam. It was hot at three o'clock that May afternoon in 1935 in Austin, and the air that oozed in through the open window was honey-sweet with the scent of a flower, the name of which I cannot remember at the moment. At times it was hard to tell whether it was the bees buzzing or the professor.

I could remember all this but not who wrote Edmond Rostand.

"My lord," I exclaimed, "am I losing my total recall?"

A TOTAL collapse of the mind like this demands instant action. Considerably shaken, I got up to look the matter up in the dictionary of names. Then I discovered that I couldn't remember where I had left the dictionary of names.

Forcing myself to relax, I went to the icebox and drank a quart of tomato juice. I pondered the matter. Then I saw a jar of jalapeños in the back of the icebox, and I ate one. This apparently triggered my instant recall. Suddenly, I remembered. Nobody wrote Edmond Rostand. He wrote *Cyrano de Bergerac.* Anybody knows that confusing the two names was perfectly natural. Both men had big noses — I think.

I remember the exact words that the professor used in saying that Rostand was a romantic while some other French playwright, whose name slips my mind at the moment, was not a romantic.

It was good to know that my total recall was intact. I ate a couple of radishes which somebody had thoughtfully cleaned.

I COULD have checked the thing easily. Our *Cyrano* is a thin blue book with silver lettering, and at our house we sensibly classify the books according to the color of the binding rather than by author or title. Anybody can remember the color of a book, but most people can't spell some of the authors. Also, most titles begin with "The," which isn't much of a clue.

I didn't need to check, though. I found some sardines and longhorn cheese and made a double-decker sandwich. I ate it and went back to bed.

Total recalling can wear a man out.

A FAMILY TREE

ABOUT twice a year I get a leaflet offering to furnish me with a Crume family tree and also a coat of arms for only twenty-five dollars. This shows the gumption and aggressiveness of the Crume family. It takes most families several generations to acquire a family tree.

Our dad's Uncle Charlie said that we once had a family tree, and Uncle Charlie could remember clear back to his grandfather's day.

Uncle Charlie said that we had the family tree but that the ancestor of our limb of the family once climbed out on the limb and sawed it off behind him.

This has happened so many times in our family that I am persuaded it is the truth.

Uncle Charlie was never known to measure the fish he caught too carefully or to minimize the size of the varmints he shot, but he could not invent a family trait like this.

Uncle Charlie said that all good family trees, like all other good trees, are started by nuts. If they prosper, they continue to produce nuts, each of which is capable of starting a family tree. If you are going to pick a man to start a family tree, said Uncle Charlie, always pick a nut.

COUSIN DAVY AND THE RATTLER

ONE thing wrong with the Remington Arms Company naturalists is that they're out to revolutionize nature knowledge.

Here is a handout that says, "A rattlesnake has, on the average, two (not one) rattles for each year of its age."

This, darn it, changes the thinking of people for thousands of years. If the snake's rattle doesn't represent a year of age, what does it represent? Furthermore, this casts a shadow on all rattlesnake records of the past. Cousin Davy, a relative of my grandmother, formerly held the record for oldest rattlesnake killed. By rattle count, this snake was a hundred years old.

All this happened on the root family homestead in Boone County in the Ozarks eighty years ago. Cousin Davy was trying to get rid of the pesty bald eagles, which were worse than mosquitoes that year. While he was engaged on a cliff in a bowie knife duel with a bald eagle of twenty-foot wingspread he felt something drop at his leg.

He looked down and noticed a gigantic rattler curling about his leg. Because of his position and the way the light fell, he instantly knew that the snake had more than a hundred rattles.

COUSIN Davy was in desperate straits. He only had two hands. He was holding off the twenty-foot bald eagle with one and grasping his bowie knife with the other. He only had two feet. One was tramping around trying to get rid of this enormous hundred-year-old snake, and the other was firmly anchored in this sheer cliff, holding them all up.

Naturally, he had to act. He threw his bowie knife at the eagle's head. He missed, but in dodging, the eagle lost its grasp and fell, knocking the hundred-year-old snake off Uncle Davy's leg and into the abyss below. This was how Uncle Davy happened to kill this hundred-year-old snake.

Of course, the eagle also knocked Uncle Davy loose from his perch, but in falling he managed to catch some kind of rooted herb between his teeth which restored his strength. He got out of it somehow or other, I forget which.

Uncle Davy was always able to prove every detail of his story by the scar on his bowie knife.

WELL, the point of this whole thing is that if Remington nature people are right, all this work and bravery that Uncle Davy put in was wasted. The snake wasn't a hundred years old, after all. It was just fifty years old. Uncle Davy should have gone home.

This makes the snake much less impressive, and it makes the herb that Uncle Davy barely caught between his teeth much less powerful than it turned out to be. What is happening is that the world is now throwing away the testimony of people like Uncle Davy, who was right there in calm and untroubled circumstances on the edge of the cliff and observed what was happening. The world now wants to believe some scientist who says double or nothing.

Nobody ever heard of a yearling rattlesnake with two rattles or a yearling Remington public relations man with less than eight.

MEASURING ANIMAL MORALITY

A BATCH of printed material has just hit this desk from a Mr. G.Clifford Prout who heads an organization called Society for Indecency to Naked Animals.

Mr. Prout is leading a great moral crusade to make people put clothing on all the animals that are now running around naked as a jaybird. He holds that the constant sight of lewd, suggestive, hardly clothed animals is gradually eroding the morals of young America. It is beyond telling what unworthy thoughts those octopi are stirring up as they swim around the beaches showing all those legs. Mr. Prout wishes Big Smith overalls on all elephants. He wants tight, ivy league slacks on all raccoons.

Probably the less said about rabbits the better.

Obviously, Mr. Prout is a high-minded, disinterested man whose only goal is the public weal. This moral reform is long overdue, if for nothing else, to improve garment sales. It seems to us, however, that Mr. Prout is a lot too liberal with these animal profligates. He proposes to exempt animals under four inches in height or six inches in length from clothing.

Since when, Mr. Prout, can you measure morality by a six-inch ruler? Morality is at least thirty-six inches long.

MR. Prout may not know it, but one of the most lascivious animals in existence is the earthworm to which our younger generation is exposed daily while fishing. Of a single earthworm, the locomotive end is a boy, while the caboose end is a girl, or vice versa. Nobody can tell which end comes first on an individual earthworm except another interested earthworm.

Neither end of the earthworm is dressed for the part. Here is work to be done.

The insect people also provide certain problems. Some of them, like the grasshopper, are like the Russian athletes. If you put jumping shorts on a grasshopper or a Russian, you can't tell whether he is a boy or a girl, and that is about as moral as you can get. But there are other insects. The cockroach, for instance, is a lounge lizard type and will break into a courtship even when under the direct gaze of a human being with an insect bomb in his hand.

The cockroach can multiply faster than a chemical in a bomb can work. In a sense, his success explains the disappearance of moral values from the modern world.

Aside from this, the skunk is one of the more decent animals in the universe. How do we measure him for a pair of slacks?

IT says here that Mr. Prout became interested in clothing animals because his father's will left him $400,000 to be spent within ten years on "improving the moral climate of animals." One has to admire Mr. Prout's filial dedication.

However, he has been superficial so far. He has been trying to influence human rather than animal minds. What good is it if he persuades a female antelope to wear a sarong if she is suddenly going to flaunt it dangerously in the presence of a male antelope?

Morality like this costs more than $400,000.

THE NERVOUS HEN

THE Englishman is already well known for his ability to worry about whether the pigeons in the neighborhood park are getting enough psychiatric help. The *London Times* catches a bushel of letters every week from citizens concerned about such things as the damage that a jet plane does to a sparrow's eardrums.

Here is one that tore it, however. Here is a report which reads: "From the managing director on down, all visitors to a big poultry-laying plant near Oxford, England, are required to wear white coats to keep the hens from getting upset." It seems that a hen, at least an English hen, gets nervous when somebody intrudes on her privacy, but she thinks anybody in a white coat is her old friend, the keeper.

This shows how far the English misunderstand hens. "Pip, pip" simply does not mean the same to a hen that it does to an Englishman.

Nor do you ever fool a hen into thinking anybody is her old friend, keeper or not.

FURTHERMORE, when a hen wishes to get nervous, she does not need a human being to start her. The hen by nature is an apprehensive creature full of vague fears and alarms. Apparently she has trouble distinguishing between a human being and a weasel, which in a few cases is understandable.

She is apt to see a chicken hawk in every shadow, to sense doom in the sound of the wind in an oak tree. According to one unimpeachable source (it was my mother), one early-day hen spent a day once running around and squawking, "The sky is falling, and we must tell the king." She seems to have made quite a spectacle of herself.

The hen is the original root meaning of the word "bird-brained." You cannot blame the hen for this. She is what she is.

It seems fair enough, though, to blame people, Englishmen or not, who try to think like a hen.

THE hen may very well be the most misunderstood animal in the world. Most of this misunderstanding stems from the asinine human belief that the main business of a hen is to lay eggs.

With a hen, the egg is only a side issue. When the hen was a wild jungle bird in India, she went around laying an occasional egg here and there without much thought about it. Within five minutes, she didn't know her own egg from any other, and no hen ever wasted time trying to grade her eggs. Only the U.S. Department of Agriculture does that.

A hen's main business was to fight chicken hawks, run from roosters, try to rake up something to eat for the next meal, and generally beat the competition down here and stay alive.

No wonder she is nervous.

ANYBODY CAN SING UNDERWATER

A HANDOUT has reached me which says that frogs are able to sing underwater because they normally sing with their mouths and their nostrils closed. This, it seems to me, misses the whole point of the frog. Anybody can sing underwater. The remarkable thing about the frog is that he can sing on dry land.

Anybody who has ever fished in the backwaters and the hidden sloughs, where the game warden isn't going to spot your seine, has come upon a bullfrog sitting upon a lily pad, arm folded across his waist, giving forth with bel canto tones. One of my older frog acquaintances always sings from the limb of a willow tree stretching out about five feet over the waters of a slough. This frog sounds fully as good out of the water as he would in it.

The point is this: In the animal kingdom, it is normal to sing best underwater. Only the frog as a genus can sing well when the shower is turned off.

Any human bathroom singer can tell you that the frog does not close his nose to keep the water out. If you clamp your nose between your fingers, you produce a better tone.

THE human animal is typical of the giraffes, ostriches, and other unmusical species. He had best sing underwater if he is to avoid an inferiority complex. The exceptions are human geniuses, who probably number frogs among their ancestors somewhere, and people who cover up their voices with the guitar.

It is best for the human singer to sing under a shower rather than under the water of a bathtub, because the dulcet tones do not come out in all their purity when you are singing under bathtub water. Almost anybody, though, even if he cackles when he laughs, can sing well under a shower.

A recent morning comes to mind, this morning in fact. I went into the bathroom and rapped on the walls to test their resonance. Having turned on the shower, I did a few renditions of "Asleep in the Deep." Bel canto, by George. This is a good warm-up number because if the tiles are the right size and some of them are loose, you create the illusion of castanets. After this, I did a small classical number called "And Suddenly It's Spring."

I then sang the Prologue to *Pagliacci* down to where humming was necessary. I was overwhelmed with memories of Leonard Warren at his best and Cesare Siepi at his greenest. I finished up with a rousing "Caro Nome."

Altogether, it was probably the finest musical morning that the smaller bathroom at the Crume residence ever experienced.

THE point is not that I can't carry a tune outside the shower. I can't even find it.

This is true of giraffes, I think. The frog is a great exception in the animal kingdom. His repertoire is limited. His execution is not as perfect as mine. He is more of an Eileen Farrell singer, singing for the wonderful fun of it, than a George London.

But the frog is the only truly amphibious singer of us all.

THE GIFT OF DELICATE HEALTH

We are all entrapped in modern medical science which works twenty-four hours a day to lengthen life and wipe out all the reasons for enjoying it.

THE GIFT OF DELICATE HEALTH

THE GIFT OF DELICATE HEALTH

A MISCONCEPTION common among the ordinary uninformed populace is the belief that health is a good thing. Even science has not been able to stamp out this belief.

How many people in poor health have you known who fell off the face of a cliff while mountain climbing? None, that's how many. Statistics will prove that people who overindulge in health are responsible for more broken arms, punctured esophaguses, torn muscles, and cases of housemaid's knee than any other section of the population.

A person who is given to excessive health is likely to develop delusions of manhood and physical strength, and he may very well beat himself to death against a golf ball.

The obituary stories in the newspapers are a tipoff. Whenever a man suddenly drops dead at fifty, the stories always say, "It was a surprise because he was in excellent health." On the contrary, if you read a story about a man who has died after he reached the age of one hundred, it will always state, "He had been in poor health for many years." This shows where the peril to human life lies.

I have noticed that my own periods of illness have usually been preceded by a period of overhealthiness. Sometimes you have to stay in bed a week to get over the effects.

THE person who seems to survive best in this vale of tears and temptations to physical strength is the person whose health is always delicate. His health is always in a precarious balance, and he cannot afford to take a chance on the effort to become healthy.

Nearly any physician has such patients. He has treated them from the time he got out of medical school, and they have kept on keeping on. He cannot tell you about them because the doctor's oath of office prohibits him from saying which of his patients are goldbricking. A lot of these patients wear out three or four doctors because of the doctors' persistence in believing in health.

During my youth in West Texas, I had an Aunt Mattie whose health was so delicate that people ordinarily talked in hushed voices when she was around. When she was opposed on anything, she was likely to go into one of her spells, as they were called, and swoon, causing all manner of consternation in the household. She was fortunate in that there was always a bed beneath her when she swooned. Otherwise, she might have hurt herself.

Aunt Mattie outlived her husband, who was so blessed with health that he worked himself to death.

She also outlived all her children except one daughter who also happened to have the gift of delicate health.

I DO not believe that people should just cut out health. Moderation is the word. A little bit of health now and then is a good thing, as all who have tried it can testify. When tempted to go on a health binge and do some yard work, restrain yourself and be content with a little indulgence.

Do not put on the boxing gloves with anybody after you are twenty-five. Avoid mixing cement. Do not get into fist fights in beer halls. Or unload barbed wire. Or get into debates about who can jog the farthest.

This kind of self-discipline takes years to acquire. Even now some of us old pros find it hard to make ourselves feel puny enough to avoid exertion.

HOOKED ON WATER

A MAN has to beware of the substances and poisons that he may get hooked on today. Peril besets him at every hand. Have you ever considered, for instance, that nearly everybody who dies has just had a glass of water?

This has bothered me, especially when I wake up in the middle of the night. I lie there trying to decide whether there is any connection between death and water, and

usually I get very thirsty. I always resist the impulse and wet my parched lips with my tongue.

Gullible, trusting souls will insist that people have drunk water forever.

This is no argument. If you will check up, you will find that most of those people are dead.

There is some evidence that water is addictive.

A lot of diaries exist which tell of prospectors, otherwise sensible men, crawling on their bellies across the desert sands and yelling, "Water! Water!"

I BEGAN to be suspicious of water years ago when I found out it was made up of hydrogen and oxygen, both very dangerous substances.

In the Lariat country we had a prim, pretty young schoolteacher named Miss Wilson who taught the general science course. She had majored in domestic science in college and therefore was qualified to teach all the sciences including high school physics.

She rigged an outfit one day which consisted of a dish of water, some electric wires, and a couple of test tubes. She announced that this would separate the hydrogen from the oxygen. The class didn't especially approve of this. Anybody who was separating water was threatening the supply to the livestock.

"Now," said Miss Wilson, lighting a match, "when the hydrogen is exposed to fire, it will explode."

It did, too, and the fragments from the test tube cut her hand, and the explosion burned it.

"Oh, damn it," said Miss Wilson, thus ruining her reputation for primness.

Mitts Fitts had some woolfat in his saddlebags. He ran after it and anointed Miss

Wilson's hand with it. No permanent physical damage was done.

Her reputation for primness, however, was never restored.

SOME may argue that water is addictive but that it does no permanent harm. You would ask what happens if the oxygen and hydrogen separate while you are drinking it. Suppose there is a spark from your cigarette in your throat.

Oxygen does not exactly blow up. As a matter of fact, people who fly airplanes and have hangovers occasionally use oxygen to restore themselves to a sense of reality. If you introduce a little fire into the oxygen, though, it cures a hangover pretty permanently.

The old-timers had the idea. Stay dry.

A PROGRAM OF PHYSICAL EXERCISE

AT regular intervals you ought to start a program of regular physical exercises. I do. This is the reason I am wearing this bandage.

Starting a program of physical exercises makes a man a better human being. It humiliates his spirit and macerates his confidence. People end up by being able to tolerate him, which is something that cannot be said of most men these days.

The first thing to do when taking exercise is to lock the door. Somebody might peek. Then get right down to doing twenty pushups. This is the routine where you lie face down on the floor, place your hands at your shoulders, stiffen your back, and push yourself up twenty times.

When you do your first pushup, you will probably find that nothing has happened.

Although you have pushed, you are still lying there on the floor. Don't worry. It is something they have done to these confounded modern floors, made them so slick you can't get a purchase.

Just try five times to push yourself up once and then quit. Reach around there and get the loose end of that muscle in your back and kind of jam it down where it used to be. Then get up.

If you can get up, heck, you've got it made.

WHEN you first regularly start your program of regular exercise, you will probably start doing it to the snappy military cadence of "Hup-Tup-Hree-Four." After a couple of minutes, you will find that you have slowed down and are pacing it to the sounds of "Onnh . . . Onnh." Don't let it bother you. It merely proves that you got rid of the false amateur enthusiasm and have become an old pro regular exerciser.

Also, resist all inclinations to become philosophical. There is an exercise, for instance, where you lie on your back, stiffen your legs, and raise and lower them without ever letting them touch the floor. After one or two groans, you will inevitably start thinking about why they put muscles in a place that is only used for eating. Resist this tendency toward deep speculation, or you will find that you have stopped exercising to think.

I find it useful at such moments to remember the punk who put a car spotlight in my face the night before. In the pure anger at the recollection, I often can do ten pushups without even realizing it.

WHEN you are about halfway through your daily exercises, you may find yourself thinking that you might have a heart attack. Stop indulging yourself in false hopes. It is better to promise yourself a treat when you have done all the exercising. Tell yourself, for instance, that once you are done you will have an extra martini.

You will find that the exercise is worth all the trouble. Within a week, you can tell a big difference in yourself.

For one thing, you cough a lot louder.

AND NOW, JOGGER'S HEEL

IT was bound to happen. The mad mania of jogging for exercise is catching up with the American jogger. A Chicago doctor has reported the appearance of an ailment known as "jogger's heel." It is similar to baseball finger, swimmer's ear, housemaid's knee, and drunkard's elbow.

Those of us who regularly engage in violent exercise could have predicted this. I, myself, have calcium of the thumb from lifting chess pieces.

Now this doctor says jogging for a mile or more on pavements breaks down a fibrous fatty pad on the human heel, causing scar formation and pain.

There is a great moral to be discerned here. It is that, no matter what you do, the human body has something in it that will break down.

ACCORDING to the doctor, the fibrous fatty heel pad acts as a hydraulic system for the normal, sane human being who does not jog. It cushions the shock of walking. It is sufficient for short runs, such as dashing for the bus, for an occasional standing high jump of six inches, or for carrying weights such as the picnic beer.

Persons who regularly run the jogger's heel-toe gait break down their fibrous fatty pads, and then they have had it.

The doctor has them soak their feet. You wonder whether it mightn't work better if he had them soak their heads. He gives them whirlpool treatments, orders rest, and then suggests that they take up sprinting, which requires running on the ball of the foot.

This is undoubtedly fine therapy for the fatty pad, but it is going to result in a condition called sprinter's heart.

I ONCE knew a college sprinter whose heart had become so accustomed to speed that it wouldn't work except when he was running a 9.6 hundred. This created a great problem for him later when he went into business. The last time I saw him he was running around a brokerage house at a 9.6 pace. He never had time to slow down and become vice-president.

The average human being would be best advised to leave his health alone. The average human physique greatly resembles a ten-year-old wreck of an automobile and should be so treated. If it is working, don't disturb it with pills or violent movement.

No matter how much new paint you put on it or anything you do to it, you can't trade it in anyway.

MAN'S NUDE

NUDE bathers are causing quite a stir these days. An examination of the subject reinforces what I have felt for a long time; the average human body is not a fit receptacle for the human being inside.

I usually feel this way when looking into the bathroom mirror in the morning. Here is this hale human body which has endured famine, pestilence, and even the bawlings out of admirals. Here it stands, its shoulders at slope, its chest caved in, its midsection pooched out, its eyes pouty and glaring.

This body is not a fit temple for the noble soul inside, its grand generosity, its magnificent scope and depth, its obvious superiority to all other human beings.

If my friends who know my art and scope, as Shakespeare has so kindly put it, could see my physique, they wouldn't believe it. I am not overly scandalized by nude bathing. It is not the bathing that betrays the average human being; it is his nude.

WHAT TO DO ABOUT DANDRUFF

IT says here that a New Hampshire skin specialist says that you should not eat nuts or butter or drink coffee if you are bothered by dandruff. His theory is that dandruff is caused by too much oil in the skin and that oily foods compound the problem.

Although we do not know this skin specialist, we can say with certainty that he is a bald man. He knows nothing about dandruff, which is not caused by oily skins. Dandruff is caused by hair. A Beatle-type man who is bothered by dandruff and wants to get rid of it can do so very easily by shaving his head. Many a prematurely bald man would be glad to give half his life's savings if he merely had the chance to have dandruff again.

Dandruff is the normal sloughing off of dead skin cells. When there is a good healthy head of hair to catch it, dandruff accumulates. It is actually the sign of hair health. Very often, in a fifty-year-old man, it is the only way you can tell a real head of hair from a toupee.

The man with a white powder on the collar of his chesterfield obviously has hair that he grew himself.

THE one thing to do if you have dandruff is to stop combing your hair. People then will never notice it. It is significant that dandruff became a social problem only after men began to smooth down their hair with that greasy kid stuff or else that nongreasy kid stuff.

In the old days, men tried to get their hair to grow out and tangle up and form a mat so that it would protect them if they were hit over the head. This was the reason that the Indians and the Franks of Charlemagne took scalps; it removed part of the enemy's protective armor. The football players of the 1898 University of Texas team let their hair grow and mat and used it for helmets.

In those days, nobody was bothered by dandruff. It couldn't get through the hair. The only time that a man ever knew that he had dandruff was when a small flour-colored cloud formed around his head after he had run head-on into something.

In those days, girls in search of a husband did not ask whether a hairy man had dandruff, but they were quite likely to want to know whether a baldheaded man had money.

THERE are certain wise rules that a man ought to follow if he wants to live a peaceful life. One is to turn the man down who wants you to bet at odds of 7 to 1 on a long shot. All life, in Damon Runyon's phrase, is still 6-5 against.

Another rule is to beware of the man who tells you to give up a food. Most middle-aged men have at least a half-dozen things mildly wrong with them, each calling for the abandonment of four or five foods if you listen to the wrong doctor. All that this line of treatment leads to is a stomach cramp.

If a man has an irresistible appetite for pecans, something in his nature demands pecans. What he gains in fewer flakes of dandruff by giving them up he will lose in a damaged psyche.

THE ART OF NOSEBLOWING

THE American Medical Association has recently issued a press release on how to blow your nose. It shows how thoroughly Americans are now being cared for in this scientific age. You used to have to wait until you got into Miss Tilly Simpson's second-grade hygiene class to learn all these secrets.

The AMA says that you should blow with both nostrils open, not closed. This seems to be scientific enough. If you let go while the nostrils are closed, the backfire may explode through the middle ear, the AMA says. You might hear double or something. This advice is well and good, but it leaves out Miss Simpson's main admonition for good health, which was, "Don't save your handkerchief." A handkerchief saved for two or three weeks was the main threat to human health in Miss Simpson's eyes.

Actually, she never needed to worry. At our age, we never blew our noses. For hours on end, we would forget that we ought to. Anyhow, in one of the playground fights, you would get clouted up the side of the head sooner or later. This was wonderful for clearing the sinuses and even toned up the middle ear for an hour or two.

Also, a middle ear that has been chastised with the fist severely enough in early life is not likely to give way before a nasal backfire.

ACTUALLY, the art of noseblowing is all but lost. Like many vigorous folk arts, it has become the victim of genteelism. Although the kids were too young to care much for this elaborate art, the men of the Lariat country in our day had perfected it to an astounding degree.

An old-timer about to engage in the practice on the high baldies would first heave up his chest and contort his face in preparation. He would then take out a big red bandanna reserved for the purpose and wave it vigorously around in the air. He did not do this to attract attention. He was clearing out the accumulation of dust of the last hour or so.

He would then place the bandanna to his nose and sound off. Distant cattle would raise their heads from grazing and gaze in his direction. The sound was not shrill and piercing like the whistle of a diesel locomotive. It was mellow and sonorous like casual thunder. Afterward, the old-timer would methodically replace the bandanna in his pocket and arrange his face in a look of blessed relief.

Men specially gifted at this art were widely recognized. They were all nicknamed Honk.

ON a second examination of this press release, it seems to me that AMA has been issuing statements without enough research. What is the AMA recommendation, for instance, for blowing the nose while running into a strong wind? This problem has bothered many a last-place quarter-miler.

Also, noses are different. Some have bad gaskets. My nose has a slight mountainous ridge of bone in it that blocks the passages so that I have to lower away the right shoulder and blow a curve. One of AMA's own members has certified that the bone is there and has suggested that he go in there with a chisel and create another Mount Rushmore.

This seems rather extreme, but the doc says we ought to do it because someday I might want to breathe.

THE TAILORED LENS

ONE of the minor catastrophes hanging constantly over the head of modern man is the chance that he may lose or forget his spectacles.

This happened to me during the week. At such times, a thick gray haze blots out the physical world and all in it. The sounds of ordinary life and ordinary business seem from beyond it disembodied and strange. The name you are trying to read in the telephone directory becomes a thin black line bounding around on a sea of milk. Voices, voices, voices come to you, each chuckling as it offers to lend you its glasses.

When you are in this shape, about the only physical thing you are capable of is driving a car.

In part, I blame the medical profession for man's present plight. It has succeeded in persuading people that the same pair of spectacles, or pairs no more different than the hardware store can carry, do not work alike for all people. As a result, modern man is lost without his tailored-to-measure lens.

As a result of the tailored lens, modern man has lost entirely the talent for squinting, which is the only way to make out without glasses. If you squint long enough, someone will read it for you.

IN our childhood in West Texas, things were different. Astigmatism did not exist then. Neither did nearsightedness, ophthalmia, or cataracts. People then had only two kinds of eye trouble, "weak eyes" and "strong eyes."

Furthermore, "weak eyes" was just as derogatory in connotation as any other thing weak. A man did not lightly confess to weak eyes; he squinted. When he was by himself, he might make use of his or his wife's spectacles, but in public he would no more wear spectacles than he would wear spats. There were a few exceptions to this general rule of etiquette. It was all right to put on glasses, for instance, to find a verse in the Bible proving to another man that the tenets of his particular church had damned him eternally to hellfire. It was all right to wear spectacles when signing for a telegram, because there was no telling what fine print was up there ahead of the signature.

But usually you did not wear glasses. When faced with something that had to be read, many men dodged the disgrace of admitting their weak eyes by keeping silent and allowing people to think they were merely illiterate.

But no more. Undone by the modern lens grinder, man now stands ashamed and naked in his own weakness.

MORE than most people know, America was shaped by the lack of good spectacle lenses. The average pioneer was pretty nearsighted. If he hadn't been, he would never have had the heart to start out on the task before him. Usually, he thought he was fighting three Indians because he couldn't see the tribe beyond them.

You've often seen the pioneer pictured gazing off into the distant horizon. Actually, he wasn't looking at the horizon at all. He was squinting.

CAPTIVE OF THE CALORIE

A FRIEND of mine has been told by the doctors to cut fifty to a hundred pounds from his weight. It has been suggested that he cut out alcohol.

He has studied the subject thoroughly and reports that he cannot do this. He has found, he says, that cutting a mere ten calories a day from his diet will reduce his weight one pound over a year's time. An ounce of alcohol has about a hundred calories.

"If I cut out drinking," he said, "I would lose eight hundred pounds in a year. I couldn't take it. I would be skin and bones."

Nevertheless, he will probably go on and lose eight hundred pounds. We are all entrapped in modern medical science, which works twenty-four hours a day to lengthen life and wipe out all the reasons for enjoying it.

In a sense, modern medical science is a captive of its own inventions.

It invented the calorie. Before that time, people didn't have any calories that could make them overweight.

ANYBODY who ever grew up in a small town in the old days can recall some elderly men of truly noble physical weight, men who had to have someone put on their shoes because they could not reach their feet. When such a man wished to rise from a chair, it took all the able-bodied males of the family, hauling and pushing, to get him on his feet. These men lived on and on, probably for two or three hundred years, and perished only when there was nobody left to bring them food.

In a sense, the vitamin has done even more than the calorie to ruin the human diet. In the old days a man would breakfast off a quart of blackstrap molasses into which he would pour a skilletful of redeye ham gravy. He would stir this up with his knife and then sop it up with forty-eight or fifty-four biscuits.

He would then sit back and wish that he had something really expensive to eat like Post Toasties or canned tomatoes. He did not gain weight because he took on no vitamins. Probably he got a few calories, but he did not have time to notice them. Usually he had to pull a cow out of a bog somewhere.

In those days, being fat was a matter of pride. It showed that you had money enough to eat.

THERE is one danger in the modern weight-controlling diet. If you change a man's food, you change his temperament and his emotional climate.

George Gissing pointed out half a century ago that empires are built by men who eat beef. A man who eats beef snorts when he talks and glares at people. We would like to see the glare produced by a ton or two of Metrecal.

To a man on a well-balanced, huge beef diet, vegetables are useful frills and garnishes. Our own opinion of vegetables remains that of Beau Brummel, who when he was asked whether he ate vegetables replied that he once ate a pea.

Probably modern medical science and its diets are altering the course of history. The lesser breeds without the law are acquiring all the beef given up by those of us who dine now on cottage cheese.

THE AUTHENTIC STOMACH MAN

AN acquaintance has complained that his wife is always saying, "Eat slower. You will live longer." He wants to know whether there is any scientific basis for this.

It is a great satisfaction to report that there is not a word of truth in this saying. It is simply a superstition. I have personally tested the thing by experiment. I have eaten fast; I have eaten slow. I have lived just as long by both methods. Also, I have looked into various historical figures, and of those who have eaten fast and those who have eaten slower, the same number are dead, 100 percent.

A curious fact is that people who don't have anything to eat seem to die younger than people who eat fast.

The guiding word is eat, drink, and be merry, for tomorrow you may be eighty and reduced to milk toast.

HOW fast a person should eat depends entirely upon the person and upon how much he has to eat. It depends also on whether he has an authentic stomach. Some people have no stomach at all. They will blanch at the mere sight of a seventh fried egg for breakfast.

The man with an authentic stomach can eat anything any way any time, and he will relish it.

Nothing can bother the man with the authentic stomach. He may have forgotten to shuck the shell of the lobster. OK. It was a minor oversight. However, he is always aware that there is a limit on the time to be spent eating, and he can handle this problem one of two ways. He can take enormous bites and chew slowly, or he can take smaller bites and chew fast.

A good authentic stomach man can mix them up, however, as the situation demands. He can eat fast, or he can put a bait in his mouth that needs all afternoon to chew.

Some of the fastest eaters are lady nibblers at cocktail parties. They eat with the speed of a cockroach.

WHETHER eating fast will damage a man physically depends a lot on why he is eating fast. They say that some men cram themselves because they are trying to escape from their wives, or something else. This is fine for escaping from something else, but putting on weight is not a good way to find an escape from a wife.

Other people eat fast because they say, "Oh, boy, here is all that wonderful shrimp remoulade," and nothing bad ever happens to them because they eat in happiness. They bother people with their belching, but they are healthy enough.

A man should so live that when he cashes in his meal tickets he can weep for all the fine meals ahead that he has missed.

State of the Nation
of the Nation

POLITICS AND THE PEOPLE

People who talk of conservative and liberal shifts are talking nonsense. The grassroots American is neither liberal nor conservative. He is opinionated.

POLITICS AND THE PEOPLE

THE HUMAN ELEMENT

A FRIEND of ours holds that the Democratic convention opening today is a complete waste of time, just as was the Republican convention before it. The computers, he says, already know what is going to happen, so why not turn the business over to them while we all get to work on the problems of America, such as creating the kind of poverty in which a man can live comfortably?

In truth, politics in these United States seems to be increasingly dehumanized. Any of us old-time election workers can tell you that the voting machine took the picnic out of politics, and when the picnic closes down, the human beings inevitably depart.

It is only a question of time until the computers install one of their own in the White House all set up to push the button under the proper circumstances.

All that will be left human then will be the political oratory, which cannot be created electronically. It can only be magnified.

THE human element is already gone from our big city elections. The voting machine is inexorable. If a man wishes to exercise his sovereign right as a voter and vote against everybody, he can't do it. If he has two friends in the same race and wishes to help them both, the machine jams.

As a callow election clerk out in the Lariat country, I was once sitting by when the man who was reading off the votes for the tally clerks waved a ballot in the air and exclaimed, "Mutilated!"

It looked mutilated all right. Some voter had stricken every name on the ballot with broad, gouging strokes. He had gouged a hole in the middle of the ballot in the process. The election judge, however, looked at the ballot, recognized the handiwork, and shook his head.

"This is not a mutilated ballot," he said. "This is Uncle Benny Jenkins's ballot. He was trying to find Jim Ferguson's name in it so he could vote for him. Count it."

"How?" asked one of the clerks.

"Count it the way he marked it, a vote against everybody."

The vote affected the total not at all, but the will of the elector was done just as he intended it.

EVEN the big city voting scandals nowadays are machine-made things beyond recall. They are as nothing to the famous Miss Bee Noble case. Miss Bee Noble was a spinster who served for many years as an election clerk.

It is customary in marking a tally sheet to put down a straight mark for each of four votes and then cross them catty-cornered with the fifth mark to form a group of five. One year somebody discovered that Miss Noble had been putting down five marks and crossing them with a sixth.

You can see the uproar that broke out. The results of half a dozen past elections were suspect. Although nobody upbraided her about it, Miss Bee Noble wept gently and retired from politics. The candidates in those past elections met and had fistfights, and the whole thing settled down.

SEARCHING FOR A SUITABLE CANDIDATE

AT this time of crisis in the United States, any sensible man has to be asking himself what presidential candidates we will pick in the upcoming conventions. Obviously, the candidates have to be cleaner than a hound's tooth that hasn't bitten into a rabbit in a month.

To my mind there is only one suitable candidate, Snow White. After Ron Ziegler, it may be hard for anybody to believe in Disney-type people, but nobody has anything against Snow White. Her only fault is that she seems to get lost in the woods, but apparently this is common to American Presidents.

Furthermore, Snow White comes equipped with seven good advisers. True, one of them, Dopey, will probably get nominated by the opposition party.

She still has left Doc, who is the perfect secretary of state. All foreign affairs advisers are known as Doc these days. She also has Sleepy, who is a perfect secretary of agriculture where the people have been asleep for fifteen years. And then, among others, she has Grumpy who could step right in today as head of Internal Revenue.

If she ever got into trouble, Snow White wouldn't have to confront the Congress. She could just stop and sing, "Someday my prince will come."

This would beguile the public while she got on to the business of the country, and only later would they discover that the prince wasn't coming and that they were stuck with the bill for the whole banquet.

This kind of ability to avoid a constitutional confrontation is called statesmanship.

SNOW WHITE is the only candidate who is viable, to use the currently popular word. The candidates in the next election have to be purer than the tall candle before the holy rood, as Yeats remarked. We just don't have anybody like that who has grown up beyond puberty.

Take the case of myself. I can run this country. I know how to cut the taxes and expenses and increase the White House standard of living and discourage bribery. The simple way is to take the bribes and don't do anything; they quit after awhile.

But I can never be President. There was this stolen mule that followed me home one night. I

145

didn't want the mule, and his trust was misplaced because he didn't get any food. Nevertheless, the electorate will never believe me. Even the sheriff didn't.

The well-meaning and accidentally tainted people are not enough today.

THIS is why I think Snow White is the only possible candidate. There are many fine men in the United States who have been followed home by a stolen mule.

A BEAUTIFUL DIVING HORSE

HERE is a news release in which a man says that the Democratic party has done itself great harm by using the donkey as its symbol. The party, he says, should adopt instead a beautiful diving horse, of course.

"The donkey has earned such a bad name that it now has a dictionary connotation of 'a person regarded as stupid, foolish, or obstinate,'" says this man. As you can see, this is a fair Republican description of the Democratic party, and the man undermines his own case.

What he suggests may be subversive. Let us stick to the donkey and elephant ideals of our forefathers.

The diving horse is not an American Symbol. In his general downward trajectory, he more nearly resembles The Great Leap Forward of another country.

THE donkey is admirably equipped to represent the Democratic party just as the elephant is the natural symbol of the Republicans. As everybody knows, The Elephant Remembers. He has to remember a long time back to keep up his hopes of winning. In any given election year, the elephant is burdened with a mahout named Goldwater or something with whom he does not wholly agree.

In the forest of voters, the elephant is unable to see the trees for the trunks.

Now, consider the donkey. By rippling his shoulder muscles rapidly, he is able to create the illusion of Getting the Country Moving while his feet stay in the same spot. The donkey is gifted at dodging all obstacles to get to the feed trough, and once there he is almost impossible to get out. The donkey cultivates alliances with his front half and kicks them apart with his hind quarters. His foreign policy thus is always forward-looking.

If there is a better symbol of the Democrats than the donkey, it surely isn't the diving horse.

THE horse is showy, beautiful, and tractable. He excites envy, which is no way to attract votes. The donkey looks like us common men. He is homely, always faintly threadbare, and given to spots of dandruff, obviously a safe character who is not going to take us on any dangerous dives.

If we had to choose between the donkey and the horse, we would elect the donkey and make the horse go jump in the lake. That's what he does naturally.

CONSERVATISM AND LIBERALISM

AN old West Texas boy confessed to me the other day that he was puzzled by present-day politics. After looking over the Rockefellers, the Harrimans, and the Kennedys, he said, he has decided that a liberal is anybody with more than ten million dollars. A conservative, on the other hand, is likely not to have more than two cars to his name. This was not the way he heard it, says my friend, when he was growing up in Hermleigh, the Queen City of the Scurry boondocks.

Indeed things were different at Hermleigh and Lariat. The main liberal of my boyhood was a county attorney named A. P. Dosier, a large, portly, and loud man who could never resist making a speech when in the presence of three people. The liberal-conservative battle in those days was fought every Sunday morning in the Baptist church, where A. P. Dosier would usually make five speeches during the Sunday school convocation and two more during the collection. All his speeches were directed full face at the town's main conservative, Mr. Tom Estep, an elderly moneylender at 10 percent who considered twenty-five cents quite enough to pay for any church service.

During each speech, A. P. Dosier would loudly offer to give the church twice as much as Mr. Estep.

Of course, A. P. Dosier didn't have it. But what he was doing seemed safe, and he was performing the classic function of the liberal. He was trying to give from those who had it.

IN contrast, they who have nowadays are quite willing to give from those who have not. Things are mixed up because the philosophic soil from which liberalism and conservatism grew is all torn up.

The old-time liberalism, for instance, was deeply rooted in the values of the Christian faith and its ideas of good and evil. The liberal knew how impossible it was for a rich man to get into the kingdom of heaven. He was grieved by the plight of the rich man's soul and was only too willing to help him to salvation by giving away his money.

Similarly, conservatism was rooted in the philosophy of Locke and Adam Smith. The conservative believed in such things as free enterprise, laissez faire, and high protective tariffs. He believed that the good things of the past should be conserved and protected. So, when the liberal started handing around people's money, the conservative undertook as a civic duty to get hold of as much of it as he could and conserve it for the future.

Some people argue that the Rockefellers, Kennedys, and such worked a neat gambit for self-protection and took over liberalism.

I REJECT this cynical idea, however. As I said, the philosophies in which the two political theories were grounded have broken up. It is a tribute to the human skull. The hardest philosophy, when tried on enough human heads, will shatter into bits.

The human being does not fit easily into a syllogism. For instance, I personally have noticed that I always vote liberal but I think black reactionary. This is as it should be. A man ought to have balance.

Maybe you're wondering what happened between A. P. Dosier and Mr. Estep. Well, the thing went on until Mr. Estep one day got mad and offered the church a thousand dollars.

Conservatism ran roughshod over liberalism again.

RUNNING A CLEAN CAMPAIGN

THE Candidate came into the office and said he would appreciate my vote and influence. He offered me a card and a small leaflet listing nineteen points of progress under his program.

"I am running on the issues," he said. "Unfortunately my opponent is a sorry, evil, misbegotten wretch who will not debate the issues with me. You know, of course, that he let his mother starve in 1956. Imagine a ninety-eight-year-old woman who died because she was put in a convalescent home where she didn't get enough to eat."

I said I couldn't imagine anything like it, and he said that was the trouble with the voters, no imagination.

"Also," said The Candidate, "a teacher has told me that one of his kids has two heads. I cannot document this personally but this teacher is reliable. She teaches algebra."

I said a lot of people were two-headed about algebra, and he said he never touched the stuff himself.

I ASKED what the issues were that he wanted to debate.

"Honesty in government is one," he retorted. I said that neither he nor his opponent had ever held public office, so there didn't seem to be any honesty in government involved.

"Yeah, but if he had been in office, there would have been," replied The Candidate.

"If you had checked into this, you would find that he still owes twenty-two payments on a Frigidaire that he bought two months ago. This stock has been fluctuating ever since, and there is a conflict of interest here if I ever saw one. Anyhow, I defy you to find one case where he has ever said whether he will be honest or dishonest."

All this was beside the case, said The Candidate. He just wished his opponent would discuss the issues and quit slinging mud.

It was unfair to turn a serious campaign into a vicious battle between personalities.

I ASKED whether he had any more issues that he wanted to discuss, and he said he was for lower taxes. His opponent, he said, has steadfastly refused to take the opposite side of the proposition and argue the issue out.

I told The Candidate that I was in favor of no taxes at all, and he said that I was sound but unrealistic.

"If you didn't have any taxes," he asked, "how on earth would you pay public servants?"

I confessed that this was a problem, and he observed that most of us never thought things through.

His opponent, he added, consistently refused to make a stand and fight.

"The minute I came out against busing," he said, "he came out against it."

I finally agreed with him that the candidates ought to discuss the issues, and he departed, leaving behind the thought that a man who runs a clean campaign is bound to win.

HOW TO SHAME THE POLITICIANS

THEY say there is a lot of immorality today in politics, which is probably true, politics being generally a pretty good mirror of the human animal. The human animal never accepted morality until he was herded into it, and he is always trying to escape. An immoral thing is usually something done by somebody else who got caught. Immorality in another man is likely to be your own lovable quirk of character.

Years ago, out on the high baldies of West Texas, Bully Means was accused of not handing out the trading stamps he had advertised to his customers unless they demanded them. Bully's argument was that if the customers didn't ask for them, he had no right to force the stamps on the customers.

The Primitive Baptist minister, who was the only man who could bring Bully to his knees in repentance once a year, asked Bully whether he didn't think holding back the stamps was immoral.

Bully was incandescent in his indignation.

"Immoral?" he roared. "What has my holding back the green stamps on people got to do with girls?"

Since the touchstone of morality to him was girls, he was a very moral man. He had a large, possessive, and angry wife who managed to keep tabs on him just about all the time. She once called the county sheriff and had him arrest Bully, the town banker, and two prominent merchants for playing penny ante in the back of the filling station after midnight.

Considering Mrs. Means, Bully had more compulsions to be moral than most men.

I HAVE already decided that I cannot change up morality on the national level and that I will just try to rearrange my own morality, painful though that may be. If enough of us do this, maybe we will shame these politicians into practicing our saintliness.

First, I have resolved never again to use the company's paper in the pursuit of private projects except in emergency circumstances where I have a chance to make five dollars or

more quick. When it is necessary for me to use this paper, I will mail the company an anonymous letter enclosing a quarter and saying that I took a newspaper from an honor box. This takes care of the morality of that.

Also, I will never again give the managing editor inflated reports about all the work I have done in a given period. I just won't mention it, and he will usually be too busy to ask.

I will not again tell anybody that I taught John Galsworthy how to write.

When I join the Boy Scouts again, I will not weasel about the Scout Law except that part that says a Scout is brave. This always was a lie so far as I was concerned. I am an authentic coward.

These are stringent reforms, but stringent moral measures are needed now.

IN return for my stringent sacrifices, I would like people to notice my morality more and to compliment my new halo. I would appreciate it if people didn't come around saying, "Sir, this credit card you offered us is two years out of date." This isn't a matter of morality. It deals with chronology.

Also, ducking out on my part of a tab is not morality. It's economics. And walking a red light when no policemen are around isn't morality. It's irresistible.

THE GRASS-ROOTS AMERICAN

ANYBODY with any sense knows that the TV commentators and the eastern press do not represent the thinking of the American people. This has always been true. These TV and press folk are bright people, well educated, well read, intrigued by new and imaginative ideas. They keep themselves sopped up with all that free cologne and other graft. They are trapped in their own minds.

They make the mistake of thinking that an American has to be properly informed, the definition of "properly" being the nut of the argument, before he can form an opinion.

An American can form a firm opinion on any subject without any information at all.

THE TV commentators all spend too much time on airplanes and too little time traveling on buses. They could learn a great deal by coming down out of the clouds and mixing with the crowds at the bus station. American grass-roots opinion rides the Greyhound, not the airways. The boys in the plane are too often riding high on the company expense account and busily impressing each other by referring to important people by their initials.

The bus rider is still a traveler with time to kill, strangers to talk to, and nobody to impress. He usually has a unique life experience which he is glad to share. He has pretty well sized up the universe and is not reluctant to pronounce judgments.

Anybody who rides the bus has to discover that American grass-roots opinion is really an almost impossible snarl of filaments growing out of infinite influences, few of which come from Washington or TV. The bus riders usually agree on two things. The coffee which they have experienced is awful, and every tradesman around is out to gyp the poor traveler. On other matters, they think different things, or think the same thing for different reasons.

You find a number of people who oppose some government proposals simply because the Lord did not intend it that way.

Others don't like something because they didn't do it that way when they were a boy. Some approve of a measure because Abe Lincoln would have done it, or Teddy Roosevelt, or FDR.

People who talk of conservative and liberal shifts are talking nonsense. The grass-roots American is neither liberal nor conservative. He is opinionated.

THE politicians and the facile men of the media would not even consider this sort of thing public opinion, but as some have discovered before, it can turn on you and crush you.

The man who spends a while at the lunch counter in the bus station will discover that grass-roots opinion can be stubborn, bigoted, and appallingly ill informed. But he will also discover that it is nearly always shrewd and is sometimes in an odd and simple way very wise. It is the kind of wisdom that Washington could use, but, of course, when a man gets elected, he starts riding airplanes.

PREDICTING THE WINNERS

SEVERAL people who are impressed with this writer's uncanny ability to pick the winner of a football race have lately suggested that I turn this talent to predicting the winners of the spring elections. These people misunderstand the problem. Politics is not a twenty-two-man scrimmage like football. It just looks like it.

Football is an exact science. Winning depends on having the right man at the right place at the right time. In politics, the wrong man can often be at the right place at the right time and win. Predicting a football race is also an exact science. You merely read all the sports experts to find out what the logic of their thinking is and what teams they have picked. Then you pick a team which fits in with their logic but which they overlooked in deciding who is going to win.

Like most other people, sports experts use logic to justify what they do but make their decisions on a hunch.

It is impossible to explain a politician by logic, however. There are no hunches to spot and throw away.

IT is this which makes politics proof against us prophets. There is no real expert opinion to be wrong. Anybody who has studied the problem knows that a lot more political experts have predicted the results right after the vote is in than seemed to before the polls were open.

It is the same with voters. Any politician who has won an election quickly finds out that more people voted for him than the election crews managed to count. The average voter may cast his vote however you may guess, but he keeps an open mind about who he is for until he finds out who wins. There is nothing wrong with this. After all, our society in the United States is pluralistic. A man ought to fit himself in with his times. Similarly, any losing candidate is bound to wonder whether he really got all those votes or not.

This shows the virtues of the American democratic system. The losing candidate seldom makes a peep because he is pretty convinced that somebody was crooked on his side.

Predicting and betting on politics is for the monied and reckless few. A man with a small bet to wager would be well advised to put it into something with a smaller but surer return, like horse racing.

THE best that any prophet can do on politics is an educated guess, and it is this sort of thing that has brought American education into disrepute. Years ago, out in West Texas, Judge John Patrick McGill was told that one of our townsmen, Timothy Carter, had said he could make an "educated guess" about something.

"Tim," said the Judge, "is giving himself airs."

Eight years ago I personally made educated guesses on all the political races from public weigher to governor and missed them all. It sort of took the education out of it.

The only thing you can do about politics is to take a resigned attitude. What will be will be.

THE INAUGURAL ADDRESS

CERTAIN great themes run through the inaugural addresses of all the Presidents from Washington on.

For one thing, the skies over the country are always lowering and dark at the moment of the speech, but a dim light of hope can be seen on the horizon. We can do anything if we will but march ahead united. The United States desires nothing on earth so much as peace everywhere, but don't tread on us.

We must help the poor, fit the blind with a new cork leg, and lift up the afflicted and the gross national product. We must go ahead and never turn back, or we will falter.

Our new President handled the old music in a new arrangement very well in his recent inaugural address. If he used more violins than trumpets, it is probably a good thing in these times. The trumpets have been calling pretty regularly lately.

None of this is meant cynically. After all, anything as majestic as an inaugural can never be trite.

An inaugural is a ritual. It is an old and cherished possession which is brought out and admired once every four years.

AFTER all, what would we have a new President say when the topics he has to deal with are all too familiar? For one thing, on any inauguration day the skies over Washington are dark and lowering, and if the new President sees some faint light of hope ahead, it ought to be mentioned.

Also, the American people tend to think problems can be solved; but problems, like computers, are getting ahead of mankind. In part, the American people believe this because they have mistakenly located the problem outside the human being. They have identified a problem as a set of circumstances which bedevils human beings.

Actually, the problem is inside the pigheaded human being himself; and if the government removes the outside circumstances, the human being will get himself a new set of circumstances to clothe the problem.

Solutions, furthermore, are like pills. They attack problems, but they start up other things. We solved the farm problem of the 1930s and created the city problem of our day. If we respond to the first cold gestures of friendship from the Chinese, will we have the Russians back at our throats?

I am even skeptical of the negative income tax.

It sounds like a good idea, especially for me, but what happens if there isn't any negative income tax?

THE American people do not progress by marching abreast forward. They get ahead by floundering around in circles out in the woods and edging, maybe, a little toward the promised land.

I am not against inaugurals. It does seem to me that they could coordinate the clerics more so they wouldn't cover the same ground in their prayers, but this probably infringes on religion. If a man wants to cover the same ground, he should be allowed to.

And, like everybody else, I am right now on our new President's side. I'll bet he solves some problems, but I'll also bet he'll leave more problems than he found. Problems and pollution are taking over the world.

STATE OF THE ECONOMY

The man who robbed from the rich and gave to the poor was a much better redistributor of wealth than the government. Instead of robbing from the rich and giving to the poor, the government robs from the middle class and gives to the rich and the poor.

STATE OF THE ECONOMY

HOW TO HANDLE A BALANCE OF PAYMENTS

THE dollar is again losing value internationally, and the economists are telling us all not to get worried. Some of us are replying, "Who is worried?" We don't have any dollars.

The problem is that the U.S. has an unfavorable balance of payments, and the experts are worried. Many of us have lived with an unfavorable balance of payments personally all our lives, and we know how to handle it. Let them sweat. They are holding the bag. They are the ones who are supposed to worry. Those of us who owe the balance trip our way gaily through life like the grasshopper before autumn and build our house of sticks against the big bad wolf.

It is a law of life that the man who has money coming to him is supposed to be worried, not the man who owes it.

In the matter of an unfavorable balance of payments, it is more blessed to give than to receive.

ON a personal basis, of course, I never receive polite statements saying, "Sir, your balance of payments is unfavorable." My statements say, "Please remit."

Still, it might help if the United States made no response at all to this kind of statement. From a personal point of view, I have never received any consideration from a letter acknowledging that my balance of payment is unfavorable. However, if I write back, "Are you sure?" I usually have three months while the other side considers.

The man with an unfavorable balance is actually a favored customer, usually, but he needs to drop by occasionally and look at the favorable man's merchandise as a reminder. This reminds the guy that holds the balance that a problem is there.

If you go into a place, having always paid cash, and ask for an item, the saleswoman is likely to say, "Find it yourself, buster." But if you have an unfavorable balance of trade in the place, the word mysteriously gets around by way of runners and electronic intercom systems, and a vice-president comes down to see what he can do for you.

Maybe you will suggest that you ought to cut off your trade until you can get paid up. In the Goldwynian phrase, he is horror and struck. This will cut down his volume, which will cause him to be fired when the next comparative sales statistics are posted.

He will urge you to increase your unfavorable balance and work out a long-term way of settling it.

NONE of this works out the way Ben Franklin recommended, but it works.

What this country needs is a good debtor President. The Presidents all pay on the first of the month, which is a heck of an example for a nation that doesn't.

The President should subtly suggest that he will stop buying things and cut down on the allowances for our soldiers overseas until we balance the payments.

The other nations will start begging him to increase his unfavorable balance of payments.

If I understand it.

THE PIGGY BANK MENTALITY

AS you may have noticed, the stores in the East are upset this Christmas because of a shortage of nickels, dimes, and quarters to make change. Some expert up there has blamed piggy banks. If people would break open their piggy banks, he says, there would be plenty of nickels, dimes, and quarters in circulation, and commerce could flourish unabated.

It is probably a good thing that these big stores ran out of money here right before Christmas. Now they will know how the rest of us live and maybe be a little more lenient with their charge accounts. However, it was high time that a real expert put his finger on the piggy bank problem. If there is one great threat to the American way of life, it is Thrift.

Thrift dries up the juices of trade. It makes everything come out in even dollars instead of ninety-eight cents, and the average housewife is reluctant to step over into this higher expense bracket.

The piggy bank encourages Thrift. It has all the appearances of being a devilish invention to sabotage the American standard of high living and allow the Russians to close the gap.

UNFORTUNATELY, many careless parents allow their kids to play around with piggy banks in their tender years. Before they know it, the child has caught the habit and is unable to break it. All his life he does irreparable harm to the American economic system and to his household collection of gadgets.

The federal government itself is guilty of contributing to the piggy bank mentality. It ought to take the cork out of the bottom of Fort Knox and put all that money back in circulation. The money is certainly doing no good where it is. It may make a nice jingle when the President shakes it, but it isn't working. Maybe it's just a coincidence, but ten-dollar gold pieces have been scarce around our house ever since the government set up Fort Knox. It hinders our making change.

Thrift is a Shining Ideal, like quitting tobacco. It is impossible of attainment, and ought to be kept in the world of ideals and abstractions the way people keep the Sermon on the Mount.

Unrestrained thrift causes something called inventories to pile up and shrinks something called new orders.

IF I've said it once, I've said it a hundred times; the mainspring of the American economic system is not the hope of gain, because the average American doesn't have any. The mainspring is debt. Nothing keeps the average man working hard, with no absenteeism after his sick leave is used up, like the need to make the next installment on something or other.

The piggy bank strikes at the very mainspring of the American economy. It ought to be abandoned, or at least be made of china. None of the locks on them ever work when the paper boy demands his pay. A restraint of trade that can be broken with a hammer often turns out to be no restraint of trade.

A PARABLE WITH NO APPLICATION

THE economic situation was the issue back there in 1095 A.D., and Pope Urban II's administration seemed to be in trouble.

There were a lot of people living below the poverty level. Even liege lords of castles customarily slept on straw piles on the floor. The horrendous Normans had been soothed by intermarriage, and a lot of unused plant capacity was lying around in the form of walled castles. Unemployment was up, too. There were thousands of unemployed knights in Europe who were becoming bellicose. Occasionally, they even staged demonstrations and robbed honest burghers of their belongings.

Urban II decided on a new policy. He decided to export the only surplus he had,

unemployed knights. He called his party workers together at Clermont and proposed that a crusade or two be sent to Palestine to liberate the Holy City of Jerusalem and smite the infidel.

Apparently, he did not mention that this would remove the unemployed knights from Europe and inflict them on the Saracens, which would be quite an affliction indeed.

THE West then vaguely knew that the East was a land of fine silks, expensive perfumes, very pretty harems, diamonds, and that jewel beyond price, pepper. Pepper was needed to preserve meat.

The great lords, men of war and statecraft, were immediately interested. They thoroughly understood the profit motive. However, certain orators like Peter the Hermit were sent out to carry the campaign to the people and met with unwanted success.

The people did not understand the profit motive, but they perceived immediately that pepper ought to be redistributed, and they wanted their share. By the thousands they took off for the land of silks and pepper. As they passed through Europe, the local inhabitants who had been robbed of their possessions decided they wanted their share of pepper, too, and came along.

By the time of the second crusade, even the church chroniclers were noting an unusual number of thieves and robbers among the pilgrims.

In this the chroniclers noted the work of the hand of God in redeeming these lost souls and turning their arts and skills against the Saracens.

THESE wars dragged on for about two hundred years without proving anything except that there was not enough pepper to go around.

Toward the end somebody had the idea that youth, bright, smart, and energetic, could put the world right where the old folks couldn't. A youth leader named Stephen of Cloyes got the youth rally started, and soon thousands of children and teen-agers left their homes on the Children's Crusade to right the mistakes of their elders.

The older ones got sold into slavery, mostly by Italian shipmasters. The children were mostly killed. The Saracens saw no point in keeping an imported child who would need a lot of food and training before he could become a slave.

This crusade proved that old people are just as dumb as the kids.

The Children's Crusade is supposed to be the root of the legend of the Pied Piper of Hamelin.

This parable has no application to our present problems, of course. We don't have any Pied Pipers leading the young, we don't have any unemployed knights, and we have more pepper than we have meat.

A DOLLAR IN MY HAND

NEARLY every day now some important person is worrying in the public prints about how the dollar is really worth only fifty-five cents.

The whole thing leaves me greatly unagitated. I have noticed that the dollar is only worth something when there are no dollars around. When there are plenty of dollars for everybody, the dollar is almost not worth reaching for. It is just a small subdivision of the large natural law that I never win. Worthless or not, though, I still like a dollar in my hand. Better a half dollar than a whole nothing.

HOW TO REDISTRIBUTE THE WEALTH

IF anybody knows how to locate that man who always robbed from the rich and gave to the poor, have him get in touch with me. I am going to need him in a hurry.

Robin Hood was one of those men. He always robbed from the rich and gave to the poor. So was Jesse James, the man who killed many a man and robbed the Danville train. Jesse gave so much to the poor that he had to rob more and more from the rich, and this was his downfall.

When robbing a train, Jesse would sometimes come upon a five-year-old orphan who had only five mothers with him.

"You folks get over there out of the way," he would tell the orphan and his five mothers. "You cannot afford to take part in this robbery."

He would then proceed to rob from the rich, which was anybody who owned a gold watch or who was patronizing the news butch. Many a middle-aged man with a gold watch craftily cried that he was an orphan who had never had a mother and was shot on the spot.

Jesse James could see through subterfuges like this.

He would say, "Bust up this gold watch and give the proceeds to the poor."

THE man who robbed from the rich and gave to the poor was a much better redistributor of wealth than the government. Instead of robbing from the rich and giving to the poor, the government robs from the middle class and gives to the rich and the poor.

This is the way it maintains what is called the silent majority. The middle class isn't very silent.

For this reason, probably, the people who cavalierly redistributed the wealth never did much good in politics. I can find no record that his popular acclaim ever made Robin Hood king of England. Similarly, Jesse James was never nominated for President. This is hard to understand. He had a popular following which invented and sang songs about him.

The explanation probably is that when a man who is poor is given something which has been robbed from the rich, he is likely to say, "All right, no more robbery. This belongs to me."

This is the attitude that will restore law and order to the country.

IT is important that I get in touch with the modern people who rob from the rich and give to the poor because I am just about out of money.

It is not my own hide I am thinking about. I am thinking of the condition of the national economy. It has been bolstered for years by the things that I have bought on credit. I don't particularly need anybody to rob anything from the rich for my benefit because I already have the merchandise, but hundreds of business firms will probably go bankrupt because the rich have all the money I need to pay off.

We need an authentic Robin Hood to take charge of our government and rob from the rich. This Robin Hood then would accumulate the money to put the whole business picture back in focus and would divide the funds as

follows: "One for the poor, one for the middle class, and two for me."

This way we can keep our looting at home instead of letting the foreign oil states get in on it.

HOLD YOUR BREATH

AS you may already have noticed, the cost of living has taken another big jump. Since we already know from the government economists that inflation is being whipped, something else must be causing this rise.

It could be that people live too much. Maybe it is getting too expensive to live every day of the week. If the average American family just cut out living one day a week, it would cut the family budget by about 14 percent by my figures, which I refuse to swear to because of the unpredictable nature of arithmetic. If the family would stop living on the day it invites somebody to dinner, it would save even more.

It would cut the cost of everything except pet food, which goes on whether people live or not.

BETTER A DEBTOR'S PRISON

WHAT this country needs is a good debtor's prison where those of us who are broke can get some nourishing food, a dry, warm place to sleep, and a color TV.

At the moment, I am not broke. I have the better part of ten dollars socked away, so everything looks rosy for the indefinite future. But things can change overnight. I remember once when a boss told me that times were bad and he could no longer pay for my services, although I hadn't been delivering any services really for about two months. This is an inconvenience when you have a date that night.

With more and more people attaining unemployment, we are going to need debtor's prisons to keep up the American standard of living among a large percentage of our population.

After all, most of these people faithfully paid into the system until they went broke. They then patriotically went into debt to keep up business volume until even the credit managers started noticing the size of their debts. These poor unfortunates are then thrown out on the street.

This kind of treatment offends the conscience of all civilized people and even causes the natives to be restless.

Better a debtor's prison.

After all, stone walls do not a prison make, and iron bars often keep out the burglars who bedevil good people who have not yet made it to bankruptcy.

WE don't want any debtor's prisons in this country like Old Fleet was in London two hundred years ago, not us debtors. It was jam-packed with bankrupt people, even bankrupt pickpockets. The wardens tortured the prisoners and bilked them of any valuables that might be sent to them.

If a prisoner addressed a guard as anything except "Sir," the prisoner was thrown into a dungeon vile where earthworms waved at him from the walls, and the prisoner was kept there until he shaped up.

We debtors will not allow this in the United States. While it might not be oppression of a minority, because most people now are in debt, it is undoubtedly cruel and unusual punishment and will make the Supreme Court mad as the devil.

All we American debtors want is simple quarters with a coilspring mattress, perhaps a rocker, and, of course, the color TV.

IN the old days, when the English wardens had stripped one batch of prisoners of all they had, they would report the prison was overcrowded. The British government would ship a bunch of the stripped debtors off to a colony somewhere so that some debtors with more financial resources could be put in prison.

At that time the world had vast areas of land containing no people at all, just natives, and the debtors would be told to burn their credit cards and would be shipped out. In these new lands, the debtors often learned new tricks like training kangaroos for circuses and became richer than their creditors.

As everybody knows, debtors settled Georgia. But for debtors, it still might be swamp and sand land, forest and grass, populated only by Uncle Remus and a few animal characters. We would be missing the civilizing graces of Coca-Cola and the Rambling Wreck as well as the company of Georgians, who are charming people, probably because they know how to go into debt gracefully.

A GOOD, SHORT-WHEELBASE BUDGET

A MAN mature enough in years to have a little sense is likely to wonder how on earth his dad made out in the country store without the benefit of all these taxes. What has happened, he asks.

It may be that budgets have become too high

159

priced, and we have all become addicted to them. The federal government can't afford its budget. The state has overbought in this field, also. The counties, cities, and school districts have all gone in for luxurious budgets which they are reluctant to give up.

What we need probably is a good, short-wheelbase budget with no optional equipment.

But who would be caught out with that?

OUTRUNNING INFLATION

WHILE the economists fiddle, inflation burns. The solution is plain before our eyes. Make money move so fast from hand to hand that inflation never gets a chance to devalue it.

What we need to do is annul all money in existence and replace it with bank notes that are valueless in thirty days after they are issued. Also, they would become valueless at the moment they were presented at a bank. This would force people to move their money fast ahead of inflation. It wouldn't discommode the average citizen, whose money fades like the April zephyrs before he can touch it very well.

It would have a beneficial effect on all those fat cats who have stocks and bonds and real estate. They wouldn't dare sell their holdings, and because they couldn't be sold, the value would be deflated to the good of the country.

It would also enormously increase consumption and create jobs. "For Pete's sake," the husband would tell his wife, "let's go on and buy that car before this money gets worthless." The auto company would be in a hurry to pass the money off to a steel company.

Probably, a whole lot of this money would vanish into advertising, which can pass money faster than most businesses.

But the point is to move money so fast that inflation never has a chance to catch up with it.

THIS new thirty-day currency would have worldwide effects. Here is the ruling sheik in an Arab oil country, and he opens his payment for the month.

"Ye Allah," he exclaims. "This money is going to be worthless in a month. Take a plane. Take American Airlines. Buy something with it. Buy secondhand shoes or anything."

The United States balance of payments would turn around overnight because everybody would want to send the money back.

The NATO countries would probably react violently. "What do we want with all this money that goes dead in thirty days?" they would say. "Let them get their troops out of here."

This might even send the Russian ruble up to a price where the Russian nation couldn't afford it.

This is the plain logical solution to the problem, but the President and the Congress will never consider it.

HOW would this affect the average man? Well, the price of lettuce wouldn't go any higher because they have pumped as much air into a head of lettuce as lettuce will stand.

It would be very hard on the paper millionaires but not hard at all on the hard millionaires. It would take all the air out of our economy and get it down to a dollar-and-cents basis.

I figure that it would lead to a renaissance in the arts because a whole lot of people can't get rid of that much money in thirty days. The symphony orchestras would probably be oversubscribed, especially considering that the high rate of money turnover will drive up the high-level income taxes.

People might give more to private colleges, too, if they can clear the money in thirty days.

You do see how simple it is, don't you?

TAXES FOR ALL

A FRIEND dropped by the office this week. He was pretty set up because he says the income tax people are thinking of a new standardized form which will save middle income people who have few deductions a great deal of money.

"They have finally found out," he said, with a dreamy look in his eye, "that the middle-class man pays all the tax."

"It is true that I did," I told him, "but I resent being called middle-class. I am actually an impoverished aristocrat."

"I know oil men who pay less income tax than you or I do," he retorted.

"Yep, but for every dollar they save in tax they spend five on accountants and lawyers. It depends on whether you want to put your dollars into highways and schools and bombers or into accountants."

Taxes, I reminded him, are the price of progress.

He thought this over. "I notice from my last returns," he commented, "that Progress seems now to be running out of control."

HE said I was not sufficiently alarmed about the welfare of the country. The government, he said, was going to double up on Social Security taxes in January. Steadily the tax bite on every man's income was getting larger. What, he wanted to know, was going to happen when the federal government began taxing me for more than I make?

"Obviously, you are ignorant of the laws of economics," I told him. "This is the last firm hope of this country."

I pointed out that the federal government, when it begins taxing a man for more than he makes, will have to pay back the money. When it begins taxing most men 40 percent more than they make, this flood of returning federal money, poured into the economy, will probably set off a prosperity explosion the like of which we have never seen.

"I must be ignorant of economics," said my friend, "because I don't understand this. However, it is obviously true, and I believe I will invest in a few more growth stocks."

The power to tax, I pointed out, has become the power to balloon things.

"I SHUDDER to think what would happen," he said, "if the government stopped this all of a sudden, and the scheme collapsed. The wrong people would profit. I would not have a dime."

I argued that nobody would profit if the government shut down this economic perpetual motion machine. Industry, I said, would lose its markets, and the laborer would lose his job. "What we need," I said, "is tax reform."

"It is too late to reform taxes now," he replied. "The only remedy is to electrocute them all. They should have been spanked and corrected when they were little."

He added that I was a traitor to my class for not wanting to shift the main tax burden to some other section of the population.

"It is best not to worry about it," I told him. "In the future there will be plenty of taxes for all."

TAXES MAY BE DANGEROUS TO YOUR HEALTH

A FRIEND who reports on business news spends a lot of his time drawing graphs and noticing trends, and the other day he spotted one.

He discovered that there is almost an exact correlation between the increase in taxes and the increase in cancer.

This is probably a scientific breakthrough of the first magnitude. True, as the doctors are always saying, the tests up to now are inconclusive, but the implication seems clear either that taxes cause cancer or cancer causes taxes, probably the first. After all, anybody who knows anything knows that constant irritation of a tissue often causes cancer, and if there is anything more constantly irritating than taxes, I would like to know what it is.

We are now forming a task force of one half of a stenographer to find out whether taxes also don't often cause heart failure, especially around April 15.

But while we are doing this research, we call upon everyone with willpower enough to shake this tax habit. Better be safe than sorry.

WE also call upon Congress to invoke the General Welfare clause on this. Probably Congress will be too timid to do much in the beginning. After all, there are a lot of vested interests involved in the tax habit, along with some who have no vests.

The least we could expect, though, is that Congress would require the Internal Revenue Service to print on its Form 1040: "Warning! The Persistent Paying of Taxes May Be Dangerous to Your Health."

Having got this done, we should undertake a long-range program to eliminate taxes and the resultant health threat from our scene. We should set up an operation on the Texas border to see that none is smuggled in from Mexico. Probably it is too late to save the habitual payer of taxes. He is already hooked and can never shake the habit. But we can warn the young by public service TV ads that the kid that starts paying taxes inevitably gets in deeper and deeper until there is no hope.

Over the years, taxes may well have damaged the ordinary person more than morphine.

ALTHOUGH nobody can prove conclusively that there is a link between taxes and cancer, it seems more likely than a link between cigarettes, DDT, artificial sugar, or any of the other substances now being wiped out.

After all, plenty of people have used tobacco, sweeteners, and pesticides for years without getting cancer, but I have never known of a cancer patient who didn't pay taxes.

One of the healthiest men I have ever known was a chain-smoking diabetic who sprayed crops for a living. He had never turned in a 1040.

It will probably be hard to rally public support for wiping out taxes, but we should try.

FROM ENERGY TO WASTE

A government commission studying the matter has said the United States in ten years is going to run low on energy. When this happens, they needn't come whining to me. I don't have any to spare.

FROM ENERGY TO WASTE

HOW TO CONSERVE ENERGY

A GOVERNMENT commission studying the matter has said the United States in ten years is going to run low on energy. When this happens, they needn't come whining to me. I don't have any to spare.

As I get it, we are going to run low on oil, gas, coal, electricity, and all the other sources of energy. Gasoline for your car is going to cost about two dollars a gallon, probably. A kilowatt of electricity may be bid up as high as a dollar. Obviously, people will have to change their habits. Probably everybody will have to go back to the old hand-operated can opener. A householder may have to walk from the back to the front of his lot instead of riding in his car.

Those of us who have always conserved our energy and have taken a dim view toward the prodigal waste of energy by people like city editors and managing editors are not going to waste any sympathy on them.

The best way to respond to the energy crisis is by not responding. Don't move unless it is for purposes of comfort.

ANY high school physics student can tell you that there are two kinds of energy, potential and kinetic. A potential energy who is sitting in his chair and dozing represents a mysterious and powerful force. Once the energy gets up and starts walking, however, once it becomes kinetic, it is soon wasted.

The expenditure of energy is usually futile. Take a can of Henderson County blackeye peas, the world's best even if they are grown in West Texas. Look at the useless waste of energy.

The energy used in picking them is necessary, of course. But vast amounts of human energy are then used in stuffing them into a can. Electrical energy is expended in moving the can down a belt conveyor to the capper. The capper is driven by most vast amounts of energy. The can is then plunged into a boiling cooking vat, powered itself by vast amounts of energy. More energy is expended in pasting on the labels.

Leaving aside the energy used to haul the can of peas from Henderson County to your local store and put the can on the shelf, more energy is expended by your electric can opener.

And what have you got for the expenditure of all this energy? The same confounded pea that the man picked from his patch in the first place.

THIS crisis is a thing that we as citizens can do something about. When tempted to be energetic, resist the impulse.

If you have to travel from the back of your yard to the front, neither travel there in your car nor walk. Conserve your energy. It is going to become liquid gold. Probably the caller is just somebody collecting for Infant Mental Thrombosis, anyhow.

As some of us have always known, energetic people are going to become the ruination of us all.

ENERGY CRISIS

THE nation is getting unnecessarily alarmed over something called the Energy Crisis. I have had an Energy Crisis for years. I do not like to get up in the morning.

I cannot tell that this has affected the nation's economy in the slightest. The measure of the energy you have is not necessarily the measure of the work you are going to have to do. You may just have to do the same work with less energy. It's harder but still necessary.

Once when I had a very bad Energy Crisis, the office sent out another reporter to peer through my bedroom window and report.

"He looks dead," our friend reported.

"Nonsense," declared the managing editor. "He is just having an Energy Crisis. You go back out there and tell him that, whether he has any energy or not, he had better get his tail down here and get his work out."

It is amazing how much work can get done when you have no energy at all.

REARRANGING OUR PRIORITIES

THE Canton Street boulevardier dropped in at the end of the week. He draped his flop-brimmed panama over the "in" basket on the desk and said he had been trying to learn how to work flint.

"It is the coming thing for tools," he said, "because the human race has just about dug all the iron ore out of the earth that was ever there."

I said maybe the human race would find another source of iron. The moon, I told him, is supposed to be very rich in iron.

"It'll be a lot richer after we get through leaving all that landing equipment up there," he replied somewhat grumpily.

He said his work with flint is not going very well. He is not discouraged, however, and expects eventually to make his fortune with it.

"All innovations proceed slowly," he said.

I told him that I had noticed the same thing the last time I put in for a raise.

HE said that the trouble with me is that I am materialistic like all other Americans. The bleeding hearts in the Senate keep saying that the country must reevaluate its priorities, but the real need is for each individual to sit down and rearrange his own priorities.

There is something wrong with and not much future for a people, he said, which spends more on automobiles than it does on feeding starving children, more on tobacco than it spends for schools, more on iceboxes than it gives to its churches. There is something awfully wrong about a fat cat who expects portal-to-portal air conditioning for himself but thinks first graders are all right in a sweltering room.

Each individual, said the Canton Street boulevardier, should spend some time in sweet and solemn thought and redirect his spending toward things that benefit the human race.

"I am going to do this myself as soon as I get my color TV," he promised.

I protested that shifting all this money around was probably going to impede progress.

THE boulevardier snorted. Progress, he said, is merely painting yourself into a corner. It is the business of using up your basis for existence. Look at the dinosaur, he said. The dinosaur ate up all the smaller animals.

Did I ever notice, he asked me, that starvation in the United States has progressed in direct proportion to the amount of land that we have buried under the concrete of airports and streets? When all that land was producing, food was so common that saloons gave it away.

Probably the land wouldn't be used for food even if it were unpaved, I argued. It might just grow up in bushes.

Don't bet on that, he said. The human race would move in on the land because it is constitutionally incapable of leaving nature alone.

He is probably right. I have to go home now and chop the wild rye out of the St. Augustine.

WHAT RUINED AMERICAN CITIES

A FRIEND of ours came by the other day to gloat over the mess that everybody is making out of the country now, and he said the

financial ruin of American cities began with the invention of sanitary sewers.

"If New York City didn't have any sanitary sewers, they wouldn't have any welfare problem today," he pointed out.

The development of sanitary sewers made necessary the installation of pipes and the development of the plumbing trade, this latter leading directly to the development of Big Labor, our friend declared. And when you have pipes, you have to have running water to put in them. As soon as a man has running water in his house, he has to have ice water to impress his friends. This meant the development of the refrigerator and the beginning of the electric industry, without which no power shortage is possible.

The need for running water made dams necessary, of course, and when you needed dams, you had to have the Army Engineers.

"And there," said our friend with some satisfaction, "you have the beginning of the Giant Bureaucracy."

I said I thought the postal department was the beginning of the federal bureaucracy.

"THE postal department ain't a bureaucracy," he countered. "Danged if I know what it is." It is, he said, a Benjamin Franklin invention, and none of Franklin's inventions ever worked in the long run. Even lightning won't work every time you send up a kite with a key tied to it.

The damage done to the cities by sanitary sewers is incalculable, he said, getting back to his main subject. Once you got Big Labor into it, Big Business had to get in. This meant bankers, and when you get bankers into something, you have had it.

To build sanitary sewers, the cities had to begin voting bond issues, none of which the people wanted. They voted for them because they didn't understand them. Can you imagine, asked our friend, an ordinary man voting for a bond issue if he knows he has to pay for it?

"If the cities didn't owe any bonds," he added, "they wouldn't be in any financial crisis."

They wouldn't be having to vote more bonds to build new sewage plants if the sanitary sewer hadn't created pollution, he declared.

THE sanitary sewer had done its worst damage, perhaps, to the American character, our friend said. It has dampened the American's sense of independence and discouraged the use of his private initiative in this field.

"When a man starts to move now," argued our friend, "he is likely to ask whether there are any sanitary sewers instead of whether there is any free land where he is going."

Only a general collapse will restore the American system of values and correct the kind of tunnel vision that thinks the sewers have to be kept operating, and the collapse is coming.

"She's gonna blow, boy," said the visitor as he departed. "I seen the same thing in 1929. There'll be empty office buildings standing in the streets."

SPURIOUS REMEDIES FOR CRIME

CRIME and violence seem to be bothering everybody these days, and most of the remedies don't make much sense. This is par for the course. Government remedies for anything under the sun seldom make sense.

According to the news reports, crime went up 120 percent, or something like that, under the Republicans. Obviously, the Republicans should not get credit for this. Anybody with any sense knows that the Republicans are not any better at crime than the Democrats. The remedies that are offered are the spurious things. They say we need more policemen. When you increase the police force, you increase crime because more people get caught.

It is the same with stronger new laws. You increase crime this way because there are more laws to break.

It is important to remember that the human being always remains the same criminal at heart however you shift the laws and the officers around.

DOWN THE ANTICRIME RATHOLE

THE Canton Street boulevardier dropped by the office the other day, flourished his hickory walking stick angrily, and declared that he was fair put out. He had just read where Congress was about to drop a bunch of more billions down the anticrime rathole.

Spending public money to fight crime, he said, is pointless because it just turns loose more money from which the criminal can take his percentage. A fair share of it will end up in the slot machines.

The way to cure crime, he added, is not to turn loose more money but to get rid of it. Back when he was a boy on a North Texas farm, said the boulevardier, they were never bothered by crime because they had nothing that big-time crime could use. True, his dad did hide the ax when they went off on a fishing trip, but they

167

left everything else unlocked and figured that if somebody carried it off, he deserved his fate.

"People nowadays have too many valuables," he said. "Pickpockets are encouraged because everybody has an electronic peanut cracker in his pocket. If people didn't have any jewels, there never would have been any diamond thieves."

I told him that I was lucky. I had nothing. I didn't have anything to worry about even if my bank was robbed. He said humph.

SPENDING billions against crime won't work, he added, because some criminals are going to be in there helping spend it. The cause of crime is inside the human beast.

"The trouble is that people have forgotten original sin," he declared.

I asked him what kind of sin that was.

"I don't exactly know," he answered, "but it was original."

Organized crime exists, he added, only because crime has become endemic in American society, not just among criminals but among so-called decent citizens. He didn't say "endemic." He said, "Nobody cares what's right or wrong, just whether they can get away with it." Last summer, he added, two expensive lawn sprinklers were stolen from his front lawn.

"Teen-agers don't steal lawn sprinklers," he thundered, "no matter what the FBI's statistics say. These were taken by some of my good church brothers who found them handy."

"Why are they blaming the admitted, honest criminal when everybody else is mixed up in it?" he asked.

SO-CALLED decent citizens cheat their insurance companies, he went on bitterly, and pride themselves on getting a new roof or a new car out of it. They lie on their income tax returns. They run a red light when they think nobody is watching. Just that morning, a salesman type had run a red light and barely missed hitting my friend. Reputable banks back hoodlum enterprises. Reputable companies take hoodlum backing.

"Yeah," I said, "and ordinarily decent pals sometimes cheat at poker."

He turned a baleful eye on me.

"Cheating at poker," he declared, "is not criminal."

A MATTER OF RECORD

THEY have a record on you, brother, and if you could see it all, it would curl your hair.

A record is filed on you when you are born. It is tactful enough not to say that you were warthog-ugly, but it tells how much you weighed stark naked and records the parents responsible for this act. When you join the Cub Scouts, an item is made in the record, and if you are stupid, the record puts down how long it took you to make Lion.

When you start to school, they give you tests and put the results into the record. They do not say you are a moron. They say your IQ is 40. They do not say you are mechanically deficient or artistically dull. The entries add up to a mere sigh.

All through school, records are entered on you about your slothfulness, your lack of neatness, and your failure to cooperate with constitutional authority.

MAYBE you enter the service right after this. Into the record go your fingerprints and a photograph fully as good as a police mug shot. The military keeps a running record of offenses, but the military is shorthanded and seldom has time to enter minor good jobs. Once out, you are really in the records.

Year by year, the Census Bureau finds out how much you make, how many TVs you have, how many cars you operate and whether they are expensive or just heaps, whether your house has a bathroom, and how many pets you keep.

If you ever got publicly drunk, that is in the record, and if you and your wife had a fight, it is going to stay there.

By going to old city directories, anybody can find out year by year where you lived, what menial job you held, and the year that your first wife's name changed. If they want more about the divorce, they can go to the courthouse and there read all the lurid sins of which both partners were guilty.

If your youngster gets in trouble, it's on the record, and if one of your uncles says the government is less than it should be, that is cross-referenced into your file.

The credit bureaus have records which show what kind of deadbeat you are, how long it takes you to pay your bills, and whether you can really afford what you're buying.

And, every two years or so, the opinion polls come by to enter into the record what you are thinking.

THERE are all kinds of other records on you, and you can't get away from them. It's on the record when you were christened and when you were baptized and how niggardly you have been at the collection plate.

If you've ever contributed to a political party out of power, that's on the record. When you die, it's a matter of record whether you had cirrhosis of the liver.

At death, a human life looks like a compact box of records neatly tied up in red tape.

Some people still object to the FBI and Army intelligence, of course.

These people think the agencies are going to invade their privacy.

BUGGED FOR POSTERITY

THEM as has gets. Most of us have never been privileged to have a bug put on our telephone, while the high and the mighty apparently get them by the dozens from the fawning wiretap industry. The worker has to make out with a plain, underequipped telephone which connects him with one person at a time. In contrast, his boss often sends his voice out on five or six different lines at the same time.

This didn't bother me much until I learned the other day that the tapes from these wiretaps are really made for the sake of posterity. It gives one to think. If a man does not leave any tapes behind him, for instance, how will posterity ever know that he did anything? Every human being knows instinctively that the other people of the world are unimportant. Just as firmly he knows that he is a person who should be preserved for posterity.

He wishes, for one thing, to leave behind the philosophy he has distilled from experience. He wishes to remind posterity that the problems that confront mankind are the same from generation to generation — blondes, redheads, and brunettes. He may wish to advise posterity

169

to take a few wooden nickels now and then; the wood is worth more than the money.

Of course, a man runs the risk that his tape will show that he never did or thought anything, but I intend to edit mine so that it will present me in my true greatness.

IT is a wonder that George Washington got remembered at all, considering that he never left any tapes for posterity. People do remember certain important things about Washington. They remember that he stood up in the boat that time and that he delivered a farewell address.

A few tapes might have established him more firmly with posterity, however, provided that posterity would be willing to take the rock music tapes off the recorder and listen to Washington. Also, tapes would have cleared up several controversies involving Washington. Did he once throw a dollar across the Rappahannock? Did he or did he not chop down the cherry tree? Could he tell a lie? If he couldn't, how did he get elected?

One thing is certain. Our tapes will prove that none of our generation ever threw a dollar across a river. It isn't that heavy.

ABRAHAM Lincoln managed to score with posterity, too, without the help of tapes. If he had left tapes, he might loom larger today than any recent president. Tapes would have cleared up a few things about Lincoln too. He was the president who freed the slave owners and left the slaves to shift for themselves. Did he really mean to do this? They say he once got a man acquitted by proving that a witness could

170

not have seen a midnight murder by moonlight because it happened in the dark of the moon. Was it the dark of the moon, or did Lincoln have the only almanac in the courtroom?

These few instances attest to the ennobling influence of tapes to the reputations of public figures and even ordinary men.

I am therefore searching for a bug for my telephone. If other people are allowed to have bugs, I am entitled to one. I am just as buggy as anybody else.

I do not demand a new bug. A secondhand one in good working condition will do.

OLDSTERS IN THE WAY

A GREAT deal of thought has been turned of late to the problem of what to do with our aged people. They seem to be in the way.

Some of our state officials want to kick them off our highways. The federal government seems to want to lock them up in convalescent homes and kill them with Medicare.

A lot of the bright young men up in Washington are talking about taxing Social Security payments, apparently on the theory that the power to tax is the power to destroy.

I hope that our Texas congressmen do not fall for this temporizing approach. I hope that they will face the issue squarely and avoid these piecemeal measures.

There is only one forthright solution to the problem of the older people. They must be shot.

SOME sentimentalists will object, but logic dictates this.

Take the composite old-timer of our time. What has he done? He has, of course, already kicked in his share on the highways that his kids want to keep him off of. Probably he has reared and educated one or more children, some of which are serving in Congress and the state legislature and debating what to do with him. He has served the country in one or two wars. He has built the schools that are now burgeoning. If he was a farmer, he has cleared the land and out-starved the drought and readied the fields which now grow such handsome federal subsidies. As a city man, he has built the businesses that his sons now run with so much more flair.

But the question isn't what has he done. It is what has he done lately. Obviously, the old man hasn't picked up the tab for any of his kid's bills in years. Why not get rid of him?

We need to face this issue squarely. Too long have we been held back by younger people who feel a false sense of shame at what they are doing to their elders.

We have to remember the injunction: Honor thy father and thy mother that their days may not be long upon the earth.

THERE is no escaping the fact that the senior citizen is holding up progress. When he looks at a space shot on TV, he wants a rerun so that he can check it. His Honda put-puts at a speed which allows the hair of his grandson to settle straight to the shoulders.

In a liberal, humanistic civilization like ours, we have to consider that the old man and the old woman stand between us and the future, that they can no longer write a significant check, that they drag on the economy by being nonproductive.

We cannot afford to be a sentimental, communist country like Russia.

WHAT TO DO ABOUT TRASH

THE Canton Street boulevardier dropped in the other day, cleared off a large flattop desk so he would have room to deposit his hat, and said he thought the TV sages were being awfully gloomy about the space program. He said one fellow was almost in tears over what to do about all the trash being created by our technology.

"The man can't see beyond the end of his cue card," thundered the boulevardier. "We have already solved the problem of industrial wastes and all other kinds of waste, thanks to the space program. We have the soft goods. We have the hard goods. We have the technology and the know-how.

"All we have to do is load three or four junkyards on top of a Saturn rocket and fire them off into the sun."

I said I thought he had a wonderful idea.

"There are few bigger," he admitted.

It would be particularly good for ridding the earth of radioactive wastes, he added. "Let 'em be radioactive up there," he said with a wave toward the ceiling.

AS soon as possible, he said, the United States ought to line up a few old obsolete Saturns and then organize a worldwide clean-up drive.

There could be national slogans like "Bully for Bulgaria" and "Hurrah for Halmahera." The U.S. government could let drop a rumor that the Russians were trying to accumulate a larger trash pile than ours to show how their standard of living was higher. The Russians could accuse the capitalist imperialists of artificially creating trash.

The Chinese could spur their trash people on by warning about the Soviet revisionist bandits.

It would be a great thing for peace and good will, said the Canton Street boulevardier, because all the peoples on earth could contribute. A lot of the earth's peoples don't have the means to take part in most common undertakings, but they all can contribute trash.

"Even the Yaks," he said.

"The Yaks?"

"Yeah, that's that bunch of naked Communists in the Philippines."

"I think that's Huks," I told him.

He said this was a minor detail and had nothing to do with the grand design for garbage disposal.

I SUGGESTED that the cost of shooting the world's trash into the sun might be pretty high, and he shook his head scornfully.

"You ever figured out the fuel bill on all the world's incinerators?" he demanded.

I hadn't.

But I suggested that maybe we could get the beer companies to pay for the shoots by buying TV time. Probably, our technology was such that we could work out a way to have the sun show "Budweiser" across its surface on the day when Bud financed the trash load.

"Now you're thinking constructive," he said.

He left with the plea of being tired. Working out the details of a big idea, he said, is exhausting.

WAR, PEACE, AND
THE STATE DEPARTMENT

Man's only hope for peace probably will be, as Great-Aunt Martha put it, the last trump, and she didn't mean spades.

WAR, PEACE, AND
THE STATE DEPARTMENT

THE INSTITUTION OF WAR

THE conduct of foreign policy in our times seems a great deal too much like walking a high wire in the dark with no safety nets beneath it.

A U.S. secretary of state inches along in the blackness, aware on the one hand of the restless hordes who would gobble us up and on the other of the thing that punctuates the final sentence of civilization with a boom. If you misstep either way, you splatter.

So far, our leaders seem to have performed very well, walking with great care. Prudence has been the watchword, and we have evidence that the other side is acquainted with prudence.

But this is the discouraging thing.

Sooner or later, a man is going to come along who will say, "Not only can I stay on this wire in the dark, but I can do it on a unicycle while eating a banana."

There is always a smart aleck every twenty years or so in the human crowd, confound it.

WAR is an institution of the human race, like religion and the cooking fire. Probably it's older than both. We know too little about either war or the human being to be very certain of either. War is not just competition for control of the world. At times, war has been a personal expression like poetry or the writing of scriptures on highway culverts.

At times, also, war has served a social purpose such as a sudden introduction to a wife from another tribe or the development of an improved flint arrowhead. At other times, a man can get higher rank and social status in war than he can as a civilian.

Times in history when there seems to be no reason for war have spurred on the human race to invent new philosophies and urgent needs which make war necessary.

My opinion, not substantiated by any of the sciences from A to Z, is that the basic cause of war is Man, the most mischievous of the great apes.

Sooner or later Man is going to say, "They say these H-bombs if used will wipe out civilization. We ought to test them and find out."

I NOTE signs, fortunately, that we are erasing some of the causes of war. Or so we think.

The human competitive spirit is steadily being circumscribed. It now has to meet the President's guidelines. Women used to be a prime target of war. There are now more than enough women in every country. Territory used to be another purpose of war, but our human earth has worn out to the point where the cost of fertilizer makes more territory prohibitive.

Finally, war used to be prized by the strong and courageous, the best fighters. Muhammad Ali, who admits that he is the world's best fighter, doesn't want anything to do with war.

When the captains and the kings like Ali depart, maybe war will lose all its glory.

THE GRANDFATHER SOLDIER

T HE President apparently flat overlooked one of the options he could have used against North Vietnam in the recent conflict. He could have broadened the grandfather clause.

The original grandfather clause provided, generally speaking, that residents of southern states whose people had voted before 1867 didn't have to pass the literacy and other tests set up for voters. It was designed to avoid the current problem of civil rights. As a solution to the civil rights question, it seems almost useless today.

The President, however, could have broadened the clause to provide military service for all men who voted before 1936. These old soldiers were fire-eaters all, that

being about the only thing they can eat without Tums. They would give the enemy pause. As a matter of fact, they scare some of our people half to death by their solutions to world problems.

You can imagine the effect on the North Vietnamese if they had awakened one morning and found themselves facing a whole division of Bela Lugosis.

A T the present, there seems to be a lot of prejudice against the grandfather soldier. Critics say his medical costs would be too high. This is obviously utter rot. His medical care wouldn't cost the military services anything. Medicare would pick up the bill.

The grandfather soldier could get along on about half the normal amount of food, and if he has recently been retired from business, he would be unaccustomed to eating that much. This food could be mostly mashed potatoes and cream of chicken soup, these being the main staples of the grandfather diet.

The need for dental care among these men would be greatly reduced, incidentally. In some cases, it would be nonexistent.

The grandfather soldier would have many other advantages. He has the experience of giving years of advice to the military, and because he is older and more experienced than the Joint Chiefs of Staff, these jobs might be eliminated, thus cutting enough from the military budget to give all the poor people a trip to the moon.

Also, the grandfather soldier would be a contented soldier. No matter what happened, he would know that no modern war could be anything like as tough as the one he had to endure.

THE valid objections to the grandfather soldier are mainly logistical. There is the question, for instance, of whether the country has enough good cloth to put wide enough gussets into the seats of all those uniform pants. Also, do we have stockpiled enough arch supports of various sizes properly to support the military?

Probably, we don't. There are civilian failures of this sort in every war.

Because of the supply failure of the military-industrial complex, the President may not have had the grandfather option at all.

MOLE TRAPS

AN expert was telling me the other day how the U.S. could always count on air bombardment to cut enemy supply lines, and suddenly I thought of the mole trap. I hadn't thought of it in forty years.

Probably we don't have many moles in North Texas. At least, I never saw one. A mole lives all his life beneath the surface of the ground except at noon, when he usually comes up. Naturalists have wondered why he surfaces at noon, but it is very simple. While traveling around underground, the mole necessarily has to operate by dead reckoning. He comes up at noon each day to take a sun shot.

The mole is a fat little animal, about six inches long, with beautiful soft gray-black fur. He is so round that he looks a little like a rocket without a tail, being equipped to burrow through soil.

The mole is the only animal equipped to breaststroke his way through solid earth. He has big shoulders and wide paws to throw the dirt aside.

WHEN he burrows out from his home chamber, the mole breaks the surface of the ground and makes a little mound along his path. Nowadays, people know that the mole is just hunting for worms to eat. Like the average teen-ager, the mole will starve to death in twelve hours if not fed.

When I was a boy, though, the mole was regarded as a horrendous raider of crops and grass. Besides that, the presence of the mole excited the foxhounds, thus ruining them for a good chase that night.

So, when a mole turned up in our pasture, Pete, the hired hand, was given some mole traps and told to capture this six-inch ogre. I went along as supervisor. I was about eight then, and liked to supervise everything.

The mole trap was a small upright device, about two feet tall, which had two spikes that fitted on each side of the mole hill, as the mounded trace was called. You pulled up on a small handle to compress a steel spring and cock it. The plunger on this spring was equipped with a dozen four-inch steel needles which would be driven in the ground when triggered. It had a lot more fire power than a mole.

Pete and I set one across the mole's course. "Gone goslin'," said Pete, and we went to supper. Next day, we found that the mole had dug a neat detour in a semicircle around the trap.

"Stupid son of a so-and-so," said Pete, of the master race. "Cain't even foller his own tracks."

WE never did get the mole. We set traps up and down the trace. He circled around all of them. We set traps on his detours. He apparently then followed the old straight route.

Pete finally pulled up the traps and took them in and threw them down in the yard with the air that he was quitting this chase or he could be given his time.

"This thing is so ignorant," he said, "that no sensible person could catch him."

I hope any future enemy doesn't turn out to be too ignorant to be caught.

ROCKS ON THEIR MINDS

IT says here in a news dispatch that the secretary of state has promised to "leave no stone unturned" in a search for peace. The statement betrays what is wrong in the State Department. It is probably unfair to say that our diplomats have rocks in their heads, but they seem to have rocks on their minds.

For years, they regularly have been leaving "no stone unturned" in their search for something or other, and at this late date, they should have turned over enough stones to know already what is beneath each. When you consider that the diplomats of the other side have been leaving no stone unturned, too, you can see what has happened to peace. The whole apparatus of world peace has been so busy turning over stones that it has spent no time on figuring out how not to throw them.

Why not hire several millions of the world's unemployed to turn over stones while the diplomats get together and make a deal?

SAD SACK FROM BROOKLYN

ONE thing this Castro business is doing. It is stirring out a lot of old soldier-type stories. We got this one from our old friend, Cy Wagner, who trained a lot of infantrymen in World War II.

It concerns Private Cohen, a five-foot, hundred-pound sad sack from Brooklyn who turned up one day at Wagner's camp. Private Cohen's only qualification for infantryman was desire. He wore glasses half an inch thick. Loud noises scared him. He not only dreaded to fire an M-1; he wept when he had to fire a .22. Allowing him near a hand grenade was unthinkable.

Once, during target practice, Wagner got into a profound puzzle about why Private Cohen's rifle in his hands could never touch the target while in Wagner's hands it scored repeated bull's eyes.

The solution turned out to be really simple. Private Cohen was firing at a target that belonged to a soldier two places down the line and not hitting it too well.

This experience led Wagner to start recommending that Private Cohen be put in some such place as the quartermaster corps, where hand grenades are not one of the instruments of accounting.

THE army apparently set its mind against this on the ground that Private Cohen was the very kind of man it wanted for a foot soldier — a volunteer.

In his training days, Private Cohen never qualified in even one infantry requirement. He could not even clear the first obstacle on the obstacle course. Wagner and his sergeant ran beside the private, helping him over the obstacles. When Private Cohen had to make the trip under barbed wire and over fences under live fire, Wagner went with him.

After each such performance, the rest of the company would break into a cheer. This always caused Private Cohen to weep because they were making fun of him. Wagner, who had long ago learned that his sad sack was doing his best, had learned a convenient remedy.

"What's your serial number, Private?" he would demand.

After Private Cohen had recited it, Wagner would say, "It shows you are a volunteer. All these other men," with a sweep of his arm, "are draftees. You're the only volunteer in the outfit."

"That's so!" Private Cohen would respond hopefully and get back to doing his best.

WHEN it came time to leave the camp, however, Private Cohen was a little fearful about what would happen to him. Wagner reassured him.

"When they see your record, where you haven't qualified for anything, they will transfer you to quartermaster corps," he said.

Many months later he got a letter from Private Cohen. He had been through the whole Italian campaign right up in front and that day he had been out on patrol. The Germans had pinned his patrol down with machine guns and 88s.

The private wrote calmly that they had tried to head for some trees and that one soldier who had tried to run had been killed instantly. Private Cohen had remembered that Wagner had taught him to crawl. He was able to move into the trees in safety.

Wrote the man who was deathly afraid of guns: "I still haven't fired my M-1, and I hope I never have to."

Said Wagner, this day: "If I could, I'd give him the Medal of Honor."

COMMUNICATIONS BREAKDOWNS

ONE of the wire service nostalgic pieces about Pearl Harbor this year said that the communications breakdown that led to that disaster is impossible now because Admiral Harry Felt commands all the services in the Pacific. This statement itself is one of the best examples you ever saw of a communications breakdown.

Communications breakdowns go on in the military services every day. They are caused by a thousand things. If the admiral will pardon the reference, he isn't any better at it than some radioman striker. I could write a book about communications breakdowns I have known. There was the one that slipped down behind the radio central teletype and wasn't found until three days later. There was the time that Commander Hall said, "Belay that," and I thought he said, "Relay that." There was an aviator friend of ours who radioed in one day and said, "How do I get back to the base?"

"Where are you?" asked the tower operator.

"That's what I want to know," said the flier.

Most communications failures are supposed to be caused by garbled messages, but in my day they were really caused by garbled young ensigns.

LUCKILY, communications breakdowns, even the big ones, are mostly harmless except to the subordinate officer involved. The biggest one I ever heard of happened to a friend who commanded a small ship in the North Pacific back in the old war.

One day an officer messenger who had flown all the way from Pearl Harbor appeared, handed my friend a package too precious to entrust to guard mail, took his signature, and departed. When opened, the package contained the battle plans for a big operation thousands of miles away in the Pacific. This was Hush, Hush, Most Secret Stuff. Even touching it would fry the tips of your fingers. It was so secret that there was no way for my friend to ask whether he was supposed to have it. He hid it deep in his personal safe, changed the combination, and then had the shipfitter put a big padlock on it.

At intervals, the officer messenger would fly back and repeat the operation. Toward the end of the war, my helpless friend had a complete library of these battle plans, and then his ship was swapped to the Russians. He had to get rid of this library. Though many of the operations were history, the plans were still so secret that the hair of senior officers would stand on end when my friend tried to turn the plans over to them.

My friend finally found a courageous Marine colonel who furnished him an armed guard and four officer witnesses and allowed him to burn the stuff in a supercharged furnace.

EVERY day in every office in the land a communications breakdown happens. What can you expect of something as big as the military? My advice to the admiral is to eliminate the middlemen and use the bullhorn.

Some communications break down because of garbles. One of the most frequent causes is that the sender forgets to put into the communication what he intended to say. At least one communication breakdown that I know of occurred because a small unit decided that its cryptographic materials were looking

pretty shabby and that they would use next year's.

THE CORRUPTION OF SEAFOOD CARTER

WE once had in our outfit a man named Seafood Carter. He got the name because, when asked why he had elected to join the Navy, he replied seriously that he was very fond of seafood. This became a standing joke. It was retold by our people at least once a day for four years.

Seafood was the son of an Episcopal minister. He came from the Virginia tidewater and was so polite that nobody could stand him. He called everybody "sir," including the apprentice seamen. Anybody with any sea worldliness knows that a noncommissioned man is never a "sir." In our day, he was a "mac."

When we first went out for a day at sea, we passed through the Potato Patch outside San Francisco. Everybody got seasick and rushed to the rail to get rid of his breakfast, Seafood among them.

Between retches, however, Seafood took the trouble to apologize to the people on both sides of him. "I hope," he said, "you will not think this is typical of my behavior."

SEAFOOD had other peculiar habits. He said "aboot" instead of "about." He was fastidious about his grammar and his appearance. He even carried a small pair of scissors which he used to cut off the long hairs protruding from his nose, thus giving himself a distinctly nonsailorlike appearance. Sometimes he listened to Bach on his portable radio, which, as our boatswain's mate first pointed out, was a waste of time.

You can't dance to Bach, Boats pointed out, and if you can't dance, you can't involve any girls, so what is the point in the music?

As a result of his peculiarities, Seafood had to whip somebody nearly every day to prove his manhood. He once went to captain's mast three times in a row, but he had an inborn dignity that seemed to impress officers. The captain sent word down that Seafood seemed to be taking care of his own problems and to leave him alone.

After he had whipped everybody in the company, we began to perceive that Seafood was a good old boy who had been ruined by a life in a parsonage. We started out to reform him.

IT didn't work very well. Seafood was urged to express himself always in manly, strong language. He said he didn't feel that way. We took him to a sailor's bar in town. It was frequented by the kind of girls that never showed up at the USO tea dances. When introduced to one of the girls, Seafood would always say "ma'am," and the girl would shy away. One of them said he made her feel like a creep.

It all seemed hopeless until one day a particularly mean Navy chief had Seafood move a stack of 2×4s over six feet. When Seafood had restacked them and trued each board, the chief said, "Now stack them back where they were."

Seafood waited until the chief was out of sight and then said, "Damn it to hell." That was the beginning of the corruption of Seafood Carter.

He became a roisterer whose exploits were legend as far away as Manila, and they said he became hell among the ladies, some of whom liked to be called "ma'am."

DUTCH HARBOR

ALASKAN congressmen were told recently that the Dutch Harbor Naval Station, which was "disestablished" twenty years ago, was going to be formally closed. I doubt that it will hurt the Alaskan economy.

The Dutch Harbor Naval Station has been "disestablished" almost from the beginning of World War II when it was only a weather reporting station bossed by an elderly chief radioman who stayed on and became famous as Sawtooth Dozeman of Sharktooth Shoals because of his smoothmouthed look when his dentures were out, which was usually.

With the war the Navy moved in an admiral and then tried to create the proper environment for him — docks, power plant, barracks, a barbershop, repair facilities, an officer's club which was a gem because a friend of mine ran it, and a moonshine still which somebody forgot to notify the admiral about.

By the time this setting had been manufactured, the admiral had to move on west, leaving nobody to head the general air of disgust at Dutch Harbor.

ACTUALLY, if you had to spend time in the military, Dutch Harbor was a fine place. The mountains rose in cliffs twenty-five hundred feet around the harbor. In the summer, the tops were a beautiful green, the delicate green of watercress or new lettuce, splotched with pastel wild flowers. Under the snow and ice of winter, they sparkled in the sun like fresh diamonds — when there was a sun.

The quarters were comfortable; the food was good. Everybody got his laundry and barber work for nothing, and you could buy a carton of cigarettes for fifty cents. The icy little rivers leading up into the hills from the bay were crammed tight with Dolly Varden trout. Occasionally, a gunnery type would go up and throw in a stick of dynamite. This usually produced him a couple of dozen to eat, but actually he was doing it just to let the water flow.

Still, nobody liked Dutch Harbor. It was betwixt and between. With some, it was not far enough from their wives; with others, it was too far from the girls. Some wanted to go west where the war was, and others wanted to go east where it was less likely to be. A lot of people thought the silversmithing instructor wasn't as good as he pretended.

On some nights the yellow moon over this harbor was as large as a beach ball, and the land under it was white with light, but this pleased nobody either. Without some use for the moon, what is the point of it?

ONCE we got a new captain named S. Gazze, really a good man but one who had been sent down to tighten up the base and make the officers make the enlisted men salute them again. Naturally, this disturbed a number of old friendships, but Captain Gazze was respected. He was also suspected because he was believed to like the kind of thing that was Dutch Harbor.

In time, he got his own relief. I am told that he met with the new captain on the airstrip, went through the ceremony of changing

commands, walked up into the waiting plane, and then, from the hatch, roared down the genial advice, "Burn the damn place down."

MATHEMATICS AND FOREIGN POLICY

MATHEMATICS seems to have gained a toehold in the State Department, and as usually happens with mathematics, the results are disastrous. You can never make the answer come out the way it is in the back of the book.

As a result of math, the American people have now been promised about one hot crisis in the world a month from here on out.

It figures this way. The U.S. now maintains relations with 110 countries. It is a mathematical certainty that there will be about twenty-five changes of government in all these countries each year. About half of these nations, however, are new. They are countries, places of vague states of mind who have become nations since 1945.

Most of these new nations have no constitutional means of changing a government. For that matter, some of the old ones don't either. It is a mathematical certainty that a government which cannot be changed constitutionally will eventually be changed with a Colt .45 — or the Skoda equivalent.

Usually, the U.S. is caught in the fire between the Colt and the Skoda and has to worry its way out.

MAYBE you want to know how we got into this in the first place. Okay, let them change their government by force. As a matter of fact, why not arm the natives and let them kill each other off? This would bring the quietest peace that some of these countries have known in a generation.

The experts say it is not quite that simple, and they will change channels on their differential calculus and prove it. People in these new nations, they say, have begun to expect pie with their meals. If the local rulers can't get pie money from the West, they will get it from the big, friendly banks of the Volga.

You may say let Russia furnish the pie money and good riddance, but the experts say we have already tried that in a country named Cuba. It didn't work so good. Some of the other countries which use lead poisoning as a form of legislative recall are also in our hemisphere.

If you will change your calculus into neutral here, you can see that it is a mathematical certainty that we are going to get involved.

IT was a mistake ever to let mathematics get into foreign policy making in the first place. If the State Department had been on its toes, it could have had all these crises anyhow without figuring them out ahead of time. Most revolutionists can't count very good, and if we didn't do all this figuring for them, they might not know that they are expected to produce twelve crises.

The West has been tempting the wrath of mathematics for a long time. For five or ten thousand years the West has been using math for one thing or another.

Look at the shape we're in as a result of it.

THE ONLY HOPE FOR PEACE

A COUPLE of our deeper thinkers were engaged the other day in a customary session of profound gloom over the future of the world. One said he didn't believe people were ready for peace after a lifetime of war.

This analysis stems from a faulty reading of human nature. After a lifetime of war, people are always ready for peace; after a lifetime of peace, they are always ready for war. Human beings like to feel that progress is being made.

Our other savant thought that if the governments of the earth could be convinced that we were being invaded from outer space, the people of the earth might unite against a common catastrophic peril. By the time the hoax was discovered, people would have learned to live together in peace and harmony.

I doubt it.

In the first place, the hoax wouldn't last that long; Jack Anderson would print it.

ALSO, if faced by an invasion of the Martians, each country would probably try to make a deal to help the Martians do the other countries in. It is the nature of people and states, when faced by catastrophic peril, to try to find a way out at somebody else's expense.

When the khans hacked and burned their way into Europe almost a thousand years ago, they first fought the primitive Russians. The Russians did not call on the other European tribes to unite against the common peril.

Instead, they suggested that they help the Mongols by becoming their tax collectors. The invaders had one of the most efficient tax collecting systems yet invented. If a man failed to pay enough taxes, he had a hand chopped off. Nearly everybody overpaid his taxes, and nobody asked for a refund.

Nevertheless, the khans accepted the offer. They were interested in cash, not in the bureaucracy. They wanted to get back with the

·fermented yak milk and the dancing girls. They merely reminded the Russians that collections had better be good.

So in the Duchy of Muscovy germinated the seed of the Russian nation, which still has an excellent record for tax collection.

IT is true that the western nations and Russians managed in World War II to unite against a common peril, but it was a specific case. We had the common peril surrounded, and American factories would not have been able to produce all that war material if we hadn't been able to dump a lot of it on Russia.

Man is an unlovely creature on the whole except maybe for girls. He is an undependable hope.

His only hope for peace probably will be, as Great-Aunt Martha put it, the last trump, and she didn't mean spades.

PATRIOTS, POLITICIANS, AND HISTORY

For the human race, a demon may either be black or shining, but it must be heard. It must be expressed. Politics and the law were the only expressive outlets available to the demon that was Lincoln's. Luckily, this was a shining demon. In a few words, a few acts, it all but created a new American dream.

PATRIOTS, POLITICIANS, AND HISTORY

THE SHIP OF STATE

ONE of the things wrong about the United States now is that our poets no longer write eloquent poems about the Ship of State. They devote their talents to things titled "Hummings from a Bumblebee's Wing" or some other such erotic material.

This was not true in the old days. A poet had to produce a suitable celebration of the Ship of State before he could be printed in an anthology. Here was Longfellow: "Sail on, O Ship of State !/ Sail on, O Union, strong and great!/ Humanity with all its fears,/ With all the hopes of future years,/ Is hanging breathless on thy fate!"

If you have never heard a primary school boy thunder this out in a declamation contest with properly wooden-lifted arms, you have never known patriotism.

It does not matter that humanity with all its fears and all its hopes of future years has been hanging on for about a hundred and fifty years and is getting more breathless by the minute.

The sentiment was there even if the ship wasn't.

There seems to be less dedication to hanging on to the Ship of State now and more toward trying to find a life raft.

THINGS have changed now. Our President no longer seems The Brave Pilot, and the nation no longer sails her course straight and true guided by the unerring light of Stella Polaris. For one thing, we have learned that the pole star is not necessarily always straight and true. It changes from time to time.

We have begun to doubt the value of the Ship of State, or at least to doubt her crew. It started a long time ago. William Vaughan Moody wrote about his Ship of State: ". . . I watched when her captains passed:/She were better captainless./Men in the cabin, before the mast,/But some were reckless and some aghast,/And some sat gorged at mess."

This is probably a more accurate description of the public idea of the Ship of State in recent years, certainly in the last three or four. Nobody is quite sure that the Ship of State isn't going to come ashore in his own backyard.

A Ship of State is better off out there where it isn't going to bother you personally.

THE decline of patriotism probably can be exactly measured by the decline in our use of nautical metaphors for our government.

The sailing ship especially was always to poets a symbol of freedom and grace. "Whither, O splendid ship, with white sails flying," wrote Robert Graves a long time before he wrote an apostrophe to Ava Gardner.

The metaphor has got tarnished by mechanization. It is hard to get patriotic about some ditty that says, "Come on, come on, you lousy barge, and let us write your name up large." You don't even have much room there for poetry.

Also, the United States has become less of a ship country. You can write a ballad if you like that says, "Run on, run on, O Army tank, and never mind the blasted clank." It just doesn't work.

Before we have good elocution again, we will have to get the Ship of State back afloat, and apparently nobody knows how to plug up her holes or how to sail her.

Meanwhile, we humanity with all our fears are hanging breathless.

WASHINGTON AND LINCOLN

A MAN who likes George Washington has invited me to make a comment.

"I consider him one of the very greatest men in history — all history, not just American," says the man. "I wonder what your personal appraisal of him might be, as compared with Abraham Lincoln. I am something of a nut in the opposite direction regarding Lincoln — a great man but not the super-great figure that his worshipers make out."

Although I am the equal of Washington in few other things, I can also sense a trap when I see one, and I'm not falling for it.

Anyhow, it's a little presumptuous of us lesser Americans to compare these two great ones, born of such different times and facing such different problems.

Washington, a man being steadily bankrupted by English fiscal policies as all the Virginia planters were, had to decide on this. Lincoln had to face a national moral problem.

THE one thing that can be said is that the George Washington that existed is not the one that most Americans believe in, the staid, dignified, purse-mouthed figure of the Stuart portrait. Washington was a companionable and attractive man. He loved music, and he loved the theater. He could put away a lot of madeira when he sat himself down at a table and got at the job.

It was Washington who threw the party that wrecked that Philadelphia tavern on the weekend before the Constitutional Convention.

Washington was not simply a gentle-farmer who happened to be commander in chief of the Revolutionary forces, either. He may have been a military genius. He was up to his neck in warfare on the frontier from the time he was twenty-one and apparently loved it. He may have invented the open-order infantry attack. Certainly, he was one of the great guerrilla commanders of all time, for this is the kind of war he fought and the kind he advocated in his letters to the Continental Congress.

He made use of space and shoreline to offset enemy numbers. Mao and Ho Chi Minh have acknowledged their indebtedness to Washington in their tactical treatises. We have largely forgotten the lesson.

The United States is extraordinarily lucky to have had both Washington and Lincoln.

LINCOLN without any doubt was a genius. Anybody who has taken a cursory look at his papers knows it. You can read the letters of Van Gogh, and the flame of genius burns out of them even if you had never seen a Van Gogh painting. It is so with the Lincoln papers. He hadn't as easy a choice as Washington.

And yet, from what you read in Washington's papers about the problem of the black man and slavery, you have to conclude that in this, a hundred years ago, he would have voted for Lincoln.

LINCOLN'S SHINING DEMON

FORTUNATELY, a handout has arrived just in time for Lincoln's birthday which says that Abe almost spent his life being a famous distiller of bourbon whiskey.

When Abe was twelve, says the handout, he was put to assisting his father, Thomas Lincoln, at mixing sour mash for bourbon in a distillery owned by Wattie Boone, a relative of the man who killed a b'ar on this tree. The handout says that Abe became very good at the trade and that Boone said he could be the best distiller in the land, high praise indeed in Kentucky.

"But," adds the handout, "the Lincoln family moved to Indiana where there were no distilleries, so Abe Lincoln became interested in law and politics."

What a comedown! However, when you start adding things up, this doesn't make much sense. Lincoln was also a gifted axman, but he didn't turn to law and politics just because they ran out of trees in Indiana.

Drink didn't drive Lincoln to politics any more than politics drove him to drink.

WHAT this adds up to is that quite a few modern whiskeys can't stand on their own reputations and are trying to stand on Lincoln's, or General Grant's, or maybe W. C. Fields's, who didn't enjoy whiskeys at all. He dominated them.

This handout misquotes Lincoln on General Grant. Told that Grant was a drinker, Lincoln is supposed to have asked that somebody find out Grant's brand of whiskey so that he could feed it to the other Union generals. Actually, there is little proof that Grant drank more than anybody else. He may just have liked to drench horses. Grant loved horses from the days of his boyhood, and the best instrument to use in drenching a horse is a standard quart whiskey bottle. All the reports on Grant's tippling come from his enemies, not his friends; and it wasn't some "dry," as this handout suggests, who made the complaint to Lincoln.

Anyhow, one thing that neither Lincoln nor Grant needs any longer is a biographical sketch prepared by a distiller. If Grant was as well acquainted with bourbon as they suggest, he would be bound to shudder at the thought of using part of the modern product as embalming fluid.

We ought to leave the memory of great men to stew in their own bourbon.

LINCOLN in his day would have turned to law and politics no matter how many distilleries were in Indiana. This is because the homely and yet magnificent shell of Lincoln was inhabited by a demon. Even in the tired and faded eyes of old photographs you can almost see the unreasoning flare of light that betrays the demonic presence.

For the human race, a demon may be either black or shining, but it must be heard. It must be expressed. Politics and the law were the only expressive outlets available to the demon that was Lincoln's. Luckily, this was a shining demon. In a few words, a few acts, it all but created a new American dream.

JAMES MADISON'S ONE FAULT

A DALLAS lady recently made a visit back to Orange County, Virginia, to see the grave of an ancestor, James Madison. She had always read, she says, that Madison was buried at his home, Montpelier, but she found instead that he lies in a family plot hidden in the woods three miles away. The lady wonders about this.

The only directions I have for getting to Madison's grave I got twenty-five years ago from one of those enthusiastic gatherers of special knowledge who haunt newspapermen and are tolerated for the fine enthusiasm that shines in their eyes. This old-timer told me that you go down the highway past Montpelier for about a mile.

At the time, I hadn't the slightest interest in finding the grave of James Madison. I haven't cultivated much since.

But this proves again that if you save everything over the years, something will turn out to be valuable.

I DON'T know why all the guidebooks say that Madison is buried at Montpelier when actually he sleeps back in the thickets, but I have a theory.

Madison has been called the father of the U.S. Constitution. Certainly, our Constitution reflects the political thought of James Madison more than any other man. Madison was a genius, but he had one fault. He could never live within his income.

I feel that this qualifies me particularly as an expert on James Madison.

Madison had to sell off part of his plantation before he died. Dolly, his famous wife, had to sell the whole plantation. The Madison family cemetery undoubtedly once was part of Montpelier.

All this was no disgrace. None of the great Virginians apparently was able to afford himself. It should be remembered that Jefferson, in his last years, got the permission of Congress to sell Monticello in a common lottery to satisfy his creditors, and only an indignant citizenry saved his home for him with public contributions.

Of course, the heirs lost Monticello later. The public wasn't very indignant about the heirs.

M ADISON as master of Montpelier makes an appealing man. All these Virginians were addicted to something called "scientific farming," which apparently never paid out, but Madison was busy at greater things. He was ordering new books for his library. He was writing his friend, Jefferson, to get him some apparatus for chemical experiments. He was reading Buffon and taking notes on the local fauna.

And he was going steadily into debt.

This is why I feel simpatico with Madison and Jefferson.

This Hamilton was a different kind of fish. He never had an overdraft in his life.

Madison and Jefferson do not only belong to the ages. They belong peculiarly to me.

REMEMBERING OLD CUMP

SOME local people recently got into an argument about which politician said, "I will not run if nominated and will not serve if elected." One man wants to know the name. The answer is, of course, that this was no politician. He was Gen. William Tecumseh Sherman, he who marched through Georgia and laid the base for *Gone with the Wind.*

When the Republicans held their convention in Chicago in 1884, certain people were still trying to draft old "Cump" as a candidate. His legendary reply is, "If nominated, I will not run; if elected, I will not serve." This, however, is one of those dressed-up legends like, "Send us more Japs." Old Cump's son has testified that his father's telegram read rather more like the version remembered by the local folk.

But Old Cump was Army through and through. Unlike certain other generals, he did not have to go through the act of playing Hamlet before he answered the presidential draft. Considering his experience, he might have agreed with Ambrose Bierce that politics is the conduct of public affairs for private advantage.

Or with Disraeli, who defined politics as the art of governing mankind by deceiving them. Sherman had already had his education in politics.

AMERICA has probably produced no more admirable man than William Tecumseh Sherman, and it is odd that more attention is not paid him. Sherman never did a dishonorable thing in his life. He loved his wife, Ellen, devotedly until the day she died. He loved his family. He was terrible in battle but almost foolish in his magnanimity to defeated foes.

They called Sherman the first of the modern generals because he first recognized the value of destroying the civilian activities supporting armies in the field. In Georgia, they say, his name is still a dirty word. Yet, Sherman loved the people of the South. He founded the military school that later became Louisiana State University. It has been comfortable to forget that Sherman, after his ruthless raid through Georgia, granted his Southern opponents such generous terms of surrender that the U.S. Congress raised hell.

Sherman understood war, and the need for it, and the uselessness of it when the battle was over.

HE was a roan-haired, proud, turkey-cock kind of man whose abilities might have been lost to the United States except for Grant. Sherman graduated near the head of his class at West Point. Impatient with his progress, he quit the army, and then year by year tried to get back. Had Grant not become the commander in the west, he might never have been singled out for distinction. This in a way is a commentary on Grant, who had no abilities except the supreme command abilities of being able to see broad strategy and being able to pick the right subordinates.

At any rate, in 1884 Sherman knew what he was and where he was and was contemptuous of swapping it for anything cheaper.

AN UNCIVIL WAR

AWHILE back I made some references to the Civil War and inevitably found myself right back in the thick of it. One of the people who objected says there was nothing civil, or polite, about the war.

In situations like this, my reply is always, "Send up A. P. Hill." We will fight it out along this line if it takes all summer. As a Confederate fugitive who has been hiding out in the bush all these years, I see nothing wrong with the term "Civil War." In its Latin root meaning, "civil" referred to great affairs of state before it acquired any overtones of civility.

I do not quite stand still for "The War of the Rebellion," but the South might get down to earth and get more done if it started calling the tragedy "The War in Which We Got Whipped."

But why start calling the Civil War names? Let's get on with it. We still might win.

OUR family yields to no other in its dedication to the South in the War Between the States. Everybody who was able to fight went. Also, our family probably furnished more people to the army who were unable to fight than any other.

In addition, a great-relative who was too old to get in any army undertook single-handedly to protect the women and kids from the guerrillas who were then roving that part of the Ozarks.

He did this by staying on the move constantly and replacing his horses at various farms. In the biblical phrase, he slew thousands — or at least enough to make him a hunted man. Once, when hemmed in against a cliff, he rode his horse over it. He fell into a tree and escaped damage except for a broken leg. The women of the countryside hid him in a cave and took care of him until the leg mended.

He would probably still be alive if he hadn't had a love for country dances. He was caught at one on a Saturday night and pretty well riddled.

Whenever someone mentions The War, old childhood memories with all the childhood emotional overtones come back about how the womenfolk hid the store of corn in a hole beneath the floor and the time my grandmother, then twelve, slapped a Yankee corporal.

I think my grandmother mainly hated the North all her life because he laughed.

PEOPLE are unable to look at that war rationally. If you write sometime that Grant really botched his first assignments in the west, you will get a letter saying that you ought not to blame Grant because he was drunk at the time.

You will read all the time about the military geniuses in the war. I have tried to be fair about this, but most of it is myth. With half a dozen exceptions, all the generals in the War of the Middle Nineteenth Century would have been relieved of their commands if they had been operating in World War II.

We can nevermore afford the kind of thinking and organization that went into command in that war. What we need is the unyielding spirit that permeated it.

TWO GHOSTS IN A DALLAS PLAZA

ONE sunny day in 1940, the late John McGinnis, professor of Shakespeare, master of the arts, and book editor of the *Dallas Morning News,* sat lolling at his desk in the old building at Commerce and Lamar.

The McGinnis physical stance was always one of indolence. He customarily sat reared back like this in his swivel chair. Only his roving eye told of a restless mind. The eyes this time lit on a new book on his desk, and he picked it up.

191

"This is a fine book, a surprisingly fine book," he said. "This young man will stand watching."

I took the book and looked at it. Later I read it, and it was a good book. As I remember it now, it had a red dust jacket.

It was titled "While England Slept," and the author was a twenty-three-year-old man named John Fitzgerald Kennedy.

McGINNIS had an eye for youthful talent, but if he could have looked ahead to the fulfillment of his prophecy, he would have dropped his teeth.

Who would have believed that this young man, known if he was known at all only as one of the sons of old Joe Kennedy, would become President of the United States, that he would be killed in Dallas within three blocks of the office where McGinnis then sat, and that the town would be setting aside there a plaza in his memory?

In the perspective of years, it seems strange. It seems strange, too, that all that history will remember Dallas for up to now — the actual founding of the city and the assassination — took place on the same little knoll overlooking the place where the river used to run.

In the perspective of years, too, Kennedy's book seems a little uncanny, for in it he began to speak for a generation.

THE book spoke for all of us who sat by restlessly while the war took root in Europe and began to grow.

The book was more than a book to those who read it. It was a shared experience, and a great many young men felt a quick identification with Kennedy. He was a kind of symbol. In magazines and newssheets, they followed his story in the Pacific even as they fought Japs, Germans, or boredom in their own small corners of the war. Their lives seemed parallel.

Later they watched the fledgling Kennedy steps in Congress, his surprising victory in the Senate race, and his sudden emergence as a national political figure. When he took office as President, it was as if a small part of each of his followers had gone with him. He spoke eloquently what many felt from afar.

In this, Kennedy must have been unique among all the Presidents.

It is the reason that, as the years grow longer, two ghosts will hover in the plaza in Dallas, the ghost of a President and the ghost of old hopes and dead dreams.

DEATH OF AN OLD-FASHIONED MAN

THE Canton Street boulevardier will appear here no more. A week never used to pass that he did not trudge in, perhaps leaning on his cane, deposit his great hat on the desk, and deliver himself of some opinions.

He was a hopelessly old-fashioned man. The younger people of the staff frankly regarded him as a bore. They had never heard such opinions. Men, damn it, he said, should rise when a lady comes into the room. As long as you work for a man, you owe him your loyalty, etc. Nearly always he had something to say, and if you thought about it for awhile, it became provocative. He furnished me many a good column, and I became very fond of him.

Well, the Canton Street boulevardier died awhile back, quietly and without notice.

He probably would have liked this. He felt, I think, that certain things like death were private matters.

"HE always looked like such a proud old man," said one of the people on the newspaper, and he was. It showed in his bearing. A tall, bulky former athlete, he carried himself ramrod straight and held his big square face high in the air.

He was proud of his old family and all that it had done in the history of the state, and he was literally proud of every furrow that his people had plowed across the Texas land. He was proud of a war that he was in when he really didn't have to be and proud of voting every year.

He was proud of being a law-abiding man, and once when he got a minor traffic ticket he was aggrieved at this blot on his record.

But he was an old-fashioned man with old-fashioned crotchets. He was a frank segregationist, though the idea of harming or even affronting a Negro person was abhorrent to him. It was the way he had grown up. He was low church Episcopalian and wary of liturgy or show in the church. The pope of Rome was an ever present threat to him, and a priest had to be watched.

His lifetime values grew out of his loyalties. First were God, country, and family, and right after that the University of Texas.

I WENT to his funeral, a plain, old-fashioned funeral with touches of him in it. While the people congregated, the organ played as usual, but one of the things it played this day was "America." It wasn't "America the Beautiful" or the Tin Pan Alley "God Bless America." It was the plain old "My country, 'tis of thee" that we all learned as children.

There were no flowers on the coffin when it was borne in. Instead, there was the American flag with the field over his heart where he would have wanted it.

He was an old-fashioned man, a plain man, a good old man.

He knew what he was. We knew what he was. Sooner or later, we have to decide whether we of the present know what we are.

END OF A DECADE

A DECADE ends today, and the 1960s now begin to look like one of the great weather fronts of history, a narrow time belt of confusion, violence, and strange calms before the winds of destiny begin to blow fresh and strong from a new direction.

The decade's assassinations, its rock festivals, its concern with cultish religion, its predilections for drugs, its student protests and racial rebellions, even its moon flights, now seem less facts than phenomena, symptoms of a convulsive change in western society. As the 1860s saw the end of the Christian ethic as the governing rule of western society, so the 1960s seemed to signal an end to human faith in science and its materialistic satisfactions.

Nobody knows now who the Charles Darwin or the John Stuart Mill of the 1960s is. Nobody knew what Darwin and Mill stood for in the 1860s, either.

But in the 1960s, as a hundred years earlier, man came face to face with some things.

AT least one thing became apparent. Scientific man's vaunted aim to conquer

193

nature and shape her more nearly to man's wish was not going to work. You can change nature, but you don't conquer her. The balance of nature can be upset on a giant scale as well as a small one, and the results are always disastrous.

The man who controls the weather in one area inevitably affects the weather in others. Man may conquer space and time with automobiles and airplanes, and he has learned that this can affect polar ice caps and even create new deserts. Primitive man accommodated himself to his planet. If a load was too heavy to drag up a hill, he split up the load. He did not level the hill and leave a barren.

Abundance was the hope of the reasonable and scientific civilization of the last hundred years. With the steady depletion of the earth's resources and burgeoning populations, it became apparent that man, and particularly American man, was going to have to learn to do with less rather than more. The earth has limits. It is a rock eight thousand miles thick in a limitless universe. Man draws his sustenance from an almost imperceptible crust on this rock. Really he lives from a little bit of fertile silt collected between its mountain ranges and its seas.

Nobody said much about this in the 1960s, but the race seems to have subconscious knowledge of its great dilemmas. The poor, who have never had much, riot if they sense they will have nothing.

AND so, the old society started breaking up because it had ceased to offer hope, a human necessity. It will be years before we know what came out of the 1960s, but Darwin, Mill, and their kind gave man new freedom for awhile. Something that happened in the 1960s may open a new door for our kind.

This is something we have to believe. Man never seemed to believe less in himself than he did in the 1960s.

A MAN
OF WORDS

THE PERCEPTIVE WORD COLLECTOR
THE WELL-CLUTTERED LIBRARY
TAMING THE ENGLISH LANGUAGE

THE PERCEPTIVE WORD COLLECTOR

"Faunch" and the other old words had honest material and honest shape to them. As the years go by, they will be very valuable to perceptive collectors.

THE PERCEPTIVE WORD COLLECTOR

DO-IT-YOURSELF WORD-MAKING

EVERYBODY knows what the verb "faunch" means even though it is in no proper lexicon. A man who is a-faunching is mad. He paws the ground. He whinnies. He raises cain. He is a-raring to go. Ordinarily this does not bother me, as there are few things really worth faunching about, but now a lot of people are a-faunching to know where the word started.

An exhaustive research of thirty minutes has failed to develop a breakthrough on this. H. L. Mencken's handy dialect dictionary's first note of its usage was in Nebraska about 1911, and this is surprising because the folks up there do not faunch. They sull. The dialect dictionary says that "faunch" was noted in southwestern Missouri in 1923. Jesse Stuart was using the word soon after that time, however, when he was at his mountain poetic best, in a way that indicated that it came from his father's generation, or perhaps his grandfather's.

For all anybody knows, "faunch" began in old England, probably at the time that Elizabeth got mad at Essex. In all history, she is probably the only female who was capable of faunching.

I HAVE a theory about "faunch" which is at least better than H. L. Mencken's. After all, Mr. Mencken is dead and can't argue the subject. In my opinion, "faunch" just grew up because of the hazards of the frontier.

Two things that the average pioneer could not carry with him, when he headed west to make a new little gray home eroded and worthless, were fancy canned goods and words. After all, if he had carried a supply of all the words he was going to need, it would have taken up a great deal of wagon space. Lacking a supply of preserved words, the pioneer did the only thing he could when he needed a word. He made one by hand.

This is how you got words like "whaunker-jawed." You can look at that one and see that it was beaten out of an old-fashioned anvil. Out of all this you got verbs like "outdugan" and nouns like "needments," which is self-explanatory, and "gom," meaning a real molasses-mixed mess, and "buckaroo."

Probably some pioneer somewhere ran into a wild range bull and had to describe the bull in a way that would excuse his running off. Hence, "faunch." This would have been before prize bulls began just to stand there and look at the photographer.

LIKE all the other old-fashioned handcrafts, wordsmithing has gone into a decline. People make a show out of do-it-yourself word-making now, but it isn't very good.

It is the fashion now for some toyfaced junior executive to go home and get out of his Ivy League clothes into his jump-suit-styled coveralls and make himself a word. It usually is something like "finalized." It wasn't made out of good material to begin with, and every join in it is stuffed with putty.

"Faunch" and the other old words had honest material and honest shape to them. As the years go by, they will be very valuable to perceptive collectors.

TO WOOLY AND CHOUSE

AS a boy, says a Dallas reader, he often visited his grandmother up in Grayson County when a lot of other grandchildren were around.

Invariably, sometime during the visit, she would order the older youngsters to "stop woolen that baby."

He recently visited his grandmother-in-law in deep East Texas, and she let go with the same phrase.

He has been wondering how you "wool" a baby and what it all means.

Quite likely, his Grayson County grandmother's "woolen" was merely a Texas pronunciation of "woolying." When you wooly a baby, you rough him up a little bit. You tease him. When you wooly a dog, you shove him around a little. When you wooly, you are playing rough.

This is a perfectly good old American word. It is always tagged as a colloquialism, but it has been one so long that it ought to be part of the language because it preserves a fine distinction of meaning. When you wooly a person, you don't really rough him up and you don't really tease him. It's something in between.

But I never did know of a baby or a dog that liked to be woolied.

TO wooly someone apparently originally meant just to rumple his hair, scuff him up a little. Almost from the beginnings of America, people jocularly referred to a man's hair as his wool. This is probably where it started.

When I was a small boy, it was the habit of bands of small boys to turn suddenly on one of their number. While most of them held him down, one or two would polish his scalp vigorously with their knuckles. This was supposed to be a mortal insult. If you had been woolied, you usually set off on a round of neighborhood fistfights which lasted until you teamed up with the gang and woolied someone else.

When you look back on this kind of thing, it seems to have been an unimaginatively stupid form of amusement, but then we hadn't yet invented color TV. As a relative of mine remarked on a trip to Mexico recently, "If a boy doesn't have something to do, he will invent something." She was talking about the

199

need of some Mexican kids to prove that they could outrun a Pepsi-Cola truck uphill.

The practice of woolying people apparently died out during the burr haircut years, but it might revive with these new haircuts.

THE original American had a number of precise terms which were never appreciated by the grammarians. You woolied a baby or a dog, for instance, but you never woolied cattle. You choused them. It was an unforgivable practice except among small boys trying to learn to ride.

"You kids better not chouse those cattle," our elders were always warning. It meant that we would hurry them and probably make them nervous and cause them to lose a pound or two on the hoof when they were taken to market.

To wooly a baby might be all right at times. To chouse the cattle was unthinkable.

BEATING A DEAD HORSE

A CUSTOMER has asked who first started beating a dead horse and why.

In the puristic sense, a dead horse is flogged, not beaten, but it is a pleasure to note that the dead horse that is always beaten is one of the oldest breeds of mythological horse.

In the beginning, he was not necessarily beaten. He was paid, or worked, or stabled, but however the dead horse was used, he was a symbol of worthlessness. An English parliamentarian named John Bright seems to have been the first man to flog the dead horse. This was during the last century. Two of Bright's friends had bills up before Commons,

but the House was behaving like the Texas legislature.

Originally, it had favored both bills, but as the session dragged on, it was less and less inclined to be bothered.

Bright finally made a speech in which he said considering either bill was like flogging a dead horse.

He thus gave this breed of horse its final form.

PROBABLY the oldest breed of mythological horse is The Gift Horse, which you shouldn't look in the mouth. Apparently, this kind of horse was known to St. Jerome about fifteen hundred years ago, and it has been carefully cultivated and improved upon ever since. Now the gift horse that should not be looked in the mouth comes in herds wherever men write sentences.

It is almost as common as the cows that come home before somebody does something.

The horse of another color is a completely different breed of horse and evidently a newer variety. It was known to Sir Andrew Aguecheek and Sir Toby Belch when they were teaming up on Malvolio in *Twelfth Night*. A special, piebald variety of this breed is of about the same age. It is known as The Horse of the Same Color.

There is also The Horse That You Can Lead to Water, But You Can't Make Him Drink, but this seems to be even a newer breed. Sam Johnson, the old dictionarist, seems to have entered the first literary notes on this one, though what Dr. Johnson knew about horses is hard to say. It is possible that the doctor mistook Oliver Goldsmith for a horse. There was a certain facial resemblance.

It seems unlikely, though, because nobody

ever had any trouble making Goldsmith drink.

One of the oldest of these breeds is the scriptural Pale Horse, whose rider was Death.

THESE horses are all creatures of the literary animal kingdom, of course, and there are other animals in this menagerie not to be found on veldt, on plain, on mountain, or in cages. They travel by the thousand, though, through English prose.

There are the dog who is always in the manger, the crow that has to be eaten, the whole hog which somebody (including William Cowper) is inclined to go, and the cats that for almost five hundred years have been able to look at a king.

READING THE RIOT ACT

A FRIEND of ours recently got home late by taxicab and had to lean on a lamppost for a few minutes to get his bearings. He says his wife then "read the riot act" to him, and he wants to know why people are entitled to read the riot act.

Actually, it is all legal enough and stems from the time of George I, the first of the English Hanover kings. Stories have been told that he was an ignorant man who could not talk to his English subjects. Actually, George I was quite a dude. He could talk to his ministers very well. He talked to them in French. If they couldn't understand French, they were too ignorant to be in government.

George I did not like the English. He didn't think they were very couth. The English didn't like him either.

Early in his marriage, George had suspected his wife of infidelity. Why not? Infidelity was a common disease at the time. Anyhow, his wife's suspected lover ended up assassinated, and George locked up his wife in a castle for thirty years.

Meanwhile, he cavorted around Britain with two old crows who were his mistresses. The great English lords were not indignant about mistresses. Most of them ran through four or five in a lifetime.

They just didn't like for mistresses to look like old crows.

AS a result, people began to gather in the streets and shout insults about the government. "A bas," they would shout, which is the ultimate insult to a man who speaks French.

George, though, was very thick with the Whigs. England at that time was not like Chicago in 1968. People didn't go around insulting political parties with impunity. In 1715, Parliament passed the Riot Act. So far as I know it is still in effect.

It provided that if as many as twelve people march the streets shouting insults on the king and government, they are a riot. Nine people can do it, or even eleven, but when twelve people were on hand, a magistrate was supposed to appear before them and read the following: "Our Sovereign Lord the King chargeth and commandeth all persons being assembled immediately disperse themselves and peaceably depart to their habitations."

This was called reading the Riot Act.

Anybody who continued to demonstrate for an hour thereafter was guilty of a felony.

Presumably, the hour was determined by the magistrate or by the number of demonstrators above twelve.

IT should be noted that these words of the Riot Act have to be read exactly as written. It is kind of like our present little formula advising a prisoner of his rights when he has been arrested. In England, charges of rioting have been thrown out simply because the magistrate failed to say, "God Save the King" at the end of his reading.

It is hard to believe in the days of this present admirable and decent queen that England will ever need to read the Riot Act.

People do it all over the world, though. If you are leaning against a lamppost and think that you are more than twelve, you are a riot.

KICKING THE BUCKET

SOMEONE has raised the question of what people mean when they talk about kicking the bucket.

This question comes up fairly regularly. A man who has kicked the bucket, of course, has mosied on, passed over, gone west, cashed in his chips, gone to the last roundup, or any of the other euphemisms which human beings prefer to saying that a man has sounded his death rattle.

A human being in the presence of death is, in the old word, affrighted, and he prefers some jocular term instead of the mention of the old eyeless skull. "Kick the bucket" is a very old term for dying. It is at least 250 years old, maybe 300. It was slang before the dictionary makers decided what slang was.

It has always been a favorite of unfanciful minds in love with fanciful language. Sir Arthur Quiller-Couch, for instance, told of a young Englishman who was writing an acquaintance about the death of his mother.

"Sir," wrote the young man. "Regret to inform you that the hand that rocked the cradle has kicked the bucket."

I think almost anybody would resent having "kick the bucket" put into his official obituary.

THERE are half a dozen theories about where "kick the bucket" came from, and most, to use another old phrase, don't hold much water.

The popular one is that the frame from which a pig was hung when butchered in ancient England was called a bucket and that the dying pig naturally kicked the bucket. The people who believe this have never killed any pigs. By the time a pig is hung, he has already quit kicking. He has been shot, or knifed, or hit in the head. He has been killed instantly, and later, his throat has been cut, and he has been allowed to bleed. He has been scalded thoroughly with hot water and scraped clean.

He is hung, not on a bucket but on a singletree, the tug hooks of the singletree being inserted behind the tendons of his back legs, for the purpose of drawing and evisceration.

This does not sound very good, but it is how you get your pork, and it is not as bad as it sounds.

Anyhow, the pig does not kick the bucket or anything else.

ANOTHER theory about "kick the bucket" is that it refers to the bucket on which a suicide stands when he hangs himself. He kicks the bucket out from under himself and so dies.

Being a man who demands scientific proof of everything, I have experimented with this on myself, and it won't work. The bucket is not high enough. A man committing suicide has to get it over in an instant, or he will back out. Dropping off a bucket doesn't kill you. It just suddenly impels you to get hold of that rope and pull yourself up and get it off your neck.

The whole subject is sort of morbid. Instead of kicking the bucket, I recommend that we go out somewhere and kick the gong around.

STRANGE BEDFELLOWS

A LADY who wishes to be signed "Anon" says that she has racked her brains over what it is that makes strange bedfellows and still does not know what it means. This is no wonder. It comes from the credibility gap of Charles Dudley Warner.

Politics make strange bedfellows. That's what Charles Dudley Warner wrote in 1870 in a book called *My Summer in a Garden.* People have been repeating it ever since. The trouble is that nobody believes Charles Dudley Warner ever said anything.

For instance, Charles Dudley Warner said, "Everybody talks about the weather, but nobody does anything about it." The populace decided that Charles Dudley Warner couldn't have said this, and everybody attributes it to Mark Twain, Warner's friend.

As a matter of fact, their only collaboration was a novel called *The Gilded Age,* a kind of disaster. Neither man could write a novel, but old Sam Clemens was a genius who could overcome by sheer power whatever he lacked in technique. Charles Dudley Warner was not a genius.

As a result, people nowadays think Charles Dudley Warner never said anything.

But Charles Dudley Warner said a great deal, part of which he probably should have thought twice before saying.

W ARNER apparently was a scholarly looking man, slim, handsome, craggy of head and face, and endowed with a good mane of gray hair. He is supposed to have titillated the ladies as much as decorum would allow in those days.

His mother's people came over on the *Mayflower,* and the family apparently never fully recovered from the voyage. Warner never had enough money, but he went to Hamilton College. Later, he tried working as a lawyer and a surveyor without much success. Having decided that he was going to fail at everything else, he became a newspaper columnist.

He got his job with the *Courant* in Hartford, Connecticut, because a friend owned the paper. This is still as good a way as any to get a job.

In the phrase of that day, he was always in delicate health.

In the phrase of our day, he was lazy.

B UT Warner turned out to be a really fine personal essayist, warm, witty, genial, and imaginative. He was perhaps too urbane for his job. He would write an essay on the joys of camping, for instance. Any ex-soldier or Marine could tell him that this thesis is of dubious value. He also wrote about the joys of gardening, which is all right if you have a yardman.

But he did say that politics make strange bedfellows. People still don't want to believe it. They say that a man named Shakespeare used the phrase in an obscure work called *The Tempest.*

But Shakespeare hadn't any idea of some of the political combinations we run into today.

LIES OF THE WHOLE CLOTH

SEVERAL people have suddenly again asked to know the meaning of "out of the whole cloth."

Five hundred years ago "whole cloth" was cloth woven the width of the loom. As such, it was particularly fine cloth without seams or joiner's weak spots.

The phrase had a fine, honest ring to it until the nineteenth century when tailors began to take whatever remnants they could buy cheaply and make suits out of them. After the immemorial manner of hawkers everywhere, they sought to cover up by borrowing a patrician phrase. "Out of the whole cloth," they said in advertising these suits made out of whatever they could get.

Our Yankee cousins, unfortunately, took the lead in this, but a Dallas resident who lived through the sixties finds it easy to be philosophical. At least, this is one thing that we in Dallas didn't do.

AFTER a time, "out of the whole cloth" came to mean something spurious, something fabricated out of questionable materials, something completely false.

But lies nowadays are always made out of the whole cloth. At least, the dark-colored, conservative lies, the sharkskins and the blue serges among this world's falsehoods, are always made out of the whole cloth. Nobody has yet made this charge about white lies. Apparently, the world has agreed that white lies are beautiful and are probably woven out of gossamer.

It seems odd that evidence bearing on a lie of the whole cloth does not come in whole cloth. It comes in scraps. "There is not a scrap of evidence to support this," says the speaker. "It is a lie of the whole cloth." Similarly, truth comes in shreds, not in the whole cloth. "There is not a shred of truth in it."

As a matter of fact, nobody anywhere has ever trumpeted, "This is a truth of the whole cloth," possibly because they know that truth won't stretch that far.

A black or dark-blue lie in a good herringbone weave, however, can be stretched out to cover a lot of territory.

THE loom of destiny seems to have got mixed up in recent years, possibly because of the effect of the forty-hour week among the gods. It is still possible for a man to see that the thread of evil runs through the work of his enemies, but it is hard for him to tell which bobbin the thread came from or into what loom it goes.

It may come out in woven form, for instance, as a shred of evidence rather than a lie of the whole cloth.

THE QUESTION OF "PIN MONEY"

A READER has raised the question of "pin money." She remembers that her mother used to do genteel work on the side to earn a little pin money. Did husbands, asks the reader, once refuse to give their wives money for pins? Is the phrase English or Scotch, perhaps?

Pin money, of course, is money which the wife acquires for her own use. She can spend it without accounting to anybody. The masculine equivalent is tobacco money. This is the stipend which a man withholds from the paycheck to pay for his cigarettes and a grilled cheese sandwich every noon if he can manage to stretch his tobacco money from paycheck to paycheck.

The ordinary paycheck contains very little pin money or tobacco money these days. Mostly, it is grocery money.

The practice of pin money may have been the beginning of women's lib.

AS a term, "pin money" is old in the language. According to the authorities, pins appeared in England in the 1300s. At first, they were rare and costly and were controlled by a monopoly under a grant from the crown.

One source says English law permitted pins to be sold only on the first two days of January. A wife in asking her husband for pin money was thus asking him to make an investment roughly equivalent to the cost of a modern washing machine.

An English will dated fifty years before the voyage of Columbus is said to "leave to my daughter Margarett my lease to the parsonage of Kirkdall Churche to buy her pins withal."

Pin money may have started in England, but the practice for which it is a name was evidently two thousand years older.

The Greeks apparently knew it. A king or a wealthy man might give his wife certain properties to dispose of as she liked. According to Xenophon, this was called girdle money.

The patrician matrons of Rome usually owned not only the pin money and girdle money but also their husbands. They allowed their Caesars plenty of tobacco money but would get rid of one in a hurry rather than give up the family stocks.

PIN money, or girdle money, evidently was a device by which women could be granted property in fee simple.

Blackstone said as much. He listed pin money along with other separate maintenance funds which a wife could will to her heirs without the consent of her husband.

So, it was a great day for women's lib when pin money came along.

Anybody who grew up in the country in the United States knows this. Farm women used to acquire their pin money by selling the extra eggs in town. They would then spend the money in a splurge that their husbands wouldn't have consented to, buying a fifty-cent subscription to *Comfort* magazine or a $3.95 guitar for the youngsters.

"PASSELS" AND "PARCELS"

A LADY from a Dallas suburb finally brought the question out into the open.

"I've heard of a parcel of land and also a passel of something or other," she writes. "Is 'passel' a corruption of 'parcel'? Is it a word on its own, or is it not a word at all?"

A passel of people who have been pretending that they didn't come from the country are now ashamed of the word and try to avoid using it. "Passel" is a very good word. The dictionaries don't accept it, and the experts say it is a corruption by the ignorant of "parcel." This merely shows that the experts may know all about words, but they don't know anything about us ignorant people.

They are not the same words at all. A parcel of land, for instance, is a designated tract of whatever odd boundaries. A passel of land is a whole lot of it.

Generally speaking, the old-time rancher who owned a passel of land would have been embarrassed to describe it as a parcel.

IT is not always true, but mostly "passel" refers to animate objects, as the word has been used in this country, which originated it. A "parcel" applies to an inanimate object.

Ignorant the old-timers may have been, but you never heard one saying, "There is a passel post package for you at the post office."

Everybody knew that the agency which delivered you packages through the mail was called the partial post.

It is good to note also that "passel" did not originate in the South or Southwest, the lands generally designated as those of the ignorant. It came out of Massachusetts, the land of the bean and the cod and the people who add a final "r" to "Cuba." At least, the word tracers find its first printed uses there. Significantly, the first usage refers to a "hull passel of children."

Through the years, "passel" has probably been most often applied to flocks of children.

It was not so with Great-Aunt Martha. She reserved the word for the "passel of crooks" which she found everywhere about her, ready to cheat her on the dozen hen eggs she had to sell or the pound of coffee she had to buy.

To her a "passel of children" was a "swarm of brats."

IN the history of the word, you can find plenty of "passels" of children, thieves, folks, hogs, horses, and people. You find very few "passels" of eggs, lamps, McCormick reapers, houses, idols, or anything else inanimate.

Of course, there is the line in the Western movie where the hero threatens to whip "the whole passel of you."

Generally, though, "parcel" and "passel" are not part and parcel of the whole thing.

UP TO SNUFF

A COUPLE of people have asked about "up to snuff." Originally, of course, the phrase applied to a person who was alert, shrewd, up to handling any problem that came along. It came to be applied to a product which was capable of filling its need.

"Up to snuff" is fairly old in the language. It first appeared in print in an English play in 1811, apparently, though it must have been a common phrase for a hundred years by then. Dickens once wrote of a character who was "up to snuff and a pinch or two over."

Nobody knows where the phrase came from, but Eric Partridge suggests that it originally was used to describe a person who was well aware of the dangers of sniffing snuff and could handle the product.

Probably, the phrase was first applied to a man four hundred years ago who took a first sniff of snuff and didn't blink an eye.

THE Europeans are fond of reminding us that the filthy habit was imported upon them from the New World, but once it was introduced, they went hog-wild about it.

No chronicler has ever recorded that an American Indian went around making himself sneeze delicately by the application of a dose of snuff, but the use of snuff in Europe was common in the seventeenth century and was endemic in the eighteenth.

In the beginning, a man had to powder his own tobacco leaves, and every snuff user carried a pocket rasp for the purpose.

Some filthy rich people who wouldn't be caught dead chewing a slippery elm switch will pay fancy money these days for those rasps.

Snuff has been a manufacture, though, for a long time, and more care and work is probably put into the making of a good snuff than into any other tobacco product. It often takes months of fermenting, perfuming, and flavoring to produce a good rappee, and even the Scotch snuffs take time and care.

Yet, snuff is a dirty word in the United States. You do not see any girls in bathing suits using it on TV.

This is because a lot of finicky people are ashamed of their grandma's habits.

SNUFF has an ancient history of accomplishment. It has fostered the growth of great civilizations such as that in old-time East Texas, which produced more oratory and less cotton per acre than any other civilization in history.

When the snuffboxes at the desks of U.S. senators in Washington were full, you had peppery, fiery senators like Clay, Calhoun, and Webster who could fire up a good snort at a President and make it resound throughout the land. All that senators do now is sniff at a President. They don't have any discharge.

The phrase is dying out and being corrupted. An older woman at a retirement hotel was telling an elderly gentleman in the lobby recently that she didn't feel well. "I'm out of snuff," she said.

He gallantly produced a can and offered her a dip.

THE ORIGINAL HORNSWOGGLE

A DALLAS man wants to know about "hornswoggle." Where did the word come from and why. "Hornswoggle" is a special case as words go, of course. Everybody knows instantly what it means, but nobody knows why.

Like so many other strange and apparently pointless things, "hornswoggle" comes right out of Kentucky. Anyhow, that is where the word first left its trace about 1830. At the time, it meant the act of greatly embarrassing somebody. Probably they had to change the meaning when another joker invented "discombooberate." Anyhow, "hornswoggle" came to mean hoodwinking somebody.

In 1856, it was used in politics to describe what the presidential candidates are now trying to do to each other.

As to what the original "hornswoggle" was, nobody apparently knows. Maybe it was an early-day animal that became extinct. It could have been a pioneer instrument that has died out like the ash-hopper and the mother-of-pearl inlaid back scratcher.

The experts are always saying that Americanisms are picturesque, but I would like to see them explain the picture in "hornswoggle."

"HORNSWOGGLE" came out of a period in history when the American people were exuberant. They went around making new words the way they plowed new fields. They had just whipped England a second time and were possibly in the mood to murder the King's English.

Partly, this was necessary. If you go into a new country and see something strange that

207

you never saw before and you can't go look it up in the dictionary, what do you do? You give it a name. Thus you have created a neologism, which merely means that you have used fresh language.

Part of it was necessary, but there is evidence that some of those pioneer characters sat around on the bench in front of the town store and made new words just for the heck of it. It was a kind of catch-as-catch-can Scrabble with no holds barred.

This went on and on, and by 1850, Americans were already noticing that the people of the British Isles didn't know how to speak English.

"Hornswoggle" turned out to be a good word, though, so good that we hornswoggled the English into using it.

Yet, though everybody uses "hornswoggle" and it has been with us at least 130 years, the dictionaries still label it "Slang" in italics that show their contempt.

OUR own stand is that sticks and stones may break our bones, but italics will never hurt. Good slang is good language. The creator of authentic slang is like the creator of authentic jazz. He sends you.

The making of fresh language takes vitality and gusto. Shakespeares can do it. Lesser and more worn-out writers duck the job.

WHAT! SAM HILL?

A CUSTOMER has asked the origin of the phrase, "What the Sam Hill?" Everybody, he says, uses it half a dozen times a day, and nobody knows what it means.

Nobody knows for certain where this phrase came from, though it probably did not come from the Latin. The *Dictionary of Americanisms* says that it was in print in the United States as early as 1830 and that "Sam Hill" is an American euphemism for "hell."

This is an odd statement. Sam Hill used to live at Portales, New Mexico, thirty-five or forty years ago, and from his appearance you wouldn't have said he was a euphemism for anything.

Furthermore, the word "hell" itself was a euphemism to the old-timer. He knew a lot better and stronger words to describe his plight at any given moment, and he only used mild expressions like "hell" when he did not wish to offend the sensitive ears of the ladies.

To me, "What in Sam Hill!" still conveys more shock, surprise, and interest than "hell."

I WAS about twenty-one years old before I ever knew the proper expression was "What in Sam Hill," or "What in the Sam Hill," if you're a purist. My generation out on the high baldies always thought it was, "What! Sam Hill?" This was what people usually said when the advanced thinker of Portales was mentioned.

Sam was a man who had made a lifelong career of part-time work and then had retired. He was a thin, wispy man with watery blue eyes and a whitish yellow walrus moustache that looked frayed at the ends. Sam had about twenty acres of sandy land in the Portales country with one irrigation well on it, which in itself marked him as an advance guard agriculturist because, in that arid country, it was believed that water applied to this land would leach the soil.

Sam had schemed out a scheme to make a fortune by raising sweet potatoes for the market. He didn't make a fortune, but he did make a living if you consider a constant diet of sweet potatoes a living. Sam had hundreds of advanced ideas. He wouldn't let a tractor on his land because, he said, all that steel smashed the minerals in the soil. For the same reason, he wouldn't let anybody work it with a shod mule.

A barefoot mule at the plow was all right provided Sam's wife couldn't work the crop by hand.

"There's just something about hand-done work that is prettier than anything else," Sam would argue.

FOR a long time, I thought Sam Hill was the one that people were referring to when they asked, "What in . . .?" But, of course, the *Dictionary of Americanisms* was right.

Sam Hill wasn't even around in 1830 when the phrase was first printed. Indeed, it is hard to imagine that anybody like him ever was around before. Still, I find it impossible when someone says "What the Sam Hill!" not instantly to wonder what preposterous project Sam has on tap now.

Most people probably have similar automatic reactions to the phrase. You might say, to each man his private Sam Hill.

ALL STOVE UP

A REPORTER who keeps up with the news from the Central Texas farm and ranch country was writing his regular weekly epic the other day when the purist behind his shoulder chided him for using "stove up."

"Stove up," said the purist, "is not in the dictionary." I would like to know what this has to do with it. Going to the dictionary is a poor way to find out the meaning of "stove up."

The best way is to ride a horse.

A lot of things are not in the dictionary. You would not look in the dictionary, for instance, if you wanted a cuff link for your shirt. There is no point in putting into the dictionary a term like "stove up," for which everybody knows the meaning before he looks it up.

It does not mean, as the purist suggested, "stove in." "Stove in" is something for which you lay the blame on the coxswain. "Stove up" is the horse meaning of the term.

"STOVE up" is obviously good colloquial English. Even Webster admits that "stove" can be a past participle of "stave," and when Webster admits something right out without making you look up ten more long words, it is really something.

Most people who have tried to deal with "stove up" have been long on theory and short of experience. The *American Thesaurus of Slang,* for instance, equates the term with such classical English expressions as "done up," "jiggered up," "pooped," "corked out," "flaked out," "pegged out," "shot," and "did to a frazzle."

In the first place, "corked out" does not mean "done up" or "did to a frazzle." The last two mean "fatigued" or "worn out." "Corking out" is the practice of sneaking off and getting in a little sack time even when one hasn't done any work. "Flaking out" is the nautical form of corking out.

Anyhow, "stove up" doesn't have anything to do with these. In a man who is stove up, the ball ends of his knee bones and elbows have busted backward through the sockets so that he does not really walk. He crips around.

He has no teeth, so the surface of his chin is clamped firmly against the end of his nose. Since his eyes have gone bad, he squints one and flutters the other when he works up a glare.

IT is really wonderful when you consider that all this confusion came from a Sanskrit word for something that stands upright, whence "staff" and "stave," as in a barrel, and "stove" which is what you do to a stave.

Of course, nobody knows whether a boat is stove in because one of its staves is busted or because a stave was used to bust in one of its staves.

But it is wonderful that the human race used all these languages and all this trouble to describe a stove-up old cowboy.

TEXAS SHINNERY

THE other day a Texas lady was telling some people about some undeveloped land near the West Texas metropolis of Seminole and mentioned the shinnery on it. Her listeners immediately hooted at her.

"Shinnery," they said. "What's that?"

The lady was further embarrassed when she went to the dictionary and couldn't find the word.

Probably the lady had run into a bunch of those swamp rabbits who have moved into Texas from the swamps and foggy bottoms of the unhealthy East. Certainly no old-time Texan would have behaved so. The old-time Texan was too polite to hoot at anybody. He

210

worked on the theory that you ought to listen to strangers because any stranger might have something, maybe a gun.

The old-time Texan preferred to listen with straight-faced politeness while a stranger made a fool of himself and then tell it all over the countryside.

ANYHOW, the lady looked in the wrong dictionary. "Shinnery" is in Webster's Unabridged as a perfectly good word, a term describing a patch of low, thick brush but applying particularly to a patch of shin oaks.

The shin oak is a tree three feet tall, more or less. It isn't a bush or a shrub. It is a real tree and a real oak and is typical of the lengths that West Texas will go to, to get a little attention.

Years ago it was sometimes known as the cussing oak, and a staunch Baptist deacon of the Lariat country, a rancher, used to have a stock prayer that included a line, "Lead us not into shinnery or catclaw bushes."

Nobody apparently knows how the shin oak got its name. It is shin high and is hard on the shins, if that means anything. Webster seems to suggest that the name may be a shortened version of "chinquapin oak," which is another name for the pint-sized forest monarch of the plains. The *Dictionary of Americanisms* says "shinnery" is related to "chiniere," a French word which has something to do with a collection of small oaks. The meaning isn't clear here in *French Made Easy in Five Minutes.*

But "shinnery," sometimes spelled "chinnery," was in respectable books and magazines at least sixty years ago.

AT any rate, people like our Texas friend ought to stand their ground against ignoramuses who sneer at words merely because they exist solely in the Texas vocabulary.

After all, there are things in Texas that can only be described in the Texas vocabulary — if you intend to be polite.

The Seminole country is probably the center of the world's shinnery forests, and the word came right out of the country. It is a very good word. The rest of the world may persist in the delusion that great oaks from little acorns grow, but Texas keeps its eye on reality.

The shin oak acorn is just as big as any other.

DUNCE'S COMEDOWN

ANY time you're worried about making a lasting mark in human history, it would be well to remember John Duns Scotus. He was, according to the *Britannica,* the greatest British medieval philosopher, and he is remembered all right. His name gave us the word "dunce."

It couldn't have happened, apparently, to a smarter guy. He was born about 1265 at Duns, Scotland, thereby acquiring his surname. He was educated at Oxford and taught there, in Paris, and in Cologne. According to one source, "in a disputation on the Immaculate Conception of Jesus Christ by the Virgin Mary, he displayed so much ingenuity and resource as to win the title Doctor Subtilis."

He was for most of his life the main opponent of Thomas Aquinas, and some say the Thomists started the idea that the "dunsmen" were thick between the ears because of their inflexibility in argument.

It would be 550 years before Pope Pius IX settled in 1854 that argument about Immaculate Conception, and the question meanwhile produced some fine oratory and minutely fine logical distinctions.

IT is hard for a mere modern layman who doesn't get a chance to meet many angels or seraphim to follow Duns Scotus's theories. At the time, of course, it was important to determine how many angels could stand on the head of a pin.

One thing that Duns Scotus was dead set against was the theory that each angel was a complete species.

But if you study the summaries of Duns Scotus's philosophy prepared by the experts, it is hard not to feel that he was a primitive forerunner of what we have since called the scientific method of thought. He drew, for instance, a strict line between the rational and the irrational. He held that the existence of God was basically unprovable, and that the nature of God could not be understood by mortal men.

He seems to have been insisting on recognizing the difference between the measurable and the immeasurable. The historians of philosophy say that he first drove the wedge between philosophy and religion, thus permitting the philosophers to take off on their own.

If so, Duns Scotus certainly didn't mean to. He was a good Franciscan and tried to appropriate everything he could to the Kingdom of God.

MOST scholars in the field think that "dunce" came to be a designation of ignorance rather slowly. Apparently "duns," "dunse," or "dunce" originally referred to a very learned, if very academic man.

Apparently, people gradually began to apply the term in fun-poking to an especially ignorant person. It came to apply to the youngster who wore the conical dunce's cap in the schoolroom until recent years. Teachers seem to have discovered that this was damaging the child's psyche about the time they got tired of whipping irritable parents.

"Dunce" is a heck of a comedown for a man who was one of the most influential thinkers of his time, but it shows what can happen if you really care about what the future thinks of you.

CAUGHT IN THE WEWOKA SWITCH

A RECENT customer at the Wewoka Switch Motel up in Oklahoma has kindly furnished us with an explanation of the phrase, "Caught in the Wewoka Switch." This is very startling because I didn't know anything was caught there; and there are very few things of this kind that I don't know, if you will pardon the expression.

About 1890, according to the motel's postcard story, the Rock Island Railroad set up an area switching yard in Wewoka, and merchants within a forty-mile area would send wagons in to pick up their goods. When a merchant ran out of anything at his store, he would tell his customer, "Yes, I have it, but it's in the Wewoka Switch," meaning that he couldn't get right at it.

With an oil boom in the 1920s, freight hit Wewoka like an overgrown tornado. In addition to all the oil field supplies, drilling rigs, pipe, etc., merchants had at times to quadruple their stocks.

The original patrons of the Wewoka Switch had to compete with new consignees from a whole Oklahoma area.

IT was a mess, they say. Freight that was lost in transit to other places was often found in the overgrown piles of shipments at Wewoka. Things got to the point where the railroad started looking for any missing piece of freight there and ordered a rubber stamp that said "Search Wewoka Switch" for the waybill of any missing item.

The oil field workers picked up the phrase and, it is said, carried it all over the world except to me. "I'm caught in the Wewoka Switch" came to mean that the speaker was in a tight, a bind, or even a dangerous situation.

One suspects that most of us at the moment are lost in the Wewoka Switch.

AT this stage of our human experience, the Wewoka Switch begins to have philosophical meaning for the human race, and the time may come when every human being ought to have a rubber stamp reminding him to "Search Wewoka Switch."

It is a common household experience to know that you have something but don't know where it is. A plethora of freight moves through your living room into some siding and is lost when you need it. The average man also knows vaguely that there were things he meant to do with his life. At age forty, he doesn't know where they went to.

Most of all, every human being knows that there are truths that transcend human experience, but in our day it is hard to know where they are.

We don't mean to change The Prayer, but maybe it would be all right for some of us just to wish that we may be preserved from temptation, delivered from evil, and saved eternally from being lost in the Wewoka Switch.

ALL'S WELL THAT ENDS WELL

IN a sense, every oil field derrick that you glimpse from the Texas highways is a monument to a sixteenth century English hangman.

His name was Derrick, too. He was a soldier under Robert, Earl of Essex, when that petulant and mercurial favorite of the first Queen Elizabeth took and sacked Cadiz in 1596. During that Spanish campaign, Derrick found himself in danger of being executed for rape; but Essex pardoned him, little realizing that he was saving the man who would later chop off his own head.

Within a year or two, Derrick was public hangman at Tyburn. Possibly he was advanced to the post on recommendation of Essex, who had a way of looking out for people who had caught his eye.

Anyhow, Derrick applied himself to his new career with such faithfulness that his name quickly became synonymous with his trade. The name was a byword among London's playwrights by the turn of the seventeenth century.

During his tenure, Derrick is reported to have hanged twenty-three persons.

MEANWHILE, the Earl of Essex was having his troubles. He really wasn't much of a military man, and most of his adventures turned out badly. After a disastrous expedition to Ireland, he returned to London, made an unsuccessful show of force against the Crown, and then returned to his estate to await the summons. It came. He was tried for treason and sentenced to death.

Because of his rank, he was entitled to something better than a common hanging, of course. He had the right to have his head severed from his body. The executioner, when Essex approached the block, turned out to be Old Soldier Derrick.

It is said that Derrick begged the Earl's pardon for what he was about to do and then botched the execution, giving Essex two whacks which did not do the job. The executioner was barely saved from a mob of the Earl's friends.

The Earl seems to have been unfortunate in the people to whom he granted favors. One of the prosecutors at his trial was a favorite protégé, Francis Bacon.

Probably Bacon performed reluctantly, too, but under Elizabeth a man had better perform.

AT any rate, Derrick bestowed his name on the principal instrument of his trade, the gallows. After a time it was applied to a simple crane.

Apparently, "derrick" in its present meaning came into general use about 1830 when European mining firms were first using drilling equipment for exploration. They needed something to pull the tools from the shaft. The first such derrick was an adaptation of the ship's cargo boom.

What does all this mean? The moral to the story is obvious: All's well that ends well.

THE WELL-CLUTTERED LIBRARY

Fast reading is supposed to save time. Sprinting through a live oak grove saves time, too, but sometimes it's pleasanter to stroll.

THE WELL-CLUTTERED LIBRARY

ADVANTAGES OF BEING A SLOW READER

IT is the fashion nowadays to hire an expert to teach you to read faster. As a hobby, this has now replaced the psychiatrist.

It may be a dangerous trend. After all, nearly all books now sell for at least $9.95. If you persist in reading too fast, you may run out of book before you have got your $9.95 worth. Theoretically, fast reading is supposed to make it possible for the busy executive to wade through more material in a day; but actually, it may just make it necessary for him to read three or four times as much just to keep his new talent busy.

One of the advantages of being a slow reader is that you don't have to read everything. A lot of things aren't written to be read, and you can take advantage of them. Much of our best advertising, for instance. It is a beautiful combination of colored pictures and fine type designed to arrest the eye and impress it with the brand name.

A lot of books nowadays aren't written to be read, either. They're written to be given to friends.

IF you're a slow reader, you can relax and enjoy the pictures and quit worrying about reading through things.

Of course, nearly everybody has to read something sooner or later, and we slow readers have worked out a few techniques of our own. Suppose you have to read a speech. The first thing to do is throw away the beginning. It is probably a joke which you have already read in the *Reader's Digest*.

Next, throw away the conclusion. All the speaker is doing here is trying to find some way to quit talking.

Then, throw away all the other paragraphs except for the first sentences. Don't worry if these sentences don't make any point; there may not have been any. If you have to write a report on the speech, you can use these sentences as quotations, and the speaker won't mind what you left out. What you used will seem to him brilliant enough.

If you find that you have to read a book, try reading it from back to front. Somewhere along the way, you will find out what it's about, often in the last line, and you won't have to read the front.

Time saved from frantic reading of this material can be spent doing something else.

OF course, some things you will want to read, and there doesn't seem to be much point in hurrying through them. Fast reading is supposed to save time. Sprinting through a live oak grove saves time, too, but sometimes it's pleasanter to stroll.

Real reading has nothing to do with time. It is an art. It requires of us time in which to savor the fit of a phrase to a thought and to drift with a sentence to its unique end. It demands time in which to test the mental temper of the author and perhaps to argue with him. Who wants to speed up the reading of Conrad's *Youth,* or the Hamlet soliloquy, or *Oedipus Rex.* What's the hurry? They're here for all time.

ON BEING A BOOKISH CHILD

ONE of the blessings of being a bookish child is that you have a few years, three or four, when you can read indiscriminately and discover books which overwhelm you for the moment and stay with you in spirit all through your life, though they are books that as an adult you could not stand to read.

John Fox, Jr. used to write them. His name came up at a coffee table the other day, and it was the first time I had thought of it in years. But when I was a boy, every cultured family owned a copy of *The Trail of the Lonesome Pine,* that copy with the red cloth binding and the photo of the heroine pasted on the front, to go along with the Bible and the *Rubaiyat.* This copy testified that the people who lived there were sensitive to the new things in literature, though not approving of the "dirty" things written by people like Theodore Dreiser.

Furthermore, John Fox, Jr. was one "adult" author who might be read safely by children. The grown-ups of that time frowned on the western novels of Zane Grey as too rough and too violent. It was felt that he might lead the nation's youth into uncouth habits such as carrying their pistols in a holster instead of the hip pocket, where they belonged.

The best thing that anybody could say about Zane Grey was that none of his heroes chewed tobacco.

AT the age of eight, the best thing I had ever read was *Hamlet.* After nearly fifty years of reading, it remains the best thing. At eight, however, I had also devoured everything that I could find by both John Fox, Jr. and Zane Grey, and I have to record that I was deeply shaken by *The Little Shepherd of Kingdom Come.* At the moment, I cannot recall one thing that was in it, though I can remember the way the page looked for every scene of the Riverside paperback *Hamlet* I first read.

But the feel of *The Little Shepherd of Kingdom Come* steals back even at a mention of the title, the utter magic of the story, the tone and the music of it. It was, of course, a hopelessly sentimental book. Fox's biographer in *The Dictionary of American Biography* has noted that he "made little contribution to thought," but at eight, I didn't have much to think about anyway. I kept his book under my pillow at night while I was reading it.

The ages of six and eight are about the only time a man may weep or exult with fictional characters, and I spent this emotion on the little shepherd.

THE real readers, I think, keep going back to the books that shaped them. We of the English tongue all return to Shakespeare and Swift. The readers of my generation go back often to Conrad, Hardy, and Galsworthy because we are hungry for them. We often go back to Hemingway and Faulkner for different reasons.

I have no intention of reading ever again a line by John Fox, Jr., but I wouldn't have missed him for anything.

BEFORE THE MAST FOREVER

ANYBODY who has ever gone to an optical company for new glasses is bound to develop a dark suspicion that the test cards used in such places are in a type especially designed to fuzz up before the naked eye and to show up brightly under a lens.

The one which lay on the counter before me Wednesday was merely a white placard covered with a faint spider web of black jiggles. My eyes are not that bad. I can see the twenty-story building across the street on a clear day any time, bare-eyed. The man finally arrived with the new cheaters and tried to fit them around the crags and gullies of my skull. Suddenly, bright and clear, the sentence lay before me:

"The fourteenth of August was the day fixed upon for the sailing of the brig Pilgrim on her voyage from Boston round Cape Horn to the western coast of North America."

I asked the man how they had happened to pick on this passage for the test card, and he smiled and shrugged his shoulders. Apparently, you were supposed to look at it, not read it.

To me it was an old friend, a friend still warmly familiar though I had not looked at it in forty years.

I FIRST came upon Richard Henry Dana's *Two Years before the Mast* in a crate of old books in an attic, and I read it there, stretched out on the boards of the floor, while the dust motes danced in a bar of sunlight that slanted lower and lower through a west window.

It was in a day when sea adventure did not come decked out with a Clark Gable type for a schooner skipper and island maidens in sarongs. In that day, it was often hard to find enough interesting books, so I read *Two Years before the Mast* again and again. The book was to affect my thinking for years. It was a long time before a sea captain did not automatically wear the horns and the forked tail of The Beast. The idea that the forecastle hands were all manly, honest fellows died just as hard.

The merchant ships of that day may have had their share of skippers who were sundowners and their share of seamen who were manly and admirable. It is a good guess, though, that seamen then, as they always have, had among their number a good many thorough bums.

Those were the years when it was the literary fashion to befriend the noble seaman, and for all I know, Dana started it.

WHEN I first read *Two Years before the Mast,* it was still supposed to be a major contribution to the world's literature, so much so that it had a volume all to itself in Dr. Eliot's five-foot shelf of books while Plato, Epictetus, and Marcus Aurelius had to share a volume among them.

That notion didn't die hard. It just faded away. A dozen writers now alive could beat Dana's narrative in the whole. He had a plain style, an uncompromising honesty, and a gift for descriptive writing and narrative which showed at their best in his accounts of shipboard life but became diffused in a long account of the California hide trade.

That eye-testing card did one unpredictable thing, however. It sold another copy of *Two Years before the Mast.* I'm going to read it again.

THE WELL-CLUTTERED LIBRARY

MR. Roy Hogg, the school janitor during my boyhood out in the Lariat country, strongly disapproved of the way one room in the high school was kept — the library.

"It's all cluttered up with books," he would say severely.

Mr. Hogg was the original do-it-yourself man. He built his own house. He decorated its walls with pictures of pine trees and mountain lakes which he had painted himself, using discarded house paints. If he had needed a book he would have written one for himself.

It is true that most of the things that Mr. Hogg did ended up not fitting some place or other. He had sawed one of the rafters of his house too short, and it was braced with a length of borrowed telephone wire that he had anchored to the other rafters. Some of his pine trees were so tall that they had to be bent on the top to fit on the beaver board that he used for canvases.

If he had written a book, he would probably have left everything out except what he wanted to prove.

Still, if you don't need a book, it is clutter, and Mr. Hogg was professionally dedicated to the elimination of clutter. The sight of it offended his sensibilities.

AS a matter of fact, our library was a clutter. Some enthusiastic soul, given the order to set up a library, had merely gone out and bought a huge mass of books and dumped them into the room, all kinds of books.

As a result, it was almost impossible to locate any information on a subject you were assigned to write about, but while hunting for the information, it was impossible for you not to find a number of books that you wanted to read.

I found dozens of them this way, some fine and some trashy. While hunting for information I never found, I discovered *Kidnapped.* I wound up reading *The Mill on the Floss, The Prisoner of Zenda,* and a hopelessly sentimental novel by William J. Locke called *The Beloved Vagabond,* a book I'd never look into now but one which I relished at the time.

This was the way a boy found Melville's *Typee* and Conrad's *Youth* and John Ruskin's *King of the Golden River.* I was beguiled away from the search for useful information by Plato, Finley Peter Dunne, David Grayson, and Christopher Marlowe.

There were hundreds of such books. I ended up devoid of useful fact, but I had a fine time.

IT is probably just as well that some of the high schools I have visited lately have taken Mr. Hogg's attitude to heart. Their libraries are not cluttered. They are well organized, and the stacks are sparsely populated by sets of the *World Book,* the *Britannica* and *Americana,* and other reference works full of information that can be paraphrased with no waste of time and turned in as a theme.

The old kind of library was a risky business from the standpoint of efficiency. There was always the danger that somebody might learn to like to read.

DEIFICATION OF THE FACT

A FRIEND of ours recently did a poll on her Sunday school class. She asked how many of her class of junior-aged people were regular readers, and every hand went up.

"What do you read?" she asked, and the answers got a lot more recognizable. A few of the kids mentioned titles of books that they were reading at the moment, but when the teacher began to question the others about what they read, she got a universal answer.

"Nonfiction," they answered uniformly.

Within limits, it turned out to be true. They certainly weren't reading any fiction, but there was some suspicion about whether they were reading anything at all.

It was telling evidence of what has to be called the New Puritanism in reading, the growth of the idea that it is a sin to read for pleasure or for aesthetic satisfaction or for any other reason except the accumulation of fact.

Partly, perhaps, this has resulted from the modern classroom which insists on teaching reading as a mechanical technique rather than a grace.

I T is true that nonfiction is the cherished literary form of our time, for good reasons or bad. Recently, John Fischer, editor of *Harper's Magazine,* wrote an essay proving

that the magazine article was the official literary form of our day, though an examination of the articles in that issue of *Harper's* turned up very little literature.

The manager of a leading Dallas bookstore testifies that any reasonably good nonfiction book far outsells a good novel. For one reason, it stays on the bookstore shelves and sells over a period of a year, while a novel is dead in thirty to sixty days.

Yet, there is more fiction in some of these fact books than there was in anything William Faulkner ever wrote. We have popular studies that sell in the thousands on the man in the gray flannel suit, the suburban set, and the affluent society that were mostly researched at the bottom of a cocktail glass. The documentation of many a "nonfiction" study of sex consists of clippings from the newspapers around the country.

One is forced to conclude that the reader is not really against fiction. He is perfectly willing to read and accept fiction if he believes it to be fact.

It is the acceptance of The Fact as a unit of measurement these days which is disquieting, that and the implied restriction of The Fact on the human mind and the human spirit.

T HE deification of The Fact in our society may very well be an indication of its sickness. For one thing, beyond a few sensually ascertainable things, there really aren't any facts unmixed with either fiction or theory. There is no Fact that you can substitute for the Puritan God.

Fiction has normally been the sign of a healthy people. Myth, legend, the story of man against god and good against evil have been the delight of people whose minds were unfettered, ranging, playful, and creative. These things deal not with the here and now but with the land on the far side of heaven toward which we aspire, though it will take a little while to reach it.

It is sad to see fiction dying among us. It may be the sign of the death of a people.

THE CENTURY OF THE NOVELIST

THE other day E. M. Forster died, and this seems as good a way as any to signal the end of the Century of the Novelist.

Almost fifty years have passed now since *A Passage to India* appeared. It is hard to believe how much attention was lavished in those days on the novelists: the Forsters, the Conrads, the Wellses, the Arnold Bennetts, the Galsworthys, the Virginia Woolfs. This list does not include the Americans: the Dreisers, the Lewises, the Cathers, the young Hemingway who was just beginning, as was Dos Passos, or the young Faulkner who had barely begun to dream. It does not include the great Frenchmen that people then talked excitedly about.

It certainly does not include the Zane Greys and the Gene Stratton Porters who had applied the technique of mass production to the novel, though they certainly had to be reckoned with.

The novelist then was a personage. He was a Lion of the Hour, a great man, a star at least as important as Richard Dix or Mary Pickford.

The appearance of a new book by one of these men forty years ago stirred up as much excitement as a current appearance by a movie superstar on TV.

ALL this began and ended roughly in the hundred years that started in 1860. It is not an accident that the great day of the novelist began with the period when the English-speaking nations had committed themselves to something called universal education, which meant that every person was to be taught to read and write.

Having learned to read, a man had to read. There was nothing else then to do in your spare time.

Dickens and Thackeray were the first to cash in on this new bonanza. Fielding and Defoe had anticipated the new entertainment field in a way, but they were both merely able tract writers using a new technique. In general, the novelists flourished after 1860, though some didn't. Samuel Butler couldn't get published until after his death. The novelist was the great entertainer of the time, though if he was a Hardy he could put considerably more than mere entertainment into his works. At the last of the cycle, a Somerset Maugham could become more than a millionaire from the revenue his words earned.

Forster wasn't exactly typical. He never had to earn a living. Neither did Galsworthy. Wells could have earned a living selling snake oil if he had had to; he was completely competent. Conrad had to earn a living writing and unfortunately never did. Bennett had the instincts of a merchandiser.

It was no accident, I think, that the great day of the novelist ended with the movies and TV. People no longer have to read to kill time, and most of them never wanted to read anyway.

FINE novels were written before 1860 and fine ones have been and will be written

221

after 1960, but the status of the novelist has changed.

In a sense, things have dropped back to normal. Only in the hundred years when the novelist could use his status as entertainer to do something important has a serious writer been able to make a living at the craft. In other times, he has had a rich man as patron, independent means, or another way of making a living.

MIXING MATH AND POETRY

A YOUNG Dallas man named William Robert King has brought out a booklet of poetry on his own called *the sleepers and the shadows*.

The lowercase letters are right. All titles are now put in lowercase because of the democratization process and the need to reduce the lordly initial "The" to the level of the common man.

Mr. King has included a preface pointing out that he has deviated from James Joyce's theme in *Finnegans Wake*, which could be pictorially represented as a sine curve, and has adapted in his own work, instead, a tangential curve because it indicates a nonsequential relationship.

All this merely illustrates why poetry has so mysteriously alienated itself from me in recent years.

I have a firm grasp of math up to "x equals 2," but if you throw in "y," it gets a little shaky.

The man who starts mixing math and poetry is dealing with the two most mysterious things in human ken, to my mind, and the mixture may well blow up.

222

IN the past, it seems to me, both schools of thought recognized the volatility of this mixture and tried to avoid the universal conflagration. The college poets of my day ran from math like the plague. They felt it would taint their muse. The mathematicians, on the other hand, hooted at the poets as inexact dreamers and were careful not to let poetic ideas creep in and corrupt the tenth root of the square of pi.

My poetic appreciation, of course, was vast and included such things as Christina Rossetti's thing about the rainbow, which can probably be expressed best as "x equals y," and things like "John Gilpin's Ride," which is probably a parabola. In those days, however, we poetry lovers consoled ourselves that we knew something which the plebeian mathematicians would never understand. They understood too darn much anyway.

Some teachers, of course, always argued that the ideas of Pythagoras, in their conception and their lean line, were absolute poetry, but they never rhymed for me.

I keep living in dread that somebody one day is going to rhyme pi with lambda and that I'll miss the significance.

I HAVE looked through poet King's book. He published it himself, which is the best way of getting a publisher for poetry in these days. I find it pretty good poetry, but I just can't find the tangential curve.

It is, unfortunately, about love of various kinds. Poets seem to let themselves sag into love as a theme all the time. This is unfortunate only because I am not adequate to judge it. Nobody my age except Robert Graves is still involved in this field.

Nobody my age is much involved in math, either. Once I had the opportunity of meeting T. S. Eliot face to face, and I came away with the impression that he couldn't add any better than I could.

OH, THE WILD JOY!

A CUSTOMER who needs to settle a bet writes that it wasn't raining rain for some poet; it was raining daffodils. He wants to know whether this wasn't Wordsworth, and the answer is that it wasn't. Wordsworth was the one who wandered lonely as a cloud. What he ran into was a host of golden daffodils, though the "golden" is put in there to fill out the line. Actually, all daffodils are the same insipid yellow.

The one who wrote "It isn't raining rain for me, / It's raining daffodils" was a character named Robert Loveman who was even more nutty. Poets notoriously have a hard time saying anything definite. After all, it might not rhyme. Loveman takes the cake. It isn't raining rain to him; it's raining daffodils. It isn't raining rain to him but fields of clover bloom. It isn't raining rain to him; it's raining violets. All this in two short stanzas.

"Make up your mind," the lover of poetry is finally bound to say. "Paper costs money."

Loveman's poem belongs to the Gee-Isn't-Nature-Wonderful-and-Doesn't-Cost-Anything School. Some pretty fine poets and highly intelligent men have fallen for this guff. Horace, for instance, knew better.

A GAIN, there is William Butler Yeats. It is well to note that he only wrote about how he yearned to go to the Lake Isle of Innisfree; he didn't go there. The tip-off to how much he knew about nature was the nine bean rows he was going to have, hardly enough to provide forage even for a garret-trained poet.

It is my observation that poets and other men discover the joys of nature and the quiet life when they begin to age and their bodies shrivel and they get bird-legged and a bowl of cornflakes suffices for what once required a steak.

Yeats's bee-loud glade would have bored him stiff after the first week if he had gone out there young enough to hear the bees.

Nature isn't so beautiful sometimes to people who have to fight her; you have to be able to take her on your own terms.

T HE nature poets are not my pet peeve. After all, a smattering of daffodils, while not a host and not golden, is all right.

Of all the schools of poetry, the Oh-the-Wild-Joy-of-Living School seems to me the farthest from the land of the living. Unfortunately, this thing was set in motion by Robert Browning. You can stand him when he writes, "Oh, the wild joys of living," though you may fear that he is going to pull a belly muscle while leaping from apostrophe to apostrophe.

Here comes somebody like Theodosia Garrison, though, trilling, "I laughed for very joy of life/Oh, thrilling hands! Oh, happy heart!"

You just get embarrassed for the people. They should have stopped before that last drink.

READING YOUR OWN AUTOBIOGRAPHY

I F you want to get a real shock out of realizing your advanced age, look down some morning and discover that you have a first American edition of *Bambi*.

This happened the other day. The books had been piled around the house so that the shelves could be painted, and on top of one stack was this volume bound in green cloth. It turned out to be the *Bambi* first printed in America.

Now, I ought to be considerably younger than *Bambi*. It seems to belong to the Middle Ages. It has been Disneyized until it has something of the feel of Rumpelstiltskin. Nevertheless, here was this book, and I remember buying it, and I wasn't any infant either. The title page says it was in 1928.

This led to a reflection that out of a couple of thousand books, more or less, accumulated over a lifetime, a man can read his own autobiography.

Every volume has a story that is part of the owner's life.

THIS first edition of *South Wind*, for instance, I got for a song from a treasured college friend in 1929 who was reduced in one month from plenty to penury. This copy of *Finnegans Wake* belongs with an old Monterrey vacation. The days that year were full of sunny showers, and there was plenty of time to lie on a bed in the old Gran Ancira and puzzle out Joyce's private language.

Here is Spengler's book on the decline of the West. As an earnest young man, I spent one autumn mastering it only to discover that nobody would then listen to me explain it, not even my favorite uncle.

Here is a book of Robert Louis Stevenson's short stories given to me by an English professor along with a stern lecture about Stevenson's weaknesses. During a dismal and hopeless year, I discovered James Thurber's *My Life and Hard Times*. It kept me sane.

I bought "Bambi" out of carefully saved nickels and dimes on the recommendation of a high school English teacher.

SHE was a pretty girl with a turned-up nose and freckles, and all the boys in high school that year suddenly discovered an interest in American literature that lasted clear through to the first six-weeks exam. The girls were less interested in "Thanatopsis" and "The Marshes of Glynn."

I read *Bambi* in a night that summer. The high plains' twilights lasted long and darkened slowly into soundless nights. Even the radio didn't work very well. One read on and on while the minutes of the night dripped quietly and slowly into the lower sands, usually until morning began to break.

It was a good time with a whole world still waiting.

TAMING THE ENGLISH LANGUAGE

Grammar is a bridle by which we try to rein the English language into a proper course, but the language has never behaved well in a bridle.
It is an impulsive, powerful beast which sometimes takes charge and runs right on through to the end of the sentence.

TAMING THE ENGLISH LANGUAGE

CONTROLLING THE COMMA

"THAT Paul Crume must be a real 'rugged' individualist," writes a North Texas reader. "He leaves commas out of where they are taught to be absolutely required — and puts them in where he damn well pleases."

I thank my North Texas friend for this expression of high admiration.

It took several years to master the comma, but by now I have got it pretty well cowed. A great many people think that all dogs and all commas behave alike. Actually, each comma is an individual and is inclined to do willfully whatever it wants unless it is controlled. Furthermore, you can teach a comma to do a lot of tricks besides those listed in the grammars if you catch it young and train it intelligently.

Most people never learn this, but I learned it early. Now, when I say "frog," a comma better sit up and beg.

This reader's letter indicates that he has allowed himself to be "taught" instead of grabbing control of the comma. It is a common tactical error.

ACTUALLY, commas are rather docile, but they are not as docile as most English teachers say. At any moment, one of them is likely to rear up and do something in a sentence that you hadn't expected. You can control them fairly easily.

The semicolon is a different breed of animal. You would be well advised not to get caught in the same sentence with one unless you have a whip. I have occasionally received spectacular results with a semicolon, but they are treacherous and unreliable. Sometimes they won't perform at all for you, and you have to throw them out.

In contrast, people have often said my work with commas has been of circus quality.

Most people never master punctuation because they get scared of these marks the minute they see them. No matter how ferocious punctuation looks, never fear. Wade into the sentence. Throw commas, semicolons, colons, and periods in all directions. Establish your authority.

If you wade right into them, these punctuation marks will never bite.

FOR the person who has not learned to train punctuation marks to do his bidding, there are a few simple rules of composition which will help him to begin.

When you are writing something and the typewriter stops, put in a period. You are probably going to start off in a different direction or on a new subject entirely, and you don't want to be trailing anything behind you.

If you haven't quite stopped when the typewriter does, put in a comma. It will permit you to turn 360 degrees and still not come unglued.

Never use a semicolon. You'll find yourself rewriting the whole sentence so the semicolon will fit in.

Never use an exclamation mark. It isn't really that important.

FROM CAPITAL "I" TO LITTLE "YOU"

A LADY was saying the other day that she found it fascinating that the monks of the Middle Ages invented lowercase letters, the little letters, the noncapitals.

It is fascinating and also a commentary on the slow progress of the human race. Humanity behaved about writing about like children do. In the beginning, few people could write, and anything written had to be very important. It was therefore written in big letters.

The young and ancient children of this world still tend to put what they think is important in big letters. A first-grader will write about everything in capitals. When he becomes a third-grader, he has learned that "dog" is lowercase but "Mama" is still uppercase.

This process goes on all through life.

For instance, when I write about myself, I use a big capital "I," but when I write about "you," you are in lowercase.

A MAN named Oscar Ogg wrote a book about twenty years ago called *The 26 Letters* which deals with all this. He implied that Saint Patrick of Ireland had a lot to do with developing small letters. I doubt this. Saint Patrick may have been guilty of many things, but a man who could scare all the snakes off one island couldn't have been all that bad.

Saint Pat, of course, was captured by the Romans in Gaul and exiled for a few years in Ireland, where he guarded sheep. Even at that time, apparently, you had to guard things in Ireland. When he got back to the Continent, he became a monk and then a bishop. All during his studies, he was determined to return to Ireland and do something to help the condition of the Irish, which is what people have been trying to do ever since.

While he was studying, a revolution was going on in the monasteries which used monk copyists. Too many people were learning to read and demanding books. Any publisher will force-feed his presses if he thinks he can make money. There is no telling how many monks just wore out or how many worn-out ones were swapped off to some smaller monastery.

Meanwhile, they were inventing a kind of shorthand version of the capital letters to be used in the body of a paragraph or sentence. This was the beginning of lowercase, or little, letters.

They say that Saint Patrick took this idea back to Ireland when he Christianized a whole people as much as it has ever been Christianized.

The Irish were supposed to have developed a pure little letter style because they were isolated from the ideas of the Continent and had only to defend themselves against druids, fellow Irishmen, and an occasional troop of British cavalry.

I DON'T know about all this. Frankly, I think little letters developed from the slothfulness of the medieval monks, who had the world's best union to date. It covered everything from the cradle to the grave except marital adventures.

"Uppercase" and "lowercase" came in with the printers, of course. The case on the upper rack of a typesetter's work rack contained the capitals. The lower case contained the little letters.

This is capital "I" in big letters bidding little "you" in lowercase good morning.

ON FOOT'S AND FEET'S

A READER has raised the question of why people in print are always confusing their "foot's" with their "feet's."

"'Foot' is singular," he declares stoutly. "'Feet' is plural. Yet, we see in print all the time something like this: 'She is five foot two inches.' . . . If 'foot' here is correct, then why not 'five foot two inch?'"

"I don't understand it . . ."

This is the proper attitude to take toward the English language. It is beyond all understanding.

The odds are that nobody understands the why of any particular bit of English usage, but there is sound reason for it, nevertheless. It is illogical, that is why.

English usage begins when the people begin using a word or a phrase a certain way. After a hundred years or so, an expert comes along and writes a book proving that you have to say it that way.

THE proper form of our friend's sentence, of course, is, "She is five feet, three inches." But it would be right to say, "She is a five-foot three-inch blonde."

This use of a number with a singular noun to form a compound adjective is supposed to be one of the few ways you can use a singular noun in a plural sense, but that shows how much the grammarians know about it. People use singular nouns in a plural sense all the time.

It is proper to write "five-foot" and "three-inch" only if they present a unit idea. "Foot" and "inch" in this case merely describe what the numbers are about. If the unit sense isn't strong, you would use a possessive. You can't do it with a blonde, but you can write "a two weeks' vacation" or "a three years' leave of absence." No hyphen here.

The person who wishes to use English well will attempt always to be as illogical as possible. Logic will inevitably betray you into the dangling participle or something.

OUT in the country where speakers are often more interested in sense than in grammar, the singular noun has often been used as a plural. If you've ever asked a West Texan the distance to some place, he may very well have said, "It's about four mile down the road."

More often than not, this kind of plural indicates an expert in some field. If a hog buyer looks at an animal and says, "It'll weigh about

349 pound," you can bet that the animal will weigh just that, give a pound or two.

Still, the usage is not sanctioned. It is suitable only for hogs and country miles.

It is illogical enough that some expert on the language may write a book one day proving that it is correct.

THE TWIN SHOALS OF "WHO" AND "WHOM"

CERTAIN captious people have lately berated us because we newspaper people have not been meticulous in our use of "who" and "whom." We can only sadly reply that this seems to be the human estate.

A human being starts out every morning facing dangers he cannot dream of; and if he could dream of them, he would quail and run back home. One of the greatest dangers is the letter he was going to mail for his wife. He may remember everything else on earth that he was obligated to do, but four days later he will be hearing his wife tell a relative over long distance, "But I mailed you a letter four days ago." In such a circumstance, playing the craven not only may be excused but may be necessary.

The last-minute utility bill that you took to town to get in before the deadline is another great danger. So is the friend for whom you were going to speak a good word at the employment agency.

To most human beings, however, there is no hazard like the twin shoals of "who" and "whom." You are almost bound to run aground on one or the other.

THEORETICALLY, the problem is easy. "Whom" is always an object, or an accusative, or whatever you call that grammatical case that takes the rap. "Whom" always is beaten upon, but "who" does the beating.

But, when you construct a good lordly sentence about persons against whom evil shall not prevail, who nevertheless are subject to assault from whoever shall wish them harm, but who manage to win out by hook or crook, those whom the lawyers worship — well, when you construct a sentence like this, you have an awful lot of objects in there. When the average person is berated for getting tangled up in this kind of grammar, he gets indignant.

"Whom is casting a stone at who?" he demands.

The fact is that three-fourths of the English-speaking peoples and about 90 percent of all writers get a queasy stomach when confronted by "who" and "whom."

I know one talented writer, now retired, who confesses that he spent fifty years at a typewriter avoiding situations where he would have to choose between "who" and "whom."

IT seems to me that all through the centuries, the main worry of the human race has not been typhus, or war, or the wrath of the gods. So far as I can remember, it has been grammar and punctuation. From his first school day, the child starts out confused about it. He may end up one of those masterful types who regard it as unimportant that they know grammar, but he'll think it scandalous if his secretary doesn't.

To some people, the so-called correct usage of the language is more important than whether

229

their bankbooks balance. Obviously, there is something wrong with their sense of values.

COUPLES

A MAN from Kilgore, Texas, has taken exception to this writer's recent reference to "a couple of days."

". . . With reference to the correct use of the word 'couple,' " he writes, "I was taught that it should never be used as a noun unless it referred to two of opposite sex. Instead of saying, 'a couple of days,' it should be, 'two days.' In one of your recent columns, you made use of the word several times when not referring to two things of different sex."

Here is obviously a man who has devoted some study to the use of "couple," and deserves an answer. Fortunately, I am an expert on nothing — especially the opposite sex, which seems to be at least half the meaning of the Kilgore gentleman's "couple."

All I know is that the construction, "a couple of hamburgers," was very well known to Holy Writ — at least, Holy Writ as it was accepted by the King James Bible translators as early as 1611.

IN the sad biblical story of Tamar, who was desired by Amnon, for instance, you will remember that Amnon pretended to be sick abed; and when his father, David, the king, came to visit him, Amnon asked that Tamar be sent so that she could "make me a couple of cakes in my sight, that I may eat at her hand."

In this same book of Second Samuel, there is a reference to Ziba, the servant of Mephibosheth, who met King David on a hill during the Absalomic rebellion "with a couple of asses saddled."

These two asses may very well have been things of different sex, but it is hard to see how the cakes that Tamar made were.

There is a similar use of "couple" in Judges, and such secular authors as Shakespeare and Francis Bacon were given to the usage on occasion, Shakespeare especially. As a poet, he was probably instinctively against reducing the language to monosyllables like "two."

All this proves nothing except that the makers of the King James Version would have known how many were a "couple of hamburgers."

And for some odd reason, the King James translators have to this day been able to write better even than some of the present college graduating class.

LIKE most of us, our Kilgore friend is probably still subconsciously under the influence of several generations of maiden English teachers who used to walk the earth like Amazons with a bow constantly drawn for obscure beasts like "ain't" and "he done it."

These were maiden ladies of very strong minds. They pruned American language up. They made Americans aware that "gosh all hemlock" was not noble language. They made the comma blunder as extinct as typhoid.

The only trouble was that what they were strongest-minded about very often wasn't true.

As a result, any character who can draft a clear memo is persuaded that that is the end of composition and that literature ought to be revised in that direction.

THE BOOK WILL OUT

A CORRESPONDENT asked how much grammar a man needs to know to write a book. This is hard to answer in terms of pecks or pounds. Any grammar that a man knows may turn out to be useful, but he needs to know really very little if he can write a book.

Some writers whom I know are scared to death of grammar and will spend a lot of time and effort writing around a situation that requires them to decide between "who" and "whom." Generally, they have an innate logic at keeping such things as tenses and numbers consistent. They also know fifteen or twenty simple principles of punctuation, but they would be hard put at any moment to list them.

Other writers are hairsplitters in the logic of grammar but never let this interfere with their writing.

G RAMMAR is a bridle by which we try to rein the English language into a proper course, but the language has never behaved well in a bridle.

It is an impulsive, powerful beast which sometimes takes charge and runs right on through to the end of the sentence.

It is not as precise a language as some, but it is capable of expressing more tones and kinds of meaning than most. It can convey more than the meaning we talk about when we say it makes sense. Its syllables and its old root words are colored by connotations which can stir the hidden pools of hate or pleasure. There can be a kind of mnemonic meaning in its rhythms.

The man who is writing a book is not trying to write a sentence that will parse. He is trying to arouse in another person a special meaning and feeling for his experience. Consequently, Nobel Prize winners and greatly esteemed critics do not hesitate to distort syntax and grammar out of all reasonable shape if it serves their purposes.

People have gone to psychiatrists after trying to parse some of William Faulkner's literature.

I DOUBT if grammar ever kept a book from being written. The book, like murder, will out. Both come from the visceral instincts of man.

All that a man needs to have to write a book is to have a book to write, and more people have books in them than is suspected. Some excellent books are always coming from the most unexpected people, and the few bad books are always coming from people who ought to know better. Some books by semi-illiterate people are even saved by collaborators who have enough sense to keep the language and the grammar of the creator.

Probably the best thing to do is to sit down at the typewriter, give the old English language its head, and see what kind of grammar comes out.

HANDLING A FIGURE OF SPEECH

A FRIEND has come up with a highly technical question of grammar. "When," he asks, "does a simile turn into a metaphor?" It is a good question and hard to answer because, in my experience, it will change in a flash right there on the paper before your eyes. It is very hard to keep a simile snubbed down even after you have roped it.

It is just one of the hazards of trying to use the English language. It is less than possible to speak and write without colliding somewhere with a figure of speech. As you can see, in that "less than possible," we have already run head on into a litotes. The average wanderer in the jungle of English goes blithely on his way unaware that there are beasts like brachylogues and antitheses crouched in the underbrush. It takes a sharp eye and a ready weapon to bag one in passing.

Don't start, but I do believe that in that "jungle" we have spotted a species of metaphor, and if we don't get off this fine figurative paragraph, we sooner or later will have to wrestle a bull allegory.

A MAN is likely to commit a figure of speech any time that he turns around. If he feels good while shaving in the morning and lifts his voice to sing, "O'er these high prison walls I would fly," he has committed not only a contraction but a syncope, a mild form of syncope, admittedly, but still a syncope. If he refers to the bathroom as the little boy's room, he is marked down for a euphemism.

If he is an old Navy man and remarks, "Rank has its privileges," he is guilty on the face of it of metonymy. What he meant to say was that an officer of high rank has privileges not granted to mortal men. Maybe he attributes a wisecrack to his favorite football tackle. He is then guilty of personification, which is the attributing of human qualities to inanimate objects.

A young woman who exclaims, "Heaven! Protect us working girls," is guilty of an apostrophe and wishful thinking besides.

ALMOST everybody remembers one figure of speech from his freshman high school English. He remembers that the bee buzzes. He knows that this is onomatopoeia, even if he can't remember the name at the moment. He also remembers that "Waste water washes, and tall ships founder, and deep death waits" is one of the best examples of another, whether he knows it is alliteration or not.

Most of us can look straight at the TV while a rancher in a range war mentions that he has hired twenty guns and not even know that we have come up on a synecdoche.

Probably the best way to handle figures of speech is not to worry about them. If you have to know a simile from a metaphor, you can always remember that "Mighty Lak a Rose" is a simile. "The Rose of Tralee" is a metaphor.

ROSES AND BIRDS IN THE UNDERBRUSH

IN English poetry, you will find dozens of pages about roses but not one that I know of about Venus's flytrap, a far more useful flower even if its perfume is a little carrion.

Much of the English poetry about roses is filled with an air of gentle sadness. It is not affirmative like Gertrude Stein's statement that "a rose is a rose is a rose."

They tell us that the fairest rose at last withers. They point out that you cannot have a rose without thorns, though some poets point out that no hand gets a thorn that didn't try to pick a rose. The sweetest rose must fade. The rose perishes; the thorns endure. The days of wine and roses don't last long. And other banal and obvious comments.

Where blow the roses of yesteryear?

Poets are the creatures most responsible for

the prolixity of roses in the underbrush of English literature. A poet mostly stays inside. He does not know the names of many flowers, and when he needs the name of a flower to complete a line, he drops in a rose.

He does not walk outside and say to a horticulturist, "I am writing an immortal line of poetry, and I need the name of a flower to put into it." The horticulturist might suggest the speckled begonia. This won't do. "I gave my love a speckled begonia" does not sound like poetry, although it ought to.

After all, the most speckled begonia must also die.

The rose now has been used so often that there is no human feeling left in the name. The rose is no longer poetry; it is a symbol of poetry.

Move over to the bird kingdom, you find that the poets have been doing the same thing to the nightingale and the lark. If you read "Hark, the nightingale," you are forewarned that you are going to run into a lot of classical allusions or some unrequited swain. You never read "Hark, hark, the screech owl," though anybody who has been out at night in the countryside can tell you that you are more likely to hear a screech owl than a nightingale.

And take a look at the common turkey buzzard. He is a lot more of "bird that never wert" than Shelley's lark.

STALKING THE VIABLE ALTERNATIVE

IT says here that a Texas senator has been talking with the French about the energy crisis, and he says they are all hunting for Viable Alternatives.

They had better watch out. So many people nowadays are hunting the Viable Alternative that it may become an endangered species.

They should remember what happened to At This Point in Time. Until the Watergate hearings this was an exotic animal known only to the powerful and privileged in Washington. When its existence became known, everybody took after it, and within a few months, it had been shot out of the language.

Before that, there was the Two-horned Dilemma. People were always being caught between its horns. As a result they have bred into existence a polled variety of dilemma. This is a dilemma that doesn't have any horns at all and is the kind of dilemma that faces the world today. You don't know how to dodge it.

It might be wise just to let wild things like the Viable Alternative run at large and not try to harness them to human uses.

THE Viable Alternative seems to be a very rare and secretive creature. At least, the people in government have been looking for a Viable Alternative for months, and they haven't found one yet.

A well-traveled friend of mine, Frank X. Tolbert, thinks he knew one once in the Rio Grande Valley. He was a wetback, and his name was Jose Viable y Alternative, but this is not a definitive sighting. Mr. Tolbert knows a million characters, some one-legged, some two-legged, and some centipedes. If this is a member of the family of Alternative, it has to have two legs. It has to be either or. If it had more than two legs, it would have to be just a Plover-dull Possibility. Furthermore, the feet on these two legs have to be pointed in different directions, or you don't have an

Alternative. If they were pointed, as normally, in the same direction, you would have a Mandate.

All the clues, as you can see, point to a Viable Alternative that is either ape or bird. I lean toward the bird theory, although it is true that many Homo Sapiens in the Washington area can run in two directions at once. The bird, however, could probably travel better sidewise, which is the way most Viable Alternatives work.

Great apes like Man have an instinct against progressing sidewise; they had rather go backward.

I BELIEVE that this bird not only has feet which run in different directions but also has eyes in the back of its head, because it is always operating from hindsight. If you object that an Alternative that runs off in two directions at once is not very Viable, so be it. That is the nature of Alternatives. That is the way the Good Lord made them.

We can only hope that while hunting down the Viable Alternatives, the Texas senator and his friends hold their fire and do not accidentally shoot down a genuine Prong-horned Dilemma or a lurking Point in Time. Probably we ought just to try to capture some Viable Alternatives. We could study them scientifically and find out how they work.

THE GOBBLEDYGOOK CRISIS

A BUNCH of English teachers got together recently at the University of California and held a Conference on Public Doublespeak. They declared that there is a gobbledygook crisis.

They properly attacked the Pentagon's tendency to call a shovel a "combat emplacement displacer" and to name an invasion as an "incursion." They deplored the misuse of language by politicians, the military brass, advertisers, and newspapermen to hide the truth.

Of course, hiding the truth is what most human beings want to do. Some of us are just better at it than others.

Any right-thinking man, however, is disgusted with the perversion of language. (That is hiding the truth, too, because any right-thinking man is disgusted only when he isn't doing the perverting.)

But, how about the contribution of the English teachers themselves to gobbledygook? It seems to me that they invented the stuff.

They didn't coin "gobbledygook," of course. That was done by an old plain-speaking San Antonio man named Maury Maverick, who was a politician besides.

It seems to me that the English teachers have put some of the best gobble into the gook.

THEY invented, for instance, the Active Periphrastic, which has haunted me for years. Sometimes I wake suddenly out of sleep in the morning saying, "What in the devil is the Active Periphrastic?" Periphrasis obviously is the act of writing or speaking around a subject rather than declaring it, but why is a periphrasis either active or passive? Worrying about problems like this is what keeps a man alive beyond his time.

The English teachers have put a little more gobble into the gooks. Take any ordinary verb like "guess." Your teacher will tell you in any given instance that it is in the indicative, the imperative, or the subjunctive mood. Why? It's the same word. I have moods; the word doesn't. If I put it down here on paper and it works, I really don't care how it feels.

"Noun" means "name," so why do we call it a noun, and "verb" means "word," so why do we call it a verb?

THE English teachers have not got to the heart of the matter, which is logical validity. All life, just about, consists of manipulating logical fallacies in such a way that you can avoid telling the exact truth without telling a lie.

If you want to use the language honestly, you can either make a statement, and make it flat out, or use the words to build an image. This is about all that language can do. And if the image you build with language is great enough, it becomes great poetry, and people love it more than any flat statement you will ever make.

This is probably because it will have avoided telling the exact truth.

If you go around making flat statements, your friends may not like you very much, and you may have to go back to gobbledygook.

NULL AND VOID

A CUSTOMER is a little hacked at the expression "null and void." He asks whether anything can ever be null without being void, and vice versa. If one stretched the imagination almost to the breaking point, it could; but it isn't likely. "Null and void" is lawyer's gibberish.

At its Latin root, "null" simply means "nothing," while "void" means "empty." These are not necessarily the same thing. The great void of space, for instance, the abysmal emptiness between stars and planets, is not a null. The void here is a nothing that is something. Generally, however, when a man says something is null and void, he means, "No good, no good, confound it, no good."

The human psyche seems to need to say the same thing twice in a single phrase. Once, out in the Lariat country, the first grade teacher asked the Woodward young'un whether his older brother was absent.

"Yes, ma'am," replied Tim. "He's absent, and he ain't here."

This got the situation stated to Tim's satisfaction, and the teacher had both her term and its definition in one place.

LANGUAGE is made up not only of words and rules and logic but of the basic insecurities of the human beings who use it.

The human being seems to feel, for instance, that one should never use one word when three or four will do. How else would you fill the nulls and voids in the average conversation? There is the common anxiety, also, that you have not been understood. I have an acquaintance, for instance, a pleasant and interesting man, who ends every sentence with, "You hear?" He converses mostly by repeating the same statement over and over and demanding each time, "You hear?" In time, a listener is bound to get the word.

The human being also is very chary of making a flat-out statement. He might not be right, and it would expose him to ridicule. I once knew a writer, a very gifted one, who could never make so direct a statement as "The world is round." In very complex sentences, he always started out by pointing out that it wasn't flat. It wasn't oval. It wasn't square or triangular. It wasn't the shape of a trapezoid or parallelogram. It wasn't a cone. By elimination and without ever having committed himself directly, he stated the world was round.

"Null and void" is merely a phrase which takes care of all possibilities in a legal matter, so that the appeals court can't pick a hole in it.

THE language is full of phrases which are a double statement of one thing. "Hue and cry" is one that crops up in the newspapers when any kind of argument breaks out. It is a fair guess that most of us wouldn't know what a "hue" was if it ran by on all four feet.

From its root, a "hue" is only a yell, and while it may not be the same as a cry, the hues and cries that come from the street all sound very much alike.

THE SEMICOLON SYNDROME

ANYBODY having dire feelings about the future of these United States always refers to himself as "the thinking few." Well, there are some of us who feel that the real crisis shaping up is not high taxes or global conflict but a waning interest in the philosophy of the semicolon, which must put us among the fewest of the thinking few.

We are not worried about the semicolon per se. It is merely a symbol, though a symbol which seems to terrify many writers. We are worried about the disappearance of an intellectual temper, a mental stance from which to view life. The cast of a man's mind is betrayed by the punctuation marks he uses.

Take the man, for instance, who knows instantly what he wants to say. He puts it down in quick, short sentences and slaps a period forcefully at the end of each. That's it. Period. No reservations or qualifications. No gradations in the valuing of ideas. Such men are supposed to speak in haste and repent at leisure, though, in truth, most of us do not have enough leisure in which to repent.

The man who is a compulsive user of dashes is a special case of this. He proceeds by short, swift hops, pausing always behind one clump of ideas until he perceives that the way is clear to another.

AT the other end of the punctuation spectrum, there is the writer of tourist sentences. Having stepped off toward his sentence, he quickly finds an unsuspected bypath, ambles leisurely along it describing in detail all ramifications, comes finally to a cloverleaf of relative phrases and crosses over his main track on the way to still another interesting if divergent idea, explores it at length until, after another maze of circular phrases, here at the end of the sentence the idea comes. The tourist thinker rarely has any need to repent. Any problem that he might be addressing has disappeared somewhere on his route along with most of his readers.

We are not considering here the literary artist. His words may drop as beautifully as Chopin notes, his phrases move about as gracefully as the measure of a waltz, or march, if he wishes, like Sousa. There are not enough of him to affect the destiny of the Republic. We are talking here about the common, ordinary thinking few.

Among the ordinary thinking few who write letters to the newspapers the semicolon man has all but disappeared.

IT is a pity. The man devoted to the semicolon seems always to have provided the intellectual balance our country has needed. He is direct but cautious, clear but indefinite. As its appearance indicates, the semicolon is halfway between the period, or full stop, and the comma, or half-stop. The semicolon user is always aware that his first clause may turn out to be wholly true, or it may require the second clause. His semicolon can then be read all through the ages as either a full stop or a half-one as the current truth demands.

Such a sentence has the quality which has permitted the U.S. Constitution to live all these years. It is precisely vague. This is the only way an eternal truth can be stated.

THE HUMAN CONDITION

FORWARD PROGRESS
SCIENCE BREAKTHROUGH
THE HUMAN CONDITION
TO TOUCH AN ANGEL

FORWARD PROGRESS

Science and its handmaiden, invention, have . . . all but created a world in which a lifetime is hardly enough for a man to keep up with what he knows.

FORWARD PROGRESS

KEEPING UP WITH WHAT WE KNOW

GREAT-AUNT Martha's youngest boy, the one called Isaac, was an inventor. As she liked to say, he always had been a little queer since the day he was dropped on his head as a baby, and his mechanical meddling with the divinely ordered universe caused her much anxiety.

For one thing, Ike put a float in the windmill water tank. With the help of a connecting line and some plowshares as weights on the end of the wooden windmill lever, he rigged the windmill so it would turn itself on when the water got low. Aunt Martha was aghast. She grieved over Ike. She ranted at him to get himself to church and, through prayer, purge himself of the Old Scratch.

"If the Lord," said Aunt Martha, "had meant for a windmill to turn itself on, He would have created a way Hisself."

Besides, she pointed out, all mechanical things eventually blow up, and they would be helpless without the windmill.

Aunt Martha held that no good was going to come of all this inventing, and time may be proving her right.

FOR science and its handmaiden, invention, have even now all but created a world in which a lifetime is hardly enough for a man to keep up with what he knows.

It is possible to argue that the world was better when man had plenty of time to think about things he didn't know. He had time, for instance, properly to propitiate the gods and to worry about shaping himself in their image. He had time to remember his dead fondly all the days of his life and time to hope for his children. He had time to muse upon the miracle of a sprouting seed and time earnestly to rejoice at a harvest.

On a warm June night, there were not only fireflies in the creek bottom but also the mystery of them and the poetry of the shadowed hills. All these things man did not know, but they were infinitely more worth thinking about than the things he knows now.

Of course, if man then lived deeply, he also lived hard. He expected only food, shelter, and the pleasures of the family fire.

SOME day computers may take up the harrowing job of remembering all that we know, so that man himself may enjoy the air-conditioned plenty which he has created and still have time to sense and ponder the universe which he knows for so short a time. The outlook is not good, though. Science seems to be creating things faster than it can remember them.

A Bell Telephone man, for instance, is creating electronic circuits which act like nerve networks. He intends to find out how the brain thinks.

When he has got the whole human brain reproduced, however, and gives it the job of thinking, he is going to find out it won't work.

Those of us who have tried to think found that out a long time ago.

THE SINGLE-MINDED ELEVATOR

AMONG the old saws cherished by the human race is one which says that time and circumstances may change but that human nature never does. This may have been true before automatic elevators.

There is evidence that the automatic elevator is changing human behavior in a radical way. The only way to keep the door of a do-it-yourself, blast-off type elevator from closing on you is to put your hand against a door edge. You have probably noticed that a number of citizens who have to stand the monsters off constantly never pass through any door now without putting a hand on the doorjamb.

It used to be that everybody walked through a door leisurely. Now, if you'll watch, you will see that a fair percentage of our people wait for a second and then jump.

Man is slowly accommodating himself to this sort of thing, but he is at the

same time losing the sense of whether he is up or down.

PERSONALLY, I have never much cared for the automatic elevator. I always liked the old-fashioned birdcage kind where you could see from minute to minute whether you were trapped between floors. These were run by old-fashioned Negro gentlemen like my friend Ben. Every once in a while you could tap him on the shoulder and ask whether you were moving.

The modern push-button elevator is a tireless, silent operator. It has a mind of its own. Just about the time you think you have mastered it and can make it take you where you wish, it takes off in a different direction with an air that says, "There is something that I forgot to do yesterday." Until the automatic elevator catches up with the requests that have been made of it in the last week or so, you move from floor to floor where you have no intention of going. Most of the time nobody gets on the elevator. It, nevertheless, courteously opens the door and holds it ready to decapitate someone. The floors between the requests fed into an automatic elevator several hours before are known as the modern Horse Latitudes.

Basically, the push-button elevator is a way of transferring all the labor to the customer. As one terribly bitter supermarket operator observed to me recently, "We refine and refine all these operations until the customer does all the work except making change. Then we give him some trading stamps and send him along."

This is the way of American progress, however. You do away with a lowly paid operator and substitute a high-priced maintenance man, and the American dream goes up at least another 98 cents.

FOR the few other nostalgic souls who like company in an elevator, I have drawn up some rules, based on experience, to handle the modern elevator.

When you step into an elevator, glare insolently at the edge of the door. This disconcerts the electric eye and causes the elevator to forget something else that it ought to have done yesterday.

Immediately that you are in, push the "door open" button. Also quickly push the buttons for one floor up and one floor down. These modern elevators are supposed to be plenty quick on the thinking, but you'll find they can't handle a complex signal any better than a fourth-string tackle.

If you have only three or four floors to go, take the stairs.

BACK TO THE HOG BRISTLE

AT the risk of setting back progress fifty years, I would like to observe that it went hog-wild in developing the nylon toothbrush bristle.

This is not a snap decision. I have thought about it a lot. The docs all say to brush your teeth up and down, not across, but I always do it both ways because I believe in being safe. I know that you brush up and down in the United States; but I might travel abroad some place where the only effective way is to brush across, and I might utterly ruin my teeth before I remembered to change over.

It is sad to have to relate that the nylon bristle does not work very well either way. If you brush vigorously across, it flips toothpaste on the mirror; and with our present modern, plastic toothpaste, you often have to get a

plastic solvent to remove it along with your transferred bad breath.

If you brush up and down, the bristles come off between your teeth; and when you flash that old Pepsodent smile into the mirror, it looks as if a moustache was poking itself out from behind your grinders.

ADMITTEDLY, my teeth have been worn very sharp on the edges by gnawing on the occasional bones thrown off by the American affluent society, but I never had any trouble with old-fashioned, unimproved bristles.

Having decided to support progress to the limit of my ability, I decided to brush with the nylon bristles in a kind of circular motion, across and down on the crevices of the teeth. This saved the mirror, but created a kind of circular whirlpool of toothpaste spray. We are now repainting the walls of our bathroom. It is a little difficult because our toothpaste is a modern brand that guarantees to keep anything from staining your teeth, and it keeps kicking the new paint off the spots where the toothpaste spattered. Our present plans are to infect each toothpaste spot with virulent dental caries and then fill.

Also, after the rotary treatment with the nylon bristles, my mouth bled most of the day. Late in the afternoon, I checked it out in a mirror and found half a dozen nylon bristles stuck in my tongue like thistles.

It was the only legitimate fuzzy mouth I've ever had.

AT the moment, I have gone back to the slippery elm toothbrush. This is a small live switch of elm, one end of which is chewed into fibers of bristlelike size. You grasp the other end of this switch and firmly rub your teeth until something squeaks. The slippery elm switch is best used with Honest or Garrett snuff but will work with salt.

My hope is that the toothbrush makers eventually will go back to the hog bristle they once used. Something about the fine swill that it was soaked in while it was growing has given this bristle a toughness and a flexibility that modern swill-less fabrication apparently does not understand.

THE SATISFACTIONS OF SLOW TRAVEL

IF Amtrak is ever going to succeed, it will have to change its policies and slow down its trains.

Some people say that the trains already arrive three or four hours late, but a late train and a slow train are two different things. To please the traveling public, a train will have to be predictably slow. The main point in traveling, after all, is to get yourself into a situation where you cannot possibly do any work. A man enjoys travel when he knows that for exactly three days and four hours, or whatever other time, he is forced to remain idle.

People tend now to think that the point in travel is to get to some place. Actually, the point is in not getting there, or at least getting there as late as possible.

The human being dearly loves to get into a situation where he is forced not to work.

He can also properly take satisfaction on a slow train in the knowledge that traveling is broadening, though nobody yet has explained exactly why.

Travel is usually pleasant in inverse ratio to the speed.

THE best of all forms of travel was probably the steamship. It traveled as fast as possible, which wasn't much. A man embarking on an ocean voyage could say, "Boy, what a waste of time. For three weeks I won't be able to hit a lick. Where is the shuffleboard court?"

He then spent three weeks in a comfortable stateroom with three regular meals of delicate viands, as they used to say, and a promenade deck where he could watch pretty women taking their daily walk. He also had plenty of time to watch the whales and porpoises and ponder the ironies of human existence.

Next to the steamship, the modern train which went out of existence about twenty years ago was the best way to travel.

A man could leave New York for San Francisco and confidently expect not to have to do any work for five days. "Since it is impossible for me to do any work for five days," he could say to his companions, "why don't we play some stud poker?"

Many a close, lifetime friendship which has lasted all the way from New York to the West Coast has been formed on trains.

The airplane is the least satisfactory way of traveling. If you travel from Dallas to Los Angeles to a business appointment, you have barely enough time to hone up the arguments you are going to use in your con game before you are there.

Air travel is not broadening at all. It is linear.

MOST of our travel facilities are designed wrong. They are built on the linear concept of travel.

We have engineered out the fifty-five-mile-an-hour speed limit, for instance, by building divided superhighways. It is unfair to expect a human being to drive at fifty-five mph on them. He can't stand the sight of all that open pavement which he wants to occupy in a hurry.

If we want to drive fifty-five miles an hour, we will have to start building highways with plenty of sharp turns where it will be impossible to drive more than fifty-five.

In the future, let us keep the human element in mind when designing our travel and leave a little time for loafing.

STEAMING BACKWARD INTO THE FUTURE

THE news is that a big corporation is working to develop a steam automobile. This is a step in the right direction, a move toward the day when mankind will live in a world of eternal fog rather than eternal smog.

The commercial frontiers which will be opened up by this new development are staggering. Any imaginative entrepreneur can visualize a vast demand for battery-driven spectacle wipers for nearsighted motorists, a revival of the moribund steam-whistle industry, a limitless market for water buckets with spouts on them and ash hoppers, probably of the plastic variety.

The public should beware of expecting the steam auto too soon, however. Its development at this time would violate a fundamental natural law which says that the nature of progress is circular.

At the moment, the steam auto would be only one step backward from the present machine, not an advance along the circle. We will have to approach the steam car from the other end.

TRUE, the auto as we know it is about on its last legs. It is too bad. The old bus was a pretty good tool while she lasted and furnished jobs for a lot of people and kept the economy roaring.

Still, it must give way to the bright millennium ahead. Within ten to twenty years, one will be able to operate an internal combustion engine only under license, having demonstrated public need, lest we strangle ourselves to death with our own air.

People already unconsciously realize this. The signs are everywhere. More and more businessmen are pulling their horses around with them in a trailer against the day when the Cadillac suddenly vanishes. Literally thousands of people are practicing jogging, hoping to get in shape to run around the traffic jam to work. The sidewalk is coming back into fashion. Some people are even learning to bicycle.

Neither the horse nor the bicycle is the immediate answer to the problem if the nature of progress is truly circular, and all math shows this to be true.

Anyhow, all math shows this when it can be warped into showing anything at all.

MASS transit is not the answer, either, because mass transit never goes where people want to go.

The joggers have the right idea. Progress has now come full circle, and the next great advance in transportation is likely to be some form of the human foot. The poor will walk as usual, while the rich will have some form of running shoe with spikes that turn into ball bearings when they want to coast.

After that will come the horse and the bicycle.

In due time, we shall work our way up to the steam auto on a sound basis, in accordance with natural law, instead of jumping into it half steam-cocked.

MOBILITY RETARDS MANKIND

FOR those of us who are so inclined, it has always seemed that the world would lose most of its problems if people would just sit still.

We hold that the greatest catastrophe to the human race is not the atom bomb but the twin team of the internal combustion engine and Henry Wadsworth Longfellow — the first because it enabled men to begin spinning wildly around this earth like sand fleas over their pencil-sized hole and Mr. Longfellow because he wrote those words, "Let us then be up and doing," with which people club a man over the head when he wants to sit down and let the world settle a little.

In my boyhood, a family had done quite a bit of traveling if it managed to spend its vacation in Galveston. Nowadays, no weekend is complete unless a man has seen Bombay or Rio de Janeiro.

But if science is so wonderful, why should I have to go to Bombay? Why doesn't science bring it to me?

NEARLY everything bad that is happening to the human race would end if each human being merely sat down and began cultivating his own garden, mainly by eye measurement.

The traffic problem would be completely solved, and the atrocious bill for highways would end. We would not have to build any more airports.

Divorce would end because marriage probably would.

Juvenile delinquency would fade away because there would be no more hubcaps.

Those of us who serve merely by sitting and waiting know that the world will eventually see that the auto, the airplane, and perhaps even the wheel have seriously retarded mankind.

TAKE a look at these high-speed inventions and see what has really happened. Our fine mobility which is so highly prized has already destroyed man's sense of place and is fast destroying his sense of family, his only reference points for determining his own identity among the gods in an alien cosmos.

The old gods were all gods of a particular stone or place. Man once knew his destiny from his people. Very soon he will be an insane man operating in a sterile and mindless world of machines.

It need not have been. There are greater wonders than Bombay in the anthill on the back of the lot and stranger jungles among the wild flowers than in the forests of the south.

BACK TO THE COTTON SHIRT

THE oil shortage may turn out to be the salvation of America. It is bringing back the cotton shirt. This shows how the human race is always making progress even when it hates it.

For several years men have been forced to wear shirts made out of coal oil or some other exotic material in petroleum. The excuse was that you didn't need to iron the shirts, and it is true that they never looked ironed. They looked as if they had been used at night as pajamas. To take care of this objection the shirtmakers promoted what they called the casual look.

It was casual all right. Some men went so far as to appear shamelessly in public in red petroleum pants.

As events have shown us, this led directly to Watergate.

Before businessmen lost their high ethical content, a casual man was one never to be entrusted with heavy responsibilities such as the petty cash drawer. You will note that since the casual people took over the drawer, petty cash isn't worth much.

The reason for coal oil shirts had nothing to do with ironing. The giant trusts just wouldn't allow any cotton shirts to be put on the market where people could get at them.

NOW a shirt manufacturer is advertising a return to the cotton shirt, or mostly cotton. As the ad says, cotton feels better, breathes, looks better. This isn't the real reason the shirtmakers are going back to cotton, however. They are running out of coal oil for shirts, and you never run out of cotton. You get a new crop every year.

Nobody has ever created anything that equaled the feel of a pure cotton shirt. Its touch on the skin is bliss. The oil shortage may also force the shirts again to be boiled in an iron kettle in the open air. Without power, we will not be able to run our washing machines. We will have to boil the shirts thoroughly in the iron kettle, punching them occasionally with a stick. Boiled shirts get ozone in them and smell like a new bouquet.

Of course, somebody will have to iron the cotton shirt, but this will increase employment without fueling inflation by creating more disposable income. Dozens of small boys also will have to split the wood or carry in the coal for the stoves which heat the sadirons of ironing, but this will keep them out of mischief. It may renew discipline within the family.

If a father has to split the wood himself or make his kids do it, he becomes much less permissive with them.

If the oil companies want to continue to help the shirtmakers, they might go into the business of growing cotton. This will reduce their excess profits faster than anything else I know.

IF you stop to think about it, the disappearance of petroleum may change our whole life for the better — morally, that is. It may return us to the good Spartan virtues of body odor and high thought.

Some wasteful men we know about now have as many as five or six shirts. The energy shortage may influence people to go back to the normal number of two. What is the use of having more than two shirts if you have to iron them?

Most of us might be better off if we had fewer shirts and more kids to split the wood.

This is the natural state of man. After all, if the Lord had meant man to make shirts out of coal oil, He would have said so somewhere in the Scriptures.

HOW TO SAVE WATER

A DALLAS man's folks, who live in an apartment in Brooklyn, have mailed him a leaflet circulated some time back by the New York City Water Department.

They were having a water shortage up there, and this leaflet showed how every person in the town could save 38½ gallons of water a day. You can save over seven gallons a day by washing dishes in a pan instead of under running water, for instance. We do not intend to run the whole list. If everybody in the Dallas area saved thirty-eight gallons of water a day, we would all probably save about thirty-five million gallons, and this would bankrupt the Dallas Water Department.

Anyhow, filling a bathtub only half full of water just to save four gallons a day seems self-defeating. Probably you just wear out the four gallons that you do use twice as fast.

The New York officials have gone at this from the wrong side of the tap. They have tried to cut off the water instead of the people.

NEW YORK CITY needs to go back to the town well. It needs to cut off all residential service and set up a common tap in every block. People would then have to tote their water home in buckets, a practice which does more to save water than anything else.

Once our family lived on the crest of a steep hill, and we had to carry water from a well in the valley below. After we had lived in this house for awhile, we noticed that we almost never needed any water. It was the rule that the person who took the last water in a bucket had to refill it, and whenever the water started getting low, nobody ever wanted any. It is fairly easy to save water when it is unwanted. This nation never had a water problem until it started allowing every house to have a hydrant. The country really started going to the hot place in a handbasket when it took up the effete practice of installing bathtubs in houses.

Back when you had to carry water and heat it and pour it into a washtub for a bath, people could go a long time without bathing.

A person who needed a bath or a shower every day was just obviously awfully dirty in his habits.

THE way to discourage the popularity of any item is to connect it with a little bit of work.

An old-time grass-roots labor leader named Carl Ameringer used to tell of a monastery in Bavaria where he once partook of the finest beer in the world. It was located on a hill. The monks had to draw the water they used from a well several hundred feet deep, so they got in the habit of using as much grain and hops as they could. Mr. Ameringer thought the worst indictment of American beer was that all the breweries were located on the Mississippi River.

At any rate, human beings don't really need water. We found that out on the West Texas plains. People were not supposed to use water except in rainy seasons. We needed it for the livestock.

IN DEFENSE OF SQUALLING

IT says here in a handout that a young obstetrician named Dr. Robert Horton of St. Paul, Minnesota, got upset awhile back because his new baby kept him awake by crying.

I had been waiting a long time for this. After all those times that he told exhausted parents not to worry about the baby's crying, it is good to see him get a dose of his own medicine. Any old-time father of five or ten kids could have told Dr. Horton what to do. The procedure with a crying baby is to get him in your arms in a rocking chair, start rocking, and also start singing in a thundering tone that drowns out the crying.

As soon as the baby sees who is boss at this bellowing business, he will stop.

Dr. Horton did not undertake this admirable bit of discipline, however. Instead, he invented a thing called the Slumber Tone, an electronic gadget which makes a small noise and puts babies to sleep instantly.

"The soothing hum is regarded by many physicians to be similar to that of prenatal environment," says the handout.

A scandalous bit of business. What is Dr. Horton trying to do, stifle the Voice of Protest in this country?

IT is my expert prediction that all this will produce is another fouled-up youngster. This baby is no longer prenatal. He is out here in the big wide world, whether he likes it or not, and he may as well learn soon as late that the only way he can change something he doesn't like is to squall his head off about it. By doing this, he soon finds out that there are bigger squallers in the world than he is. This also is a valuable lesson.

All Dr. Horton proposes to do is cut off the learning process before it starts. At the present time it ends only at the first grade.

Pretty soon we will have electronic gadgets which play soothing music to the Far Righters and the Howling Liberals, and instead of

squalling, they will settle down and become contented drone bees in the hive. Progress will then stop, because progress is generally what is left when these two quit fighting over it.

It is all very distressing. A person ought to be glad that he is given a few years on earth to squall if he wants to. It is, after all, a very interesting and beautiful place, full of strange animals all organized into various kinds of clubs. Even as a way-stop in whatever happens to the human soul, it is worth examining.

Most human males are conscious of this only about the time they discover girls.

THE male newcomer to this earth ought to be made aware early that he has come to a perilous place. He ought to be told that he prevails only by sword, mind, and spirit and that each of these has to be honed and tempered to a fine edge.

That sword business is figurative, of course. I have no intention of engaging anybody in a duel if the weapons are sharp. It is true that I am the moving spirit behind a Society for the Encouragement of Fistfighting on Public Thoroughfares, but I am only an emeritus adviser and offensive coach. I am no longer effective at fistfighting, but I am offensive as the dickens.

Anyhow, we aren't even speaking to the youngster about mind and spirit anymore. We are showing him that a gadget will do everything for him.

THE CONQUERING COMPUTER

THE National Cash Register Company has just proudly announced that it is installing New Guinea's first computer, and so far as I am concerned, this just about tore it.

Until World War II came along, New Guinea was the Dark Island where anything could happen and, according to the fiction writers, did. Strange and fearsome tribes whose warriors were ten feet tall inhabited the mysterious jungles beyond its known strands. Some of these people ate people and had a decided preference for white meat when explorers wandered within their boundaries. White women empresses, often worshipped as goddesses, ruled great tribal empires and were uniformly gracious to poor Hollywood wayfarers, especially George Arliss and Errol Flynn.

These white goddesses were seldom seen except on movie film, but there they were. You could see them bathing in mountain pools with Bing Crosby.

Happily, these movie strips always concentrate on the white goddess and devote little time to Crosby.

A NEW GUINEA where anything can happen only if it is permitted to do so by the computer is not going to be the same thing.

The world badly needed New Guinea as it was in the old days. People who do not understand binary equations, who make up practically all of mankind, needed to have left one place in the world where life was completely mysterious and completely possible, even if they would never have the money to go there.

As long as there was Darkest New Guinea, an ordinary bindle stiff had within his reach the possibility of meeting the white goddess, wooing her, and becoming emperor — or at least a prince consort with more power than Prince Philip. He faced, furthermore, a lifetime of being regaled by roast pig and dancing girls.

Possibly, New Guinea will still defeat the computer. I would like to be around when the first egghead says, "How on earth do you formulate the binary equation for two chicken bones in the nose?" In the end, however, the computer will win as the instruments of the commercial human being have always won.

Man early developed the acquisitive rapacity that will be his death and worked at it as hard as he could.

IT is hard for most of us to realize how few generations ago, perhaps ten or twelve, the earth was magic. It was new, fresh, unexplored, a constant terror and a constant delight.

Man has worked ceaselessly since then to make his earth as intolerable as possible. He long ago destroyed Darkest Africa as an idea. In recent years, he has made sure that there are no hot springs in Antarctica where people live with delight — supervised, of course, by a white goddess who needs a prince consort.

There is no longer any place to go. Man can no longer walk out of the bounds of his own kitchen middens. There is no white goddess ever waiting for him, only the sound of the computers.

There are no Shangri-Las.

SCIENCE BREAKTHROUGH

Lately science has been making a number of discoveries about the earth, each more alarming than the last. A few years ago somebody discovered that the earth instead of being round was shaped like a fat top. Any sensible person knows what happens to a top. Sooner or later, it slows down too much and turns over, mashing everything but the North Pole as flat as a dietary cracker.

SCIENCE BREAKTHROUGH

LAGGARD TIME

AS you may have noticed, science has announced that the world does not necessarily make one revolution every twenty-four hours. Sometimes it loafs along and stretches the day out. At other times it goes into overdrive. Lately it has been lagging again, and now all the world's clocks are off one-tenth of a second.

Science seems astounded by this. It discovered that the earth was loafing on the job by checking its movement against the constant vibration of atoms.

The trouble with science is that it has been concentrating too much on atoms and neglecting the larger issues such as the earth. Apparently, scientists felt for a time that they had discovered in the atom something bigger than they were.

People who live on the earth instead of inside atoms have known all along that the earth is sometimes slow and sometimes fast.

THE earth slows down markedly, for instance, when you are grubbing oak

sprouts out of new ground or unloading barbed wire. You will discover this after about the first hour when you notice how long it takes the sun to go down. The sensible human aversion to physical effort has nothing to do with this. The earth comes almost to a full stop when you are waiting for somebody to get off the telephone, too.

At other times the earth noticeably accelerates, mostly during coffee breaks and annual vacations. Back when you were courting your best girl, you'll remember, an evening was about forty-five seconds long. Nearly everybody at some time has gone to a fine party which ended a second or two after he walked in the front door. When you go on a fishing trip, the earth often spins so fast that the fish won't bite.

What is the use of wasting a lot of high-priced science on something as obvious as this?

AS a matter of fact, science has just about ruined the atom already, taking all that stuff out of it. I had just as soon science left the earth alone.

Lately science has been making a number of discoveries about the earth, each more alarming than the last. A few years ago somebody discovered that the earth instead of being round was shaped like a fat top. Any sensible person knows what happens to a top. Sooner or later, it slows down too much and turns over, mashing everything but the North Pole as flat as a dietary cracker.

Maybe that doesn't worry you, but the earth has lost nearly a quarter of that one-tenth of a second in the last month.

Anyhow, this sort of thing upsets the established order. It is disconcerting to find out that Joshua didn't command the sun to stand still, that the sun commanded Joshua to fight on.

ON ATOMS AND ALCHEMY

ORDINARILY, I understand everything about atomic science, although I don't like to keep the stuff around the house.

I understand, for instance, how the scientists smash an atom by putting it in a cyclotron and whirling it around at enormously high speed by means of electrical fields. This is kid stuff. One thing I don't understand, though. How do they find the atom to put it into the cyclotron?

Do they use tweezers, or do they blow the atom into the cyclotron off a piece of paper maybe?

There is probably some perfectly commonsense answer to this which I don't know about. It may explain why an atomic scientist, who has spent his first twenty-five years learning the trade, is usually all washed up by the time he is thirty.

Probably his eyesight is fading a little. It must take awfully keen eyes to pick out atoms.

ALL this came up because a lady introduced it into conversation the other day. She suggested condescendingly that nuclear science was nothing more than the modern form of witchcraft, and that modern man takes it on faith just as a Haitian Negro takes voodoo.

"How does anybody know whether there is an atom in the cyclotron or not?" she argued. "Maybe it is all just a good show."

With my usual great tact, I let her know that this was about as stupid a question as I had ever heard.

I know that there is an atom in the cyclotron because I was around one day when a scientist smashed an atom in it. He told me so, but I forgot to ask him how he got the atom inside.

Furthermore, I resented the lady's attitude toward witchcraft which, as everybody knows, works very well in its field.

For years people have laughed because the old-time alchemists were searching for an incantation which would turn stuff like lead into gold. Few have bothered to reflect that with so many alchemists at work on the project, some are bound to have been successful.

If some alchemist didn't find out how to work the trick, where did all the gold in the world come from?

A LITTLE hard scientific thinking would have convinced the lady in a minute that it had to be an atom that was smashed in the cyclotron.

By the definition of general science as we studied it in West Texas forty years ago, the stuff that you can't see even when you use the most powerful of microscopes is an atom. If it wasn't an atom that was smashed in the cyclotron, what was it?

Those of us with scientific minds know that for every result there is a cause. Ordinary people who do not understand this had best leave science to those of us who can handle it, and go on accepting it on faith.

THE INVISIBLE UNIVERSE

YOU probably noticed where a Princeton professor, Dr. Martin Schwarzschild, told a New York science meeting that maybe 90 percent of the universe within telescopic eyesight seems to be "missing."

My first reaction to this news was to think up a strong statement that I darn sure didn't take it.

It seems, though, that Dr. Schwarzschild has been adding up the universe, and it does not come out right. Stars, he says, do not behave right if the universe consists merely of what he has added up. He thinks that there is a "massive amount" of material out there that is invisible.

Aside from the fact that I long ago quit trying to make the universe come out right, I agree with Dr. Schwarzschild. His is a theory I have had for a long time. People have looked up there at all that black in space and said it was nothing.

Suppose, though, that it is something.

If you come at it with a space machine, something is going to get bent.

IT is no good simply suggesting that Dr. Schwarzschild re-add his figures and see if the universe comes out right when he gets the new total. A man of Dr. Schwarzschild's standing would not release figures like this without first clearing them with his wife.

He is undoubtedly right. He thinks all this massive stuff out there that we can't see may be billions of "cool" stars with light too infrared to show through the atmosphere. Also, he says, space might be all gassed up with hydrogen molecules.

I could think of several other things that the massive stuff might be — giant space monsters, old West Texas box kites, Russian dogs.

Dr. Schwarzschild plans to send up telescopes in space balloons to see if he cannot get a look at his invisible universe. However, he says, under no circumstances does he want a man in his space machine.

I find this vaguely reassuring.

The world is getting to a point where it is a blessing not to be able to get a telescope in focus.

IT is not that I am afraid of the giant space monsters. Every day here on earth we walk our way through invisible things just as fearful. There are universes beyond all telling at your elbow that you cannot know because of your rudimentary senses.

At times, I have established contact with one or two of them. When I am far gone in aspirin, for instance, the invisible ones hum Handel. Occasionally, I have been bitten on the ankle by something that wasn't the dog.

It is not that I fear the giant space monster. In matters like this, I merely prefer to keep my feet on the ground.

THE ETERNAL SMUGNESS OF MAN

ON quitting as boss of NASA, Dr. Thomas O. Paine is said to have delivered himself of an eloquent speech. In it he said that scientists are about to bring together knowledge of the cosmos and knowledge of the microcosmos, which is life. Man, he said, will be better able to understand where he fits into all this. Furthermore, Dr. Paine said it was hard to believe that among the numberless planets of the myriad galaxies there was not another planet like earth on which intelligent life like the human being has developed.

This illustrates the eternal smugness of human beings. Why does Dr. Paine assume that man is the ultimate creation of nature? Man is said to be superior to all other creatures because he can think and has invented a way of writing down his knowledge and passing it on to future men. However, most of the mess that man has got himself into came from thinking. If somebody hadn't been doing a lot of thinking, we wouldn't have created the mess in the Near East. Also, most of the learning which man has been able to write down and pass on to future generations has turned out to be mere hogwash.

At the beginning, man wrote down for his sons that a straight line was the shortest distance between two points, and later on he wrote down that a straight line is merely the segment of a curve.

And to some of us who wandered a few years back into the new math, the straight line began to seem more like a maze.

THERE is something funny about assuming that a particular arrangement of man is inherently superior to other materials.

Why, for instance, is man superior to compounds which we call life, or even to iron ore? The argument is that man is superior because he can think, but how do Dr. Paine and his colleagues know that iron ore can't think? It may just be thinking on a different plateau. Those of us who deal daily with iron products are convinced that it has a malevolent intelligence. The tipper for the lawn edger blade breaks off at the wrong time and narrowly misses cutting your throat. The gears or whatnot break down in the freezer just after you have bought five gallons of ice cream for a lawn party.

Can Dr. Paine and his people argue that they have ever tried to set up any kind of meaningful communication with iron ore? They haven't. They can't even speak iron ore. Just because they can't, they have decided iron ore can't think. I doubt that Dr. Paine can speak Mandarin Chinese, or any other Chinese, but he assumes the Chinese can think.

Why does he discriminate against iron ore thought in favor of the Chinese, who certainly do not seem any more logical?

MY own feeling is that man is not going to last much longer in this universe. He thinks too much, and every time he thinks he creates some new fatal threat to himself, a new pollution or a new politician.

When man fades away, it won't change anything much. The jays will jeer over his grave. The earthworms will try to work around his carcass. And the great substantial materials of our universe, the irons, the tungstens, and the rocks, will go on with their slow and inevitable development, thinking about one small thought each eon. Thought by thought, the limestone will transform itself into marble. The iron will go on infinitesimally purifying itself. And all will be a quiet, if not peaceful, world of planets until the sun goes up in a final holocaust and everything is turned into something grander and more splendid than human beings can even think about.

WHO FED THE KOONWARRA FLEA?

IT says here that scientists in Australia have discovered a fossil flea that is 120 million years old, and now they are hard put to find a dog to go with it.

This is the trouble with all the so-called scientific discoveries. They create more problems than they answer. The scientists have never found any fossils to indicate that any furry animals existed down there at the time of the flea. Yet, the habits of fleas are well known. Wherever you find a flea you will find a dog directly underneath him.

On the basis of this one small flea, the scientists now think animals roamed this area of Gippsland in Victoria for millions of years before anybody believed they did.

This is a thin flea to base all this theory on, but it seems sound. A flea likes company and becomes very attached to it.

AT the time of this Koonwarra flea, grass hadn't got around to inventing itself down there, and the scientists have been wondering what kind of animal could live on the ferns and the gingko trees that then covered the landscape. Obviously, the flea had to have something to live on. If we have learned

anything from all the Save-Our-Earth efforts, it is that if we have a flea, we are bound to have ecology.

This flea was not equipped to burrow down through fur, so the scientists have decided that they are looking for a bald-headed host. They think it may have been an ancestor of the bandicoot, or some other marsupial which could live on insects, earthworms, and roots.

I doubt this. All the evidence by now points to the existence in those days of a large hairless dog. Fleas are particular. They will take up with some of us while turning the majority of mankind down. It is hard to imagine a reason for a flea's existence without a dog.

If I were the scientists, I would look for a large fossil dog with no hair on his fossil. If they come upon him in stone, his mouth will be open in a snapping position.

The hairless dog is the only reasonable way to explain the Koonwarra flea's food supply. Fleas and dogs are the only animals that like to eat each other.

ABOUT all that we have discovered so far is that Australia had fleas a long time before any other country. Not many fossilized fleas ever have been found, possibly because most of us haven't been looking for them.

A couple of them have been found about the Baltic Sea. However, they are only forty million years old, and they have the physical equipment typical of fleas who feed on malemutes.

Man, they say, is only about two million years old, according to his fossils, which proves that man had fleas even before he was born.

It has always seemed that way to me, even without science.

THE THINKING FLY

A UNIVERSITY of Pennsylvania scientist has announced that the housefly may be able to think. It is high time science was catching up with such facts as this. In the past, science has held that the fly couldn't think because its brain was too small, and some of us with small brains were beginning to resent the implication.

Those of us with small brains can think all right; we just can't remember anything. Thinking has to do with ideas, not brain size, and ideas do not reside in the brain. They sort of extend out from it into space. Show me an idea small enough to put into the ordinary six-inch human brain, and I will show you an idea not worth fiddling with. Ideas float around in the air in layers, millions of them. If you've ever had one, you know what happened. It smote you right in the face while your brain was tuned to that frequency.

The finer ideas are more likely to come to small brains, which necessarily have finer tolerances, than to a clumsily made, loosely adjusted big brain.

A NYBODY who has ever lain flat on his back for several hours on a hot day and watched a fly knows that flies can think.

I, myself, have seen a large brown-bodied fly rest on the edge of a picture frame and eye the distant ceiling carefully. I have watched him figure the proper parabolic curve — in his head, mind you, not on a computer — and then sail out and do an Immelmann and light upside down perfectly on the ceiling. It is quite a trick, and I would like to see the Pennsylvania professor do it.

The human race has never been able to figure a parabolic curve that accurately.

But the Pennsylvania professor is due credit for suggesting that the fly ought to be studied. The fly merits study. Though small of brain, he is large and tolerant of spirit. Among all the flies, the housefly, the bluetailed fly, the bottle fly, the horsefly, you will find no evidence of ill will or discrimination. A fly does not mind his fellows crowding in with him on an exposed piece of cheese. It is one for all and all for one in prosperity or in penury.

Or maybe the Pennsylvania professor isn't due so much credit. Solomon said it to another scientist a long time ago: "Go to the ant, thou sluggard . . ."

T HE other animals all know a great many things that man doesn't. The fly, for instance, has an eye that is made up of a thousand or so smaller eyes. It is the original photoelectric cell, and who can doubt these days that a photoelectric cell can do anything when properly hooked up? The bat does not need to spend a thousand or so dollars for a radar set. He comes equipped with a do-it-yourself kit.

Science is doing a study now on the sea turtle to find out why he travels every year to Ascension Island. It is supposed to find out how he handles the navigation problem, but probably what bothers science most is that the turtle knows Ascension Island without a signboard. The ordinary human being doesn't.

MATING ON THE FLY

A UNIVERSITY of California insect expert discovered recently that the housefly will not mate when blown about by a wind of four miles an hour.

This scientist built a wind tunnel for houseflies for this experiment, and he worked out a bunch of flies in it before the humane society found out about it. When the wind got to somewhere between four and six miles an hour, he reported, the flies stopped flying around and started clinging to the nearest surface.

Mating, he said, is reduced to virtually nothing, and no wonder.

When you are hanging on for dear life in a hurricane, it is the wrong time to bring the subject up.

The implications of all this seem staggering, up to a point.

SCIENCE doesn't seem to have completed its homework on this subject, however. If a fly cannot mate in a four-mile-an-hour wind, how is it that houseflies mate in West Texas in a sixty-mile wind?

It is no good to say that West Texas houseflies are new settlers, immigrants from the squalor of Baltimore, Maryland, and Palm Springs, California. True, there probably are a number of houseflies from these regions with a desire to better themselves.

But many of the West Texas flies are native. You can tell because they are cross-eyed and ornerier than other flies, a result possibly of having to mate in a sixty-mile-an-hour wind.

It may be that the whole thing is a matter of relativity. If everything is being blown at sixty miles an hour, as it often is in West Texas, the mating flies are like a man who is standing still in the aisle of a bus but still traveling sixty miles an hour.

Or possibly the flies may outwit the wind by riding a grain of sand.

Whatever the reason, science should discover it and peg it down. It should not be left to the idle ruminations of newspaper writers and philosophers.

AT the moment, these wind tunnel experiments with flies don't seem to have much practical application.

You waste an awful lot of wind in twenty-four hours trying to keep a couple of flies apart.

It is doubtful whether the idea is wise, anyway. The fly is a maligned insect, highly despised. Actually, he is a kind of badge of civilization, because he flourishes best around the noble works of man. He dines from the banana peels outside our art museums and drinks from the lees in the beer cans in our parks.

If you see a string of flies, follow it, and it will probably lead you straight to the kitchen of the best restaurant in town.

TAILING RATTLESNAKES

IT seems that a zoologist named Dr. Harold F. Hirth at the University of Utah is putting radioactive wires into the tails of rattlesnakes and then tracking them with Geiger counters. A more ghastly desecration of the pure and holy boulders and dry washes of the land of Deseret could hardly be imagined.

Dr. Hirth says the tiny wires of radioactive tantalum 182 do not hurt the snakes. He and his assistants only work behind a six-hundred-pound, lead-brick wall because the wires will burn up your eyes if you look at them long. They inject the wires with special hypodermic needles, and he says they use unusual dexterity. I'll bet they do. If there is anything worse than a hot wire, it is a hot rattlesnake.

By tracking the wired rattlesnake with a Geiger counter, Dr. Hirth thinks he will be able to trace their migration habits, a ridiculous excuse.

If there is anything that will disturb a rattler's normal migration habits and send him into the far blue yonder, it is a hot tail.

DR. Hirth could have got the same results by having a dozen ranchers report the daily location of their pet rattlesnakes.

Any good rancher can tell you the name of the rattlesnake that is sounding off in his vicinity. Like radio stations, rattlesnakes buzz on different frequencies. Furthermore, rattlesnakes do not migrate very far. They find a good hunting spot and wait.

When, as children, we used to visit Uncle Uriah's ranch, he used to warn us to stay out of the mesquite around the dirt tank south of the barn.

"You might run into Old Pete," he would say.

Old Pete had a buzz deep and mellow that sounded like the bomb about to go off in a spy movie. He was an enormous snake as thick as a strong man's arm, and I always figured Uncle Uriah kept him around as a stud. Uncle Uriah had a number of other rattlesnakes. There was one called Ella in the far corner of the southwest pasture. She had a buzz with a high-pitched whine that sounded like a soprano who had run ten years out of voice.

Uncle Uriah did not keep them around out of any kindness of his heart or because, as Dr. Hirth is saying, they killed rodents. A man then preferred to kill rodents himself in his spare

time with whatever pistols and Winchesters he had around, because it was well known that a gun barrel unused soon crystallized.

Uncle Uriah kept them because a drought was likely to break out at any time, and he would have to kill a snake and turn it belly-up on a barbed wire fence to make the rain come. He wanted a good supply.

"ALTHOUGH snakes have menaced man in many ways, we know very little about them," argues Dr. Hirth in his press release.

Hogwash. Snakes have never menaced man, unless menaced themselves, except in the tales of H. Rider Haggard. It is true that certain English explorers, extremely narrow of shoulder and extremely large of sun helmet, have been engorged by pythons, but the snake probably mistook them for goslings.

An honest mistake like this may be pardoned. Maybe Dr. Hirth will make one.

SCIENCE CAN'T KEEP UP

AWHILE back the newspapers told of a man who was slowly going crazy trying to keep the armadillos from digging up his lawn. A reader from a Dallas suburb has now furnished the information that you can drive armadillos off your grass by loading the lawn with sulfur. Once they are gone, she says, you can keep them from returning by laying down a line of sulfur around the plat that you want to protect.

Probably this is unscientific, but a man who is plagued with armadillos doesn't care whether the cure is scientific or not.

It proves again that people know a great many things which science has not yet discovered.

Science eventually will get around to discovering them and making them official, but meanwhile they work just as well while they're undiscovered.

IT was several millennia after people had begun to use a good stout sapling to pry rocks with that science discovered the lever, and Archimedes announced that with a proper lever and a fulcrum to put it on he could move the world. This is a typical "iffy" scientific attitude. Science discovered the wedge and the wheel after people had been using them for years.

This inability of science to keep up with people is called a cultural lag.

It has been only three hundred years since Isaac Newton discovered that an apple, if it becomes detached from the tree, falls to the ground, though we may reasonably suppose that generations of apple-knockers had known this all along. True, Newton did figure out why the apple falls, a discovery of very little utility if you know ahead of time that it is going to fall.

People have known since the dawn of the world that a man will push back at you if you push him, but it took science centuries to find out that a force automatically produces an equal and opposite force.

Science is very good at theoretical things such as finding out why apples drop and why atoms split, but it is not very good at picking up apples or driving off armadillos.

SCIENCE, for instance, has not yet discovered that you can kill the perfume of a skunk by rubbing the anointed surface with canned tomatoes, or that carrying a buckeye in your pocket will bring you luck. I have carried a buckeye for years, and I have noticed that I have never had anything except luck, good and bad.

Science has not yet discovered that red ant stings are good for rheumatism, though thousands of people have noticed that rheumatics move with uncommon alacrity when stung.

Science scoffs at the idea that a rattlesnake will not cross a hair rope, but Uncle Ed out in West Texas knows better. He failed to scout his bed site one night before putting his rope around it, and found that he had locked a rattler in. It is the only recorded instance in history of a man doing a high jump from flat on his back.

WEATHER AND HUMAN EMOTIONS

HERE is another of those stories which says that the weather affects human behavior. What utter scientific rot!

Science is always putting its cart before us horses and claiming, by manipulating the weather, to have advanced progress by making us human beings commit suicide. The truth is that it is the other way around. Human behavior causes the weather.

Hot, unsettled weather is supposed to make human beings angry, for instance. The truth is that when a lot of human beings get mad at one time, they generate a lot of heat. This forms thermal columns, which cause hot air to rush up and chill off suddenly, setting off thunderstorms and other freak weather.

Atmospheric lows do not cause human beings to be depressed. When a great crowd of people get depressed together, they make everything around them seem low, even the atmosphere.

It is time that some good researcher determined how violent the effect of human emotions on the atmosphere really is.

THE people who live close to grass, crops, cattle, and trees have always known that their moods had an effect on the weather. When I was a boy in the Lariat country, it was a rule not to worry about a drought because it was certain to keep rain away.

In those years we had a neighbor named Uncle Mack, a fearsome man given to continual tantrums. Most people never liked to stand near him during an electrical storm because they felt that the Lord had his eye on Uncle Mack.

During one long drought, Uncle Mack looked upon his seared field and exploded. "All right, dang it," he yelled, shaking his fist at the sun, "burn 'em up, burn 'em up." Actually, Uncle Mack did not say "dang," because he had a contempt for mild language.

Sure enough, the sun did just as Uncle Mack commanded. It burned everything up that summer. This shows the extent to which a strong-willed man can affect the weather.

An unofficial township gathering resentfully considered this later and figured that Uncle Mack, by his attitude, had scared off a four-inch rain which was certain to fall.

Nobody mentioned this to Uncle Mack, of course. We were just as scared of him as the weather was.

IT is time that human beings quit associating themselves with the blanket of gases that packs around our planet and time that science quit pretending that it knows much about it.

The rain it raineth when it will. The skies cloud up as they please. Women cloud up if they think it might get them a new dress. Men cloud up as soon as they are out of the bosses' sight if they have just been reprimanded. Children cloud up without any reason at all. Dogs, being the only creatures who really feel for man, cloud up whenever anybody else does.

At any given moment, each of us is a small intense high pressure area or intense low pressure area circulating around in this atmospheric blanket that doesn't give a hoot about us.

WORRYING ABOUT A WOBBLING WORLD

A SEISMOLOGIST came right out the other day and said the California earthquake is the fault of the earth.

A lot of us prudent people have been suspecting this all along. For a lifetime we have been sailing around in stark terror on this planet which is speeding along through space at thousands of miles an hour. It is all very well for Washington to issue reassuring statements about this from time to time, but prudent people know that speed kills. That's what the ads say. That is what the Citizens' Traffic Commission has been preaching for years.

Now this seismologist says that the earth doesn't spin around and around on its axis as we were brainwashed to believe in general science. It wobbles as it spins, he says, and that might cause some earthquakes.

You can see the peril which faces mankind. If a thing wobbles, it eventually is going to fall.

It is all very well for the common herd to go helling around down the primrose path, drinking Cokes and singing roundelays, but a prudent man is bound to cower in his shelter at the prospect.

THERE was a time when the earth was solid and firm under a man's feet. Terra firma it was called. The stars and the sun might whirl around a man's head, but the earth stood still where it belonged.

All a man had to do was build his house on rock instead of sand, and he was safe.

Then the scientists started making improvements to the earth. Galileo invented the rotation of the earth around the sun, and the earth has never been reliable since. Newton added a lot of appliances to the earth. One of them was gravitation, and ever since the sun and the moon have been pushing and pulling at the earth's surface, punching it in here and puffing it out there. Anybody who has ever tinkered with a toy balloon knows what will happen. Sooner or later a bubble will appear on the earth's surface, and soon it will bust.

Like the modern automobile, the earth is overloaded now with extras like the San Andreas fault and the Milwaukee Deep.

As with anything else, the more extras you add to the earth, the more upkeep costs you pay.

WHEN the earth was flat, it was reliable. People did not really mind when they found out it was spinning, even though some of us do not like to be spun around at the rate of a thousand miles an hour. We get carsick even on the city buses.

Few people realize that the earth's spinning is gradually slowing down, probably because of the friction of the oceans. At the same time, it is wobbling. Lord help us.

The scientists all say not to worry. Nothing will happen, they say, for 100,000 years.

All we can say is that 100,000 years is small enough time to worry about what is going to happen, considering its size.

THE HUMAN CONDITION

People instinctively believe the pithy statement, for the average human being will accept almost anything as wisdom provided he doesn't have to listen to the reasons for it.

THE HUMAN CONDITION

BOUND TO LOSE

A FRIEND from the Texas Panhandle says
he is beginning to be puzzled by the
difference between something that is put away
and something that is lost.

"I know there is a difference," he writes. "At
our house things are put away so they won't
get lost. Things that are lost, at our house, at
least, like the extra keys to the car and that
letter from Aunt Sarah, the one she particularly
requested that we should read and then 'tare up
and bern,' usually show up sooner or later.

"Things, on the other hand, that are put
away so they won't get lost are just plain gone
and out of circulation. When things are put
away so they won't get lost, it don't do no good
to light no candle or invoke St. Anthony. They
are just as vanished as the dodo bird and the
snaggle-toothed brontosaurus."

*The condition here described by our
friend is part of what the poets and
novelists like to call The Human
Condition.*

T HE Human Condition is that for every
laudable human intention there is an
opposite and equal foul-up. If Aunt Sarah sends
a letter asking that it be read and that the
reader then "tare up and bern" it, the letter will
certainly get lost before the instructions can be
carried out, and it will turn up later, usually
under embarrassing circumstances.

On the other hand, a thing that is put away
where it won't get lost will never turn up,
especially if it is a record that the Internal
Revenue Service is demanding to see.

A part of The Human Condition is that the
things that you don't need are always handy to
the reach while the things that you do need are
someplace else. If you need an eraser, you find
you have a blunt-ended copy pencil, but if you
need a pencil, all that you can find is a piece of
art gum.

This is called The Law of Diminishing
Returns, or something.

*The Human Condition, in other words,
is that man is bound to lose, but he
needn't do it all in one pot. Temperance
in losing is the watchword.*

O UR friend should take the optimistic view
of such affairs. The gods have so arranged
this for the benefit of mankind. Since they have

arranged that human ingenuity will always be better than human memory, it is hardly likely that a man will ever find anything he put into a safe place so it wouldn't get lost.

The man should take comfort in this, and does. Knowing that the valuable item is in a safe place, he forgets where it is. If he could remember which safe place he deposited the thing in, he would wake up in the night worrying about whether it was really safe. He would have to go out in the backyard and dig it up and see for himself.

Of course, car keys are a special case which doesn't fall under this law. They will usually be found beneath the broken electric percolator which has been set aside for the repairman.

A SENSE OF DIRECTION

A DALLAS acquaintance heard a slight tapping on a window at his house in the Royal Lane neighborhood, and there outside was a lost parakeet asking for directions.

The millions of lost parakeets by now should have disproved finally the old myth that birds have a sense of direction. True, the mallard in the fall flies south in a beeline from Hudson Bay country to the Gulf, but this does not prove that he has a sense of direction. If you stopped a mallard and asked him whether he was flying north or south, he wouldn't be able to tell you.

The truth is that the whole animal kingdom turns its rear end toward cold weather. In a blizzard, for instance, cattle stand with their tails toward the icy wind and their heads down. The mallard is flying when cold weather strikes, of course. When he turns his rear end to the cold, he is naturally flying south.

Man is different, of course. He turns his rear end toward a fire. This proves again that man is superior to the animals.

MAN is superior to the animals, too, in having this sense of direction. Even when he doesn't have it, he knows he ought to have.

Man has a sense of direction because he is himself a kind of magnet. Anybody with half sense knows that a man sleeps better when he is lined up north and south instead of crosswise with the unseen magnetic currents. A man is like a compass needle. He is positive in the feet and negative in the head. This probably happens because a man spends most of his time standing so that most of the highly nutritious food that he eats settles in his feet.

Of course, some people spend most of the time sitting, and the highly nutritious food settles somewhere else.

Most human behavior can be explained by the fact that the human body is a magnet. A man's positive feet, for instance, are attracted by negative distances while his negative head is attracted to positive ideas. If you shove a man suddenly, he will resist with an opposite and equal force — an old law of the physics of the magnetic field.

Well, anyway, he will resist unless you are bigger than he is.

Man knows north from south. He is only deficient in knowing up from down. He is always thinking that he is going upward and onward when he is really going in a circle. Man's fate is an orbit without a sun.

IT is high time that we quit ascribing human abilities and knowledge to the animals. The plain fact is that animals don't know anything and don't need to while a lot of men don't know anything but desperately need to.

An animal does not reason. He lives from day to day on what he can snatch from the world about him. Man, on the other hand, has A Plan for his life; he lives on credit.

In one sense, the animal is becoming superior to man. Like this parakeet, he has learned that if he will move in with man, he can live as a freeloader — but some men are beginning to discover this, too.

NATURAL GRACE AND OTHER VANITIES

PEOPLE say that animals have a natural grace, but I doubt it. This natural grace is just a variation of the old magician's trick of misdirection.

A dog with a fine brushy rear-end assembly, for instance, inevitably does a lot of tail-swishing. This catches the spectator's eye. The spectator does a little lecture on the natural grace of animals. Actually, all that the dog is doing is making the best out of what he has. In front, he may be pigeon-toed and cross-eyed, but the lovers of natural graces in animals are unable to see the dog for the tail.

The bulldog, who has no tail, will hide his tail and show his teeth. This also catches the spectator's eye but usually moves him to other thoughts than the natural grace of animals.

Actually, the higher forms of animals such as dogs and raccoons are just as clumsy as lower forms like human beings, but the human being knows from experience that his fellows are clumsy. In judging them, he is less likely to be beguiled by something like a showy mane unless it belongs to a female.

All this shows that every member of the animal kingdom, from the amoeba clear up to the raccoon, comes amply equipped to appreciate his own virtues.

THIS is as true of the human being as of any other animal. If you will notice, the man who always takes off his hat to a woman in an elevator is always equipped with a spectacular hat. He wears a homburg or a derby or a white, broad-brimmed hat, or else a big floppy panama, one that will call attention to his deep, gallant bow and direct the eyes away from his big feet.

Men who wear the small, pinheaded hats now in style do not remove them when a woman gets on the elevator. If they did, nobody would notice it. A man in a pinheaded hat is more likely to kick the sides of the elevator to direct attention to his new buck suede shoes.

The man who professes to believe in a strong, hearty handshake always has hands the size of an attaché case, hands so big that you can never get hold of them and protect yourself. The man who believes in big families already has one. The moneyed man detests shiftless people who cannot match his example, and the man without money deplores the materialistic tendencies of our society.

The bookish man is likely to carry some esoteric volume around in his hand wherever he goes, and once, in a University of Texas class on constitutional law, a student showed up wearing baseball spikes as a reminder to us all that he was a fine athlete if an indifferent student.

A person who is stupid is endowed by nature to prove the worth of stupidity, and he will prove it every day.

THE man who suggests anything wrong in this would be foolish indeed. It is perfectly natural for a man with a fine, loud voice to talk incessantly, even if he says nothing. Nature demands a use of the big noses and sharp eyes it gives its subjects. A man with a big nose is naturally going to turn the conversation around to smells, and a man with sharp eyes is always going to be seeing something on the horizon.

Vanity, vanity, all is vanity, said the preacher.

Only that wasn't the whole of it. What he was really doing was calling attention to his own high moral rectitude.

SLOGANED WISDOM

A DALLAS student of human nature has noticed a change of fashion in the snappy proverbs, maxims, and other saws with which every human being seems constrained to improve his less fortunate fellows.

It used to be that we were told, "Early to bed, early to rise . . .," or "God helps them that help themselves," or "Go to the ant, thou sluggard; consider her ways and be wise." Of late, claims our friend, the mottoes have taken on a tone of social protest or criticism. They urge a man to "Support Your Local Police. Bribe a Cop Today." Or, "Is There Life after Birth?" Or, "America, Love It or Leave It."

"Personally, I am glad to have lived to see we are forgetting many of those old short, pithy sayings," says our friend. "It always irked me, when I was young, to be continually admonished by my elders with some old saw about getting up early."

Maybe. But all saws come out of the same human barrel, and they are likely eventually to have the same pickled taste.

SAWS, adages, and wall mottoes are among the most necessary of the tools of mankind.

For instance, every human being has a built-in need to give advice to other people, and ordinarily he does not have much advice to give. A kit of handy maxims and wise admonitions is the very thing to keep him occupied and the people about him uplifted.

People instinctively believe the pithy statement, for the average human being will accept almost anything as wisdom provided he doesn't have to listen to the reasons for it. "Haste makes waste" is obviously a piece of great wisdom because you don't have to reason it out. The man who reads it tells himself, "A word to the wise is sufficient," and slows down long enough for a coffee break.

People seem to react almost automatically to sloganed wisdom. On paydays, an acquaintance of ours sometimes puts out a collection can at a downtown plant. It bears a sign that says, "Save a Life," mentioning in small print that the life to be succored is his own. Sometimes he accumulates quite a kitty of quarters and small change.

King Solomon probably became a wise man because he said so many things that required nobody to think.

OUR Great-Aunt Martha out in the Lariat country believed implicitly in the capsuled wisdom of "sayings," though she seldom understood them and often twisted them into meanings that were strangely new and wonderful.

"Never look a sleeping dog in the mouth," Aunt Martha would say, nodding firmly. She knew in her bones that the worm got the early bird and that some days you would have the good luck to pick up a pin.

She was wise beyond her time.

A NEED FOR MONSTERS

IT says here that the *World Book Encyclopedia* has undertaken the job of flushing out the Loch Ness monster.

Soon, no doubt, another beautiful legend of the human race will be merely a paragraph in the *World Book* with a diagram explaining it for second graders.

This is the danger of this unreasoning, ceaseless search for knowledge. Any encyclopedia, when it has acquired a mere two dozen volumes of knowledge, grows mad with power and seeks to wipe out all nonknowledge. A very dangerous process for the human race. Often nonknowledge, when it is suddenly discovered, has proved to be more valuable to humanity than all the knowledge known at the time.

Look at Newton. He discovered that the apple falls. Up until that time, this was a piece of nonknowledge.

Look at the hydrogen bomb, once a piece of nonknowledge. It taught the human race for the first time in a hundred years to pray earnestly.

IN its misguided attempts to profane the depths of Loch Ness, the *World Book* is using all kinds of technical instruments and has even resorted to the insulting business of calling the Loch Ness monster Nessie. A monster, confound it, cannot be a Nessie.

Fortunately, the exploration is getting nowhere. One of the things that the *World Book* people are using is an underwater camera. It scans the cliffs in the nine-hundred-foot loch and photographs underwater cliffs under which could lurk great creatures, including mistakes. This camera has picked up one eel which seemed astounded and annoyed that he had been bothered, and a number of interesting strange white objects.

On examination, these interesting white objects turned out to be old beer cans.

The *World Book* people have other stratagems, noisemakers with high-pitched sounds like people being swallowed whole and low-pitched sounds like the bull Loch Ness monster. They have a small submarine named the *Viperfish*, which never has worked right. Since the Loch Ness monster always works right, you can see where this leads.

They have also tried to catch the monster with bait made of anchovy paste, crushed eels, bulls' blood, and snake hormone. Hah!

Some fishermen, these boys! Anybody knows that if you want to catch something big like this, you use dough bait.

WE glory in the continuing victory of the Loch Ness monster. The human race needs a monster. Many a night it wakes up having dreamed of one. It needs a giant which can thrust its great head out of the water and gobble up an unwary human being from the beach.

It needs the Loch Ness monster because it needs a symbol for the great dark, the measureless mysteries that lie beyond the imagination of man but are sensed, the human condition in a merciless universe where worlds may collide in our sleep.

MAN'S MATERIALISTIC HEART

FOR years Uncle Tommy Peeples lived as a guest of his nephew, Willie, on the West Texas farm that Uncle Tommy had given Willie. When Uncle Tommy died, Willie learned belatedly that Uncle Tommy had willed half of the rest of his enormous $6,000 estate to an orphanage. Willie, who had expected the whole, was dismayed.

"I don't mind a man being generous," he said, "but he ought to use common sense."

Somehow, this story always pops into my mind when I read a piece, as in the current *Harper's*, worrying about the materialism of our current society. Man is at the core of his heart materialistic. Only through earnest prayer and the rigorous discipline of self-examination does he achieve grace.

We are no more materialistic than man was in his beginning. We merely have more materialism within our grasp.

NOWHERE is man's materialistic heart more visible than in some of the symbols which he uses for his noblest institution, religion, the one aspect in which man has ever been able even to make a small statement of his wildest and most unselfish dreams.

He aspires in heaven to strum a golden harp.

He will walk on a street which is paved with GOLD. Someone may object that paving the streets with gold indicates that this base metal will be finally reduced to its proper worthlessness in the moral eye, but certain other people who want to walk the golden stairs in golden slippers have not indicated that they understand this. Admittedly, all this is a trope, a figure of speech, but it should be significant that none of us ordinary working stiffs can conceive of paradise except in the terms of primitive opulence.

The Mohammedan goes farther. He understands what all this affluence is about. He dreams of spending eternity in a perpetual oasis surrounded by complaisant New York models while he drinks the wine of paradise.

THIS is not a criticism of religion, which remains man's noblest expression of what he would wistfully, and often tearfully, want of the universe. And it is not a criticism of mankind, for God's children have always been willful and imperfect children, though bothered about it.

It is hard for a man whose ancestors not a few generations ago dug an inadequate cave for protection and found their forage from the refuse of the great lizards not to prize a proper store of wheat. It is hard for a man who never had one to refuse a golden bauble. Man's one hint of perfection has been that sometimes he wants to weep over what he is.

A TEN-CENT TELESCOPE

A READER has asked why a human being will climb seven thousand feet to the top of a mountain and then put a dime in a telescope so that he can look back down to where he came from. This is what is called a Statement of the Human Condition. At any given moment, the human being is never sure where he is. He is anxious to see where he came from. He does genealogical research. He digs deep into history books seeking to prove that he was there — or, at least, that it did happen. He is also bothered about his public image. How did he look from these Olympian heights when he was making a fool of himself down there at the corner of First and Main?

The human being is unable to believe that he has really reached the summit, the whole goal of his climb, unless there is a ten-cent telescope from which he can look back.

THE SHRINKING HUMAN BRAIN

SOME scientists now believe that the human brain is actually shrinking. This was an impression that I had, too, but I thought it was from associating with too many drivers on the expressway.

Anyhow, a Dr. Ernest Mayr of Harvard has said that man's brain reached its peak in Neanderthal man and then stopped. There is no question that the brain reached a peak in Neanderthal man, all right, but most of us prefer round heads. Wigs look better on them. Furthermore, reducing the size of his brain may be the first sensible thing man has done in a long time.

Nearly every time a man makes a mistake he has been thinking. Take the man who has to add three columns of figures, for instance. His thinking becomes so involved he is bound to be wrong.

It is hardly surprising, of course, that man's brain is getting smaller and softer. Whatever is not used will wither.

AS you may have guessed, Dr. Mayr says the human brain stopped growing because intelligence no longer pays. Quite a few of us superbrains have noticed this for years.

However, if becoming a Neanderthal man is the price of having a big brain, you can count me out. The only person interested in a Neanderthal person is another tackle who might have to play against him next week. Even the Neanderthal female blondes fail to stir up much interest in a man. Probably Neanderthal man developed that big brain because he needed it as a cushion for cracking walnuts with his teeth.

The Neanderthal man was just not a congenial type. His style of life had no grace to it. He was always thinking, no doubt, of how to get out of it, and this developed the brain muscle. His life had all the dissatisfactions of a new thing that had not been sufficiently tested. For instance, he had invented fire but not the tobacco to go with it.

A man with fire but with no tobacco can at best be called only half civilized.

THIS is not to say that modern man is the best thing that has happened along in human history. If I had my way about it, the best time to have lived would have been at the time of the Swiss lake dwellers.

By this time man's brain had degenerated to a point where politics were possible. He had stopped thinking so much and begun to indulge his sense of play, thus producing song, saga, and the bright items of art to gladden the senses. He lived comfortably in a protected village with a built-in sewage system, and ate berries and seeds and birds as well as animals, and drank tiger milk.

Mainly, though, this would have been a time when the world was new and untouched — no atoms, no nuclei, no miracle poisons or miracle fertilizers, nothing but the wind's sound in the boundless green forests and the sun-pinked clouds above the lake.

A PASSING PHENOMENON

ON TV the other morning a young woman said she became a vegetarian because she did not believe in killing as a way of getting food. This was a curious statement. The young woman looked much more intelligent than her statement and was pretty enough to attract slavering wolves.

She apparently cherishes life. She is not about to have a steer killed so that she can eat meat, but she is willing to eat a head of lettuce. But, if you think about it, lettuce is life, too. You had better eat it while it still has some life in it unless you are afflicted with necrophilia.

Plants were alive on this planet considerably before animals were, and on the whole they are more decent. They stay in place. They do not make war against each other in the Sinai peninsula. There are no vicious plants except that flytrap plant and climbing wisteria. Nobody knows whether that head of lettuce screams in agony when you cut it off, though some scientists now claim that certain pot plants weep and pine away if they are not loved by their owners.

We do not wish to overargue. Nobody knows how many bodies are caught behind those nets of grasping wisteria.

Our attitude is eat, drink, and be merry. You are using up life.

IF we have learned anything from our flights into space, it is that we live in a sterile universe. There is very little life as we know it. Life is a passing phenomenon, a fragile thing, which should be hoarded. Even a stalk of Johnson grass is a precious thing.

That is the reason we sensitive souls prefer not to cut out the Johnson grass in our lawns. Johnson grass is a form of life which must be preserved, while a steer is a peripheral form and may be devoured. Sooner or later, man, the ultimate form of life, the dictator of all life, has to make a moral decision. He has to eat. Will he destroy life and live or refuse to destroy life and die himself?

I always prefer to keep the Johnson grass and sacrifice the fat steer.

As far as life is concerned, the only difference between a head of lettuce and a human being is in the point of view.

LIFE is a very odd thing. The act of living is. We do not really know what we are or what the things around us mean. We speak of things such as mass to describe the stars and the planets or life, which is merely something that flourishes for a moment and dies. Death seems somehow to be the affirmation of life. Some say the lichens were the first form of life on our rock, and as the sun cools, they may be the last.

Some say the only basic material in the universe is something evanescent and imperceptible except when it strikes a mote or a planet, a beam of light. From this energy were all things made.

We are, they say, all brothers of the light.

PINNING DOWN DATES

A GENERATION from now every child will know the date. They will all have been drilled in it in their history classes, and they will know that at Christmastime, 1968, man first traveled to the moon. Their elders will never really learn the date as long as they live.

In a few years, you will hear arguments among the elders all over the place about whether the trip took place in 1966 or 1969. This is to be expected from those of my generation who can successfully lose forever a spectacle case within a 10×10 room in their own house. There will be one among us who is certain that men went to the moon in 1968.

"I remember exactly when it was," he will say. "It was the year that we put Bertha's teeth in braces."

For the time being, the astronauts will have to be content with having their great voyage pegged chronologically to Bertha's teeth. In time, they will have their own date set neatly into people's minds.

People of my generation have little time to remember contemporary dates. They are still trying to remember what happened in B.C.

P ROBABLY the same thing happened to Columbus, except that few people on the Spanish waterfronts really knew that he had ever departed or returned.

He did return, however, with a few trees and shrubs and a few real Indians instead of the gold from the Indies that he had promised. He also brought back a likely story for Isabella. At the time, it apparently didn't impress anybody much. He had discovered a new world and had returned. So what?

Eight or ten years later, some grandee was probably asking another, "What year was it that that guy discovered that new world? You know the guy, the one that ran his best ship aground and came back with that Spanish malarkey about a new land? Was it 1496, or 1494?"

Every schoolchild, of course, has now learned the little jingle that goes, "In 1493, Columbus sailed the deep blue sea."

This is still not as important as where in the devil I left the case for my eyeglasses.

T HE human race is ill equipped to remember important dates during its own lifetime. The best of the Greek historians once wrote that nothing worthwhile had happened in the history of the world before his lifetime, but most men feel that nothing that happened to them personally is worth recording.

There is a reason for this. The date on which man first traveled to the moon is hardly as important to most men as the date on which the income tax has to be filed. The average man is frantically trying to remember the date of his wedding anniversary. He hardly has time for the dates of contemporary history.

By the way, who were those guys who traveled to the moon?

TO TOUCH AN ANGEL

Man's ability to identify himself with things longer in time than he can ever manage is both his tragedy and his glory.

TO TOUCH AN ANGEL

REJOICE, DANG IT!

A CUSTOMER has objected that in a recent column I wrote about a "whitrock," which you sharpen your pocketknife on, and Shakespeare. A man who is acquainted with both, he says, is a schizophrene, a man without a formed character, a human goulash.

I doubt it. If Shakespeare had been fortunate enough to own a good whitrock, I think he would have written a sonnet about it. The record on Mr. Shakespeare is pretty scanty; he was too smart. Nowhere, though, is it suggested that while he was writing this immortal poetry he ever turned down a mug of stout or forgot who owed him rent. He never fell for this foolishness that because you like something you have to dislike something else.

I think Shakespeare would have said it. He would have told you that he, Shakespeare, was merely the greatest poet and the greatest writer in the language, while a good pocket whitrock was a status symbol.

At any rate, I've never felt it necessary to cut myself off from one part of the world to prove my fidelity to some other part.

I LIKE a whole lot of things that don't all add up: the smell of magnolia blossoms, the brash bravery of Johnson grass, mackerel skies, cats, dogs, redbirds that sing "cheer-cheer-cheer," mockingbirds that try to drive them off, begonias, gardenia blossoms, old rotten pieces of driftwood, pretty china, and crickets. Especially crickets. I know that these are not the cheerful tenders of your hearth of legend and that they eat your winter coat, but I love crickets. If I have a choice, I never kill one. I find some way to shunt it out of doors.

I love the poetry of Yeats, T. S. Eliot, Robert Frost, and Sandburg. And I love Horace, too, and Francis Thompson can reduce me to a kind of piety. I also like a fast horse. Sometimes I like one extravagantly, but if I never watched one on a racetrack, I'd still like a fast horse. They are beautiful. I also like good bourbon whiskey and fine tobacco and properly kept sherry and claret.

And, I think, the most beautiful of all earth's creations is a pretty, high-spirited woman, even if I am scared of them.

IF I only had to have one composer, I'd pick Beethoven, but I don't have to. I like most of the work of all the men who have made music, whether they're Mozart or Hoagy, and almost every work is near enough unique for me to listen to. I like opera as I like a bullfight. If you're lucky enough to catch a good one, you'll have something to remember the rest of your days; and I've been lucky enough in both plazas. I've been luckier than I deserve.

I don't especially admire athletes, but I love football, and I like a really good baseball game. Before bursitis, there was nothing I enjoyed more than driving a tennis ball down someone's throat.

I also love children's verse, and one in my childhood began, "The world is so full of a number of things . . ."

You don't have much time around here, and you may as well enjoy it. Rejoice, dang it, rejoice.

THE NEED FOR PRETENSIONS

I ONCE stayed at an apartment house where the manager always referred to me to other people, in my own presence, as The Sophisticate. Her attitude always seemed rather ribald and not, I thought, properly respectful to one who then was already twenty-four years old and worldly-wise.

In truth, I wasn't sophisticated, but I had to pretend to be because otherwise people would have thought I was naïve. I was much more sophisticated at twenty-four than I am at sixty-two, and with reason. At the time, it was necessary that I seem to be an urbane, overly civilized man, and if I hadn't pretended, people would have guessed at my country upbringing and my unmodern morals. Actually, it then seemed to me that I was more sophisticated than anybody else in the apartment building. I had read Rabelais and the early covert copies of Henry Miller, and I always refused to look when ladies started undressing with the shades up in the apartments across the alley.

I was already seeing my share of suicides, murders, con games, and double-dealing wives and husbands. As a matter of fact, I was running every day into things nobody had said anything about in the Methodist church back home.

The wisest way to greet all this seemed to be to wear a poker face, act blasé, and dangle your cigarette in a sophisticated manner between your fingers.

Maybe the only reason I ever started smoking was that I was afraid somebody would find out I didn't.

PEOPLE preach sermons against pretensions, quite unfairly. Pretensions are about the only shell that the young and the unsure can erect between themselves and an uncertain world. It may often be a device for preserving human sanity, and it may be a way toward human improvement. The man who pretends hard enough may find himself becoming what he has pretended to be, because the human mind reaches out for what it wants. We all can reach farther than we think but not any farther than our dreams.

This didn't happen to The Sophisticate, of course. He looks back on his early photographs and finds it hard to imagine that he ever pretended that he was handsome or irresistible. He looks back on his early work and finds it hard to believe that he ever pretended to be wise or learned. But he finds in all this a strange content.

One of the advantages of growing older is that you no longer have to pretend.

AS you age, you discover that life is a process not of attaining but of discovering yourself. The Sophisticate these days is not wise or learned or handsome or witty, but he is, in a small two-bit way, unique.

As all persons are unique and discover the things they uniquely treasure, the people whom they have met and whose minds and spirits they have shared, the favorite oaks and holly and mockingbirds, the phrase of music that strikes the pit of the stomach like a blow, the picture that delights the eye, the small, rich moments of meditation.

And the wonder of life and the joy of it.

HURRAH FOR PEOPLE!

ON a Thanksgiving Day like this it behooves every newspaperman to stop in his rounds for a moment and thank the Lord just for people.

Thank the Lord, too, that they are opinionated, pigheaded, morally not all they ought to be, unpredictable, unreliable, careless of the truth, messy, sly, suspicious, very often openhearted and generous, saintly, devilish, and usually a little mixed up. Thank goodness they are not properly respectful toward an editor's opinions and don't really believe Washington, D.C., is all that important.

Thanks especially for long-legged girls in miniskirts and people who refuse to plant turnips in the dark of the moon, but thanks for all the people, all sizes, all shapes, all colors.

Their antics, their work, their jokes and tears make our world the most entertaining round ape house ever to pass through the cosmos.

People are themselves people's best gift to people, and they ought to take time to enjoy the gift.

NEWSPAPERMEN need to be especially grateful for people. People give the newspaperman everything that he ever prints. They tattle on their friends. They issue important statements listing all the luncheon club offices they have ever held. They tip you off to stories you had never heard of and relay all the scuttlebutt from all corners.

And when all this has been published and printed, the people buy the paper and read it all eagerly. They then give you their opinions, usually not favorable, about how you handled it. They volunteer expert advice on how lousy the reporter is and make up lists of ten different ways in which the editor is an idiot. Sometimes they call for a change of congressman. They do all this for free.

They are upsetting, often irritating, sometimes inspiring, and always delightful. Thank the Lord for people, lots and lots of people. Nothing like them has ever happened before on this globe and probably not anywhere else in the universe.

How on earth would we kill time if there were not some other people around to suspect?

PEOPLE who think they don't like people ought to stop and think what a dreary earth this would be if other people were not around. It is all right to take a quick trip to an unpopulated moon and pick up a few rocks, but what would it be like to spend a lifetime there knowing that there was no other person to try to outwit?

I have spent a little time in unpopulated mountain country, and I can tell you that it is uninteresting. A mountain doesn't mean much unless you suspect that there is a couple necking back there somewhere in a hollow or that somebody is making moonshine whiskey in the woods.

So, hurrah for people! Hurrah for us all, even the politicians and the flower children.

CHRISTMAS FIRES

CHRISTMAS is the time of the evergreen tree and the crèche, but it is also the time of fire.

Long before the mystery of the Christmas tree was invented and before Christmas became a Christian holiday, mankind was lighting fires at the winter solstice to the glory of some god. The Phoenicians lighted fires to Baal. At the time the cultivated Romans were celebrating the Saturnalia, the rude and deadly people of the north were lighting fires to Woden and Thor.

It is a pretty good guess that wherever a house has a fireplace a fire will be lit this day, and the men who sit before it will be remembering other fires of Christmas — one of the great fireplaces in old houses, perhaps, with its great backlog that needed two men to carry, or the cherry-red baseburner in the plains country where gas was too profitable to waste on the people who lived next door to the wells.

The kind of fire does not matter. The fires of Christmas are mostly dreams.

THERE is something elemental about the human need for a ceremonial fire at this season of the year. It is like the moon's pull on sea waters. The Yule log itself got its name from "Jul," the old Goth's name for the winter solstice celebration, and some think it came from the Goth's name for "wheel," referring to the turning of the year.

Nearly all the gods that man has celebrated by his Christmas fires have been gods of light, even gods of the sun. Perhaps the Christmas fire is a habit ingrained into the human race by eons of wanting, of yearning again to see the good sun and the green earth. Who knows?

But the Christmas fire still works its magic. The fires string Christmases together, and sometime while sitting before the fire today, perhaps even for a moment, the fifty-year-old human child will be remembering other fires. In the flames from his chunks of oak or mesquite, he will perceive vanished faces and hear silent voices and glimpse again the wonderful toy which did not last long enough — as that Christmas never lasted long enough and has become a lonely kind of ache for an unnamed something.

The Christmas fire has become mainly a device for recollection.

ANYHOW, the fires of Christmas stretch back like beads, back, back, back — back beyond all history to a time when man was a dim shadow in a dark forest. The fires of Christmas string mankind together, no matter how often individual men try to break the string with wars, threats, and plain old beer-hall brawls.

The fires of Christmas speak out again to the gods for all mankind.

It was good of God to grant to man so simple a benediction as the fire against the cold.

THE EASTER PLACE

THEY called it the Easter Place. We moved there in the Ozarks when I was very young, too young in the beginning to go to school. After all these years, I can close my eyes and see the place more vividly on the landscape of my mind than I can now see my own backyard.

It was a hill country farmstead, a neat blue-gray house that looked out over a meadow rolling down to Terrapin Creek and the cliffs of the mountains that reared up suddenly on the opposite bank. It was an L-shaped house with a front porch and a back gallery that ran along the kitchen wing. Inside, an enclosed stair led off the kitchen to the two cramped upstairs rooms, a stair that was lined with bare boards against which the shotguns and rifles were hung.

It faced north, and to the east a long kitchen garden and orchard ran down toward a copse on the spring branch. At the lower end of it we grew cotton, not for the market but for quilts.

In the summer, the walnut trees grew tall and green around it, and in the fall the sumac flamed from the fencerows.

THE memory of the place has come back with poignance and clearness recently, as these things will without warning emerge from the mind.

It was a time when my parents were having a little rough go of it financially. At the time, they seemed to me indomitable, but they weren't very old. My father may have been thirty-five. My mother was nine years younger.

They were of an age before hope had been corroded with fatigue, before they had learned the resignation to temper ambition with what was possible.

They had long and worried talks to which a small boy paid small attention. At the time, their worries seemed unimportant. It is only after you have traveled the same way and experienced the same long, exhausting erosion of dreams that you recognize this as common human experience. Whatever a man's riches or talents, he cannot stop the wasting away of his life or the sad dwindling of his powers and his strength.

A man who has grown old enough to look back and see how this happened to his father and his grandfather — and probably all the generations before them — finds it an unsettling thing.

IT is as a symbol of this that the Easter Place comes back into the mind, the place where to two rather fine human beings came the knowledge that they faced limitations that had nothing to do with their hopes, abilities, or energies.

Some place each man comes face to face with this.

The years at the Easter Place were happy years for me, but the house that I see these days in my mind, standing high and clear on the hill in the late afternoon sunlight, is not a happy one.

It weeps.

THE RACE OF MAN

SOMEBODY dies, and then you think of it, maybe. All the richness and spiritual plenty which has been given you all your life for free. All the accumulated and wondrous things which the human race has piled up in a trash heap for you to sort through.

There are the sentences from a Conrad preface which sing like the basswood of a lute, the clear, perfect little droplets of sound that come from a piano sounding Mozart, all the rich and stomach-stirring colors that a Rembrandt or a Rubens dug out of his own insides to persuade us that he was recording reality — all this and more, too, which is vouchsafed on a human being as a blessing. All that we of the race of man have done.

Man can be sorry and mean and cheap and trashy. He usually is.

But isn't it wonderful to be a part of the race of man which has done so many things beautiful?

WE pick and cull at each other. We quibble. We cavil. It is obvious to me, for instance, that I could have outwritten Shakespeare if I had had the opportunity. A. E. Housman was obviously a sophomoric poet. "That is the land of lost content,/I see it shining plain." What idiot lines, and yet he wrote them first.

As many a critic has pointed out, Salvador Dali cannot draw a watch. They are always bent. The kind of eternal and endless landscape of the mind that sweeps back beyond the watch is still there for us to relish.

We can laugh at Swinburne's coign of a cliff between lowland and highland, and yet people still go back to read "The Garden of Proserpine."

The point is that we have so much in the past to love and cherish and so much to hope for in the future.

We are the race of man, and we're good.

WE tend to dwell on our imperfections. Probably we should. We have not yet built Jerusalem on Thames and probably never will. We have evil incarnate walking among us, as evil ever will exist among mere mortals.

But we have done some things, some beautiful things, the paintings on the cave walls and the chants to the gods sung around our primitive or sophisticated firelights. We have done some things that make life worth living to human beings, even a hungry human being.

We are the race of man, and we're pretty damn good.

THE HUMAN MIND

IT takes a man most of a lifetime to discover that the Roman Empire is not really dead.

When you were thirteen, the Roman Empire was dead. Miss Lokey said so. Miss Lokey handled ancient history when she wasn't teaching the home economics girls to bake cookies. "The Roman Empire is dead," she said, and you had no reason to doubt her. It was a comforting thought. At thirteen, anything that is dead can't amount to much and needn't be remembered beyond the next exam.

But even in that small class, two students found somehow a faint glow of life in the Roman Empire and pursued it, in desultory or professional fashion, until the Roman Empire at times came alive within them. The cynical and deadly politics of the Praetorian Guard became as real as Watergate. The sounds of the Roman imperium came back.

The human mind has the ability to call all this back, as it can call back anything from the past.

THE human mind is not a time capsule all filled with the man's personal events and time. The human mind can make images. The human being can write things down and does, especially malicious gossip about his enemies. As a result, to the extent that he is able and willing to encompass it, a man can relive the whole rich experience of the human race from the smoky Stone Age caves to the moon walk.

He can frequent the European courts which first heard Mozart. He can talk with Socrates. He can stand with Galileo before the Inquisition. He can go with Hilary to the top of the world and sail with Drake into the harbor of Cadiz. He can watch the genius of Michelangelo at work, even though he cannot know it. He can make use of every cunning tool, poem, piece of art, and bit of knowledge that the human race has left strewn along its trail into the here now and hereafter.

To the person aware of this, it seems odd that some of his fellows just want to ride their motorcycles and exist in the here and now.

SO, if the Roman Empire be a man's dish, he can live it again. He can march with Caesar's Legions and know their ration of parched grain and smell again the smoke of their campfires deep in the wildernesses of Britain and Gaul. Sometimes it will seem so real that he can hear the trumpets of the latest triumphal in a distant street.

Rome doesn't die. The man does, but Rome is beginning to live again somewhere in the mind and consciousness of another small boy.

Philippi is never really won or lost. It is always fought again.

GIVE US ANOTHER SEASON

THIS brisk autumn weather portends momentous change, of course. The year turns around us. A generation of life withers in our sight. And the condition of man changes from encephalitis to the common cold.

It is a time when man changes the disguise of his Fate. His condition is just as bad as it ever was, but it wears a new face. Last spring he labored against the syrup and insects of mimosa flowers and looked ahead to a time when they would be gone. Now, in autumn, he fights the pestilence of the mimosa beans and longs for their wintry decay. Man never just chops down the mimosa tree. That would be destroying Fate, and he paid 75 cents for this Fate years ago when it was a sapling.

The Fate in which a man finds himself at any given moment is a saddle which galls him constantly. He looks ahead to shedding it. In July, he looks ahead to a cheery December and Christmas; in December, he can hardly wait for spring. He tends to remember the Thanksgivings and Fourths of July of his off-seasons and forgets the dead car battery and the misery of mowing the lawn.

Some old-time great, probably Shakespeare, said that we always prefer to leave the mess we are in and rush into a new mess that we know nothing about. Shakespeare was a very wise man when he left out that hey, nonny, nonny stuff.

NO matter how the world changes about him and the hope that comes when the leaves change or fall, man is still in the clutch of Fate.

Fate works patiently, inexorably against him even while he sleeps. In the coldest of winter, the seed of the worm awaits the blossoming of the summer pears. In the hottest part of August, the great jet streams sweep above him arranging the ice storms and snows that will come in six months.

Considering this state of affairs, it is lucky that man doesn't have much sense. He perseveres. He keeps shoring up his little private world against the inevitable, though the props that he built a few weeks ago are already rotting at the base and the termites have started eating up his wall. Man goes on hoping. If he is a farmer, he hopes for a good crop in another season. If he gets a good crop, the longshoremen won't load it. If the longshoremen leave him alone, he doesn't have much crop.

Everything turns out to be a mixture of the sweet and the bitter, mostly bitter.

The only sensible thing for a man to do is give up.

MAN is at the mercy of the universe. You can't reach any other conclusion. It doesn't seem fair, and it undoubtedly violates the one-man one-vote principle, but that is the way it is. Man is caught in a gerrymander that he can't do anything about.

It might be better to sit back and let Fate take its course. This was the way of Primitive Man, those people who inhabited the earth up until about four hundred years ago. They did the best they could and then sat back to watch the change of the seasons, noticing the changing shapes of clouds and the subtle differences in light and deriving a satisfaction from them.

Of course, you can't do this in a city. You can see only one small patch of sky, but give us another season. Maybe things will change.

THE CONSTITUTIONALITY OF DYING

THE courts continue their gradual enslavement of the people. That judge who tried the Karen Quinlan case up in New Jersey has declared that nobody has a constitutional right to die.

We wish that people would rise up against this usurpation of legislative power. Legislatures cannot only authorize you to die; sometimes they help you along. But we fear the American people will take this latest outrage supinely. For one thing, nobody seems to be rushing forward to offer himself as a test case. For another, the courts would probably throw out his testimony on the grounds that ex rigor mortis testimony cannot be subjected to cross-examination.

It is true that the New Jersey judge is merely a state judge. The Supreme Court of the United States has not yet ruled on this landmark question. But we have no doubt that the Supreme Court will uphold the state court in this instance, even though the Supreme Court every year must hear some litigants which it wishes would drop dead, constitutionally or not.

The question will end up in the federal courts without a doubt. If you are moving from here to eternity, for instance, you certainly come under the Interstate Commerce clause.

A MAN can beat the Supreme Court if he can stick it out and the court does not know what to do. There was the famous case of Ex

Parte Milligan back during the Civil War. Old E. P., as we familiars called him, gave the courts something to do for just about half of the war.

As we remember the case, Milligan was a stubborn midwesterner who decided he did not wish to be drafted or otherwise support the war. He did not run off to Canada and cry for amnesty. He figured he was man enough to handle the situation himself. In 1863, Congress had given the President the authority to suspend the writ of habeas corpus all over the country, and Milligan was tried by a military commission, which found him guilty.

For three years, the Supreme Court flip-flopped here and there in its decisions, first saying Milligan was right and then he was wrong. After the war was over and it made no difference, the courts decided that Milligan had been right all along, which he could have told them if they had only asked.

The court only ruled, however, that a civilian cannot be tried by a military commission outside the battle zone as long as the civil courts are operating.

It did not rule out conscription, which was a good idea. How else would they have got all of us to volunteer back in the big war?

THE question of the constitutionality of dying raises some interesting questions about the basic law. We have searched the Constitution diligently and can find in it no constitutional right to be born. We are talking here about the United States Constitution; nobody can find anything in the Texas Constitution.

Since a man has no constitutional right to be born or to die, his whole life appears to be

unconstitutional, and there can be no legal basis for charging the people who do the work of Satan, the girl-chasing, the drawing to inside straights, etc., with trafficking with the enemy.

TO TOUCH AN ANGEL

A MAN wrote me not long ago and asked me what I thought of the theory of angels. I immediately told him that I am highly in favor of angels. As a matter of fact, I am scared to death of them.

Any adult human being with half sense, and some with more, knows that there are angels. If he has ever spent any period in loneliness, when the senses are forced in upon themselves, he has felt the wind from their beating wings and been overwhelmed with the sudden realization of the endless and gigantic dark that exists outside the little candle flame of human knowledge. He has prayed, not in the sense that he asked something, but that he yielded himself.

Angels live daily at our very elbows, and so do demons, and most men at one time or another in their lives have yielded themselves to both and have lived to rejoice and rue their impulses.

But the man who has once felt the beat of the angel's wing finds it easy to rejoice at the universe and at his fellow man.

THIS sense of cosmos, or angels, or the divine accommodation of a man with the universe, usually happens to a man suddenly. Angels do not take part in work for civic causes or help raise money for the United Fund. A single human heart has to long to touch an angel before it can sense one.

It does not happen to any man often, and too many of us dismiss it when it happens. I remember a time in my final days in college when the chinaberry trees were abloom and the air was sweet with spring blossoms and I stood still on the street, suddenly struck with the feeling of something that was an enormous promise and yet was no tangible promise at all.

And there was another night in a small boat when the moon was full and the distant headlands were dark but beautiful and we were lonely. The pull of a nameless emotion was so strong that it filled the atmosphere. The small boy within me cried.

Psychiatrists will say that the angel in all this was really within me, not outside, but it makes no difference.

There are angels inside us and angels outside, and the one inside is usually the quickest choked.

FRANCIS Thompson said it better. He was a late nineteenth-century English poet who would put the current crop of hippies to shame. He was on pot all his life. His pad was always mean and was sometimes a park bench. He was a mental case and a tubercular besides. He carried a fishing creel into which he dropped the poetry that was later to become immortal.

"The angels keep their ancient places," wrote Francis Thompson in protest. "Turn but a stone, and start a wing!"

He was lonely enough to be the constant associate of angels.

There is an angel close to you this day. Merry Christmas, and I wish you well.

APPENDIX: DATES OF COLUMNS

Advanced Ideas about Men's Shoes:
   September 29, 1964
Advantages of Being a Slow Reader: May 24, 1965
Advice for Prospective Boat Buyers: April 10, 1963
Against the Razor's Edge: October 25, 1964
All Stove Up: May 18, 1960
All's Well That Ends Well: June 24, 1968
And Now, Jogger's Heel: March 3, 1969
Anybody Can Sing Underwater: August 27, 1962
Art of Noseblowing, The: February 25, 1963
Asafetida: August 3, 1970
Aunt Heck: March 23, 1975
Aunt Martha and "That Man": September 22, 1963
Authentic Stomach Man, The: July 19, 1968
Average American Male, The: July 8, 1968

Back to the Cotton Shirt: September 17, 1975
Back to the Hog Bristle: September 14, 1966
Bayard's Boat: October 16, 1962
Beating a Dead Horse: April 4, 1967
Beautiful Diving Horse, A: August 23, 1964
Before the Mast Forever: September 21, 1961
Better a Debtor's Prison: June 13, 1975
Bird Rebellion, The: September 23, 1968
Book Will Out, The: December 12, 1972
Bottle Brokers: November 25, 1968
Bound to Lose: August 2, 1965

Brother Shulter and the Lord: November 26, 1970
Bugged for Posterity: July 23, 1973
Built-in Cardinal, The: April 22, 1968
Burma Shave Road, The: July 15, 1964

Calibrating Hailstones: March 13, 1974
Captive of the Calorie: February 6, 1961
Careers by Correspondence: March 28, 1960
Case of the Mauve Colored Garter, The:
   January 29, 1971
Caught between Two Fiddlers: January 12, 1970
Caught in the Wewoka Switch: December 27, 1972
Century of the Novelist, The: June 11, 1970
Christmas Fires: December 25, 1970
Cleaning the Boat: April 7, 1966
Communications Breakdowns: December 7, 1962
Conquering Computer, The: August 15, 1966
Conservatism and Liberalism: February 2, 1961
Constitutionality of Dying, The: November 13, 1975
Controlling the Comma: July 3, 1962
Corruption of Seafood Carter, The: August 1, 1975
Couples: May 28, 1963
Cousin Davy and the Rattler: June 9, 1967
Covered Wagon Trek, A: August 18, 1969
Cow-Milking Business, The: November 20, 1968
Culture Shock: June 15, 1972